SAMIZDAT REGISTER II

The
Samizdat
Register
II

edited by

ROY MEDVEDEV

W · W · NORTON & COMPANY

NEW YORK · LONDON

ISBN 0 393 01419 3

Printed in Great Britain

Contents

Introduction

The second volume of *Samizdat Register* is once again a
collection of the writings of a group of authors living in the
Soviet Union and contributing to the *samizdat* journal *XX
Century*. From the beginning of 1977 the editor of this journal,
Roy Medvedev, and the contributors have been increasingly
harassed by the authorities, while other dissidents – Professor
Yu. Orlov among them – were being arrested. Accordingly I
have assumed a more active role in helping to get their work
published abroad in Russian and in foreign languages. In
spite of this increased repression, the flow of *samizdat* work
from the USSR increased during 1977 and 1978. Several new
literary and political journals had appeared – in Russian – in
the West, representing different trends in unofficial cultural
and political developments. I do not plan to discuss here all
the aspects of this creative cooperation between Soviet and
East European dissident circles and the West, but I should
like to indicate that the comparative increase in 'New Left'
groups and individuals is probably related to the fact that
members of other groups with anti-socialist positions often
preferred to emigrate. Many of these have lost hope that the
Soviet Union could become a tolerant and pluralistic society
in the foreseeable future. Since the adoption of the new
Constitution late in 1977 the single-party system of Soviet
society has been strongly confirmed and this means the
preservation of political censorship, political control of

research and creative work and the continuation of repressive measures against any form of opposition.

At the same time a pessimistic assessment of the developments in the USSR cannot be completely justified. The political situation in the Soviet Union is undergoing some changes, albeit very slowly. The censorship system remains, but the measures against unnofficial publications abroad have become less effective. Soviet literature, art and cultural life now clearly reflect Western influences and are more experimental than they were in 1973-5. Political control has not disappeared but it has become more flexible and provides more freedoms in private life, especially in Eastern European countries such as Poland and Hungary where freedom to travel abroad has been allowed both for private and professional reasons. The economy is, of course, controlled but small scale self-employed business and services have become more and more important factors in the life of the USSR and of the Eastern European countries. The evident growth of the economic and military power of the Eastern European bloc of socialist countries, their increasing ability to operate a global policy can intensify periodically internal repressions. This new possibility of playing a more influential role in the world has, however, brought about some changes in the internal situation in the USSR. The competition and disputes between the USSR and the USA, while sharpening political and diplomatic confrontation, weakening détente and inducing some revival of the Cold War, has increased repressive measures within the USSR against political dissidents with a 'Western' orientation and also intensified Western publicity for these groups. The so-called 'Helsinki Monitoring Group' has been liquidated by arrests and forced emigration, and the same has happened with the 'Amnesty International' group and others. At the same time individual activity and attempts to criticise internal and international Soviet policy from clearly Marxist and socialist positions are more or less tolerated, which is, I believe, a reflection of the new diversity of socialist and communist movements in the world, the appearance of 'Eurocommunist' ideology and its more active influence upon developments within the USSR.

The utopian dreams of some former dissidents, A. Amalrik

for instance, predicting the collapse of the Soviet Union by 1984, have proved completely unfounded. Most of these dissidents now live abroad, and the regime which they criticised is now more stable and confident than ever; its actions are now decisive factors internationally and this will be increasingly so in the next decade. This makes more interesting and significant the position of those intellectual sources within the USSR which do not look to pressure from outside as the main factor for liberal reform, but attempt to find internal factors for political improvement and tolerance and for the reduction of tensions between East and West. Because organised political activity of any kind is impossible, the representatives of this socialist opposition work mostly through theoretical reconsideration of the history of the USSR, comparative sociology and economic analysis of negative aspects of Soviet life, constructive criticism of totalitarian aspects of the socialist system as carried out by detailed analysis of the fatal errors of the post-revolutionary period, Stalin's terror, miscalculations during the Second World War with its enormous toll of victims, post-war cultural degradation, pseudo-scientific trends in many areas of science and technology and economic mismanagement past and present. Because these attempts to understand the historical background of the current situation were based on valid factual considerations, neither the official ideological system nor the KGB were able to destroy these tendencies. Their influence could however be reduced through censorship. This is why most of such critical works have been published outside the USSR. The present collection of *Samizdat Register* represents this unpublicised but notable tendency within Soviet intellectual groups. The contributors are not only interested in criticising certain aspects of the Russian version of the socialist system but in suggesting possible alternatives which might change it for the better. Their main aim is to explain, not to the West but to the Russian people – workers, farmers and intellectuals – the nature of the sickness of their society together with its possible cure. They do not discuss their own personal troubles – the usual pattern of demands of many dissident groups, appealing about the right of emigration, travel abroad, sectarian religious activities and similar issues. They discuss the problems of people generally, the concerns of everyday life and the lessons of history which ought not to be forgotten.

I do not intend at this point to introduce all the authors. Some, like Roy Medvedev, are known in the West, some are new. When I say 'new', this does not mean young, for in Russia it is often the old who start to rethink their past life and reconsider their attitudes. This is, for example, very clear in the case of M. Bogin. A revolutionary during the Civil War, he worked in the Comintern in the thirties and carried out political work during the Second World War and subsequently. The turning point for him as for many others was the Twentieth Party Congress with Krushchev's secret speech. He started to write political essays when he was already an old man and died in 1977 at the age of about eighty. Nevertheless one can find a lot of fresh ideas in his writing. Brilliant essays by Krasikov about 'Commodity Number One' – about vodka and the plague of alcoholism – are also written by an old man, one who prefers to use a pseudonym. Some other writers use pseudonyms – it is impossible to be a free author in the USSR and also to be employed in a social, educational or research centre.

The most interesting figure among the older authors who publish their essays openly is Mikhail Yakubovich. He is eighty-eight now and lives in an old people's home in Karaganda. He began writing about fifteen years ago; before that he spent twenty-six years in Stalin's prisons and camps and has only recently completed a period of exile lasting twenty years. His main 'crime' was that he was a member of the Menshevik fraction of the Socialist-Democratic Party before the Revolution. He left the Menshevik Party after the Revolution and played an active role in the Civil War and post-war period rebuilding the economy. He was arrested in 1930 and was tried at one of the first show trials carried out by Stalin in 1931. The extraordinary story of this trial and Yakubovich's ordeal during interrogation is described in Roy Medvedev's book *Let History Judge* (Macmillan, London, 1972. A. Knopf, New York, 1971). Yakubovich's 'confession' at this trial was received after more than a month of the 'full treatment' of torture, which included such methods as beating the genitals, preventing sleep, etc. Yakubovich's case has also been described in another book which is more famous – *Gulag Archipelago* by A. Solzhenitsyn. But Solzhenitsyn, unfortunately, did not describe the 'Menshevik case' as it really was and he distorted Yakubovich's own story written as a deposition for rehabilitation. One can easily compare the full text of this important document published in Medvedev's *Let History Judge* (pp. 125-31) with Solzhenitsyn's distorted version of the same document (pp. 403-5) to realise that for Solzhenitsyn the historical truth did not mean too much when it contradicted his explanations of the tragedy of Stalin's terror.

Yakubovich does not write as a Western scholar would expect; one does not find references or footnotes. But this is not his fault. When he started to write his memoirs and essays his room was twice raided by the KGB and his manuscripts and notes confiscated. After that he began to use tape recordings and his friends in Moscow transcribed them into typewritten texts. Some of his essays were confiscated in Roy Medvedev's appartment in 1975. But they have nevertheless survived.

These examples should indicate to the readers of this collection that the essays here published were not written under the normal conditions for free academic research. These are voices of life, voices of struggle for the future.

ZHORES MEDVEDEV

Stalinism after the Twentieth Congress of the CPSU as the Reflection of Internal and International Problems of the USSR

ROY MEDVEDEV

*The situation in the USSR after the Twentieth
Congress and the reasons for Krushchev's fall*

Twenty years have passed since, at the closed night session of the Twentieth Congress of the CPSU, after the formal closing of the Congress, shocked delegates heard N.S. Krushchev's report 'The Cult of Personality and its Consequences'. Within a month, at countless meetings all over the country, the same report was heard by tens of millions of Soviet people, Communist and non-Party, and before that the text of the report, first in an abbreviated form and then fully, had been published in the foreign press.

As far back as the autumn of 1955 N.S. Krushchev had, in one of his speeches, declared to all the world that there were 'no political prisoners' in the USSR. Yet three to four months after the Twentieth Congress millions of political prisoners, who had managed to survive the terrible years spent in prisons and camps, began to return to their families. And an even larger number of honest Soviet people, who had died or been shot, were posthumously rehabilitated.

The Twentieth Congress, however, turned out to be only the beginning of a long and contradictory process of 'destalinisation'. By the end of 1956 there was a clear attempt, in the country and in the Party, to rehabilitate Stalin. The dramatic battle waged inside the Praesidium of the Central Committee

1

was almost won by Krushchev's opponents, headed by Molotov, Malenkov and Kaganovich. These people, who had formerly hated and feared one another, now united before the danger that their numerous crimes might be revealed. However, even after his victory at the June Plenum of the Central Committee, Krushchev did not raise the question of Stalin for several years.

A big and important step forward in the exposure of Stalin and his chief *aides* was the Twenty-second Congress of the CPSU. Now not only in closed but in open session, not only in a report but in the statements of the majority of speakers the theme was the numerous crimes of the period of the 'cult of personality'. And people spoke not only of Stalin, Beria and Yezhov, but of Molotov, Voroshilov, Malenkov, Kaganovich, Shkiryatov, Vyshinsky, Bagirov and some others in the immediate entourage of Stalin. The Congress resolved to remove Stalin's coffin from the mausoleum in Red Square; it was also decided to take down monuments and portraits of Stalin, and to change the names of towns, streets, squares, enterprises and institutions bearing his name. Immediately after the Congress our press carried a mass of material and documentation pursuing 'the lines of the Twentieth and Twenty-second Party Congresses' exposing Stalin and Stalinism.

Obituaries, articles and books appeared about Party and state workers, cultural and scientific figures, military commanders and diplomats, who had perished in the thirties and forties. Fiction and memoirs were published giving a truthful account of our recent past. At last, it seemed, the public life of our country would be cleared of the terrible diseases and vices of the Stalin epoch. Reality, however, was much more complex.

The new and substantial political capital which Krushchev earned as a result of the Twenty-second Congress was, unfortunately, very soon lost. The Twenty-second Congress did not put an end to the serious dissatisfaction felt in the Party and State apparatus for the many badly organised, unthought-out and hasty reorganisations undertaken by Krushchev back in the years 1957-60. In fact, the hidden opposition to Khrushchev among middle and upper Party and state echelons grew after the Congress and preliminary discussions along these lines were already taking place at the Congress itself. But during the first months after the Congress Krushchev's prestige was still very high and his personal authority increased in many respects, assisted by the new enlarging and alteration of the composition of the Central Committee. Of the 175 Central Committee members elected at the Twenty-second Congress only forty had been members before the Twentieth Congress. The exorbitant praise for Krushchev, which was begun at the Twenty-second Congress, more and more assumed the character of a new cult of personality. Krushchev became more and more aggressive, intolerant of criticism and opposition, coarse and irritable. Both the Central Committee Plenums and the Praesidium sessions turned into formalities, all major decisions were taken by Krushchev himself or in conjunction with his closest *aides* and advisers, who were not members of the Praesidium and Secretariat of the Central Committee. Krushchev even dragged his family into big-time politics. In addition, even after the Twenty-second Congress and with an indefatigability worthy of better application, Krushchev continued to think up more and more new reforms and reorganisations, causing an unstable and extremely confused situation in the country. Strangely enough, by the end of his ten-year term of office (officially proclaimed in the press as the 'great decade'), Krushchev, whose activity in all spheres was, as a rule, dictated by the best of intentions and who genuinely tried to improve the life of workers in the town and the country, had lost support among almost all sections and groups of the population.

Workers and employees in the towns were dissatisfied with the worsening of supplies, particularly the lack of many foodstuffs and the slow rise in living standards. The monetary reform of 1961 caused irritation, accompanied as it was by a concealed rise in price for many goods. Then the price of meat, milk, butter and cheese was openly raised by 25-30 per cent which certainly did not increase the popularity of Krushchev, who had recently promised to outstrip America's production of meat and milk per head of the population. In a number of cities this price increase led to spontaneous strikes and disturbances.

3

Collective farmers were dissatisfied with their drop in earnings in the over-all economy, brought about by the reorganisation of the Machine and Tractor Stations and the compulsory purchase of all agricultural machinery which weakened or ruined the financial position of many collective farms. Collective and state farmers were even more incensed by the compulsory cutback in private stockraising; in small towns and workers' settlements workers and employees were forbidden to keep any cattle for personal use. Agricultural production for the years 1959-64 stagnated and in many parts of the country the material position of rural inhabitants began to decline once more.

The artistic intelligentsia, which had greeted the decisions of the Twenty-second Congress with enthusiasm, was soon disappointed by the strengthening and increase of censorship requirements, by Krushchev's incompetent meddling in the work of cultural organisations and unions, by a series of noisy but fruitless propaganda campaigns on ideological problems. Krushchev engaged in a number of sharp conflicts with the world of science.

Krushchev tried in many cases to deal with financial difficulties that arose by taking from the earnings or privileges of one or another section of the population. Demagogic and unjustified pretexts were used to take away supplementary earnings in eastern and northern parts of the country; military pensions were reduced; a large number of officers were demobilised before their time, sometimes only a few months before acquiring the right to a higher pension for long service. On Krushchev's initiative the all-Union Ministry for Internal Affairs was abolished and many of the perks and pay supplements of the Ministry's militia and armed forces taken away.

The Party and state apparatus became dissatisfied with the increasing complication and extreme confusion of the management system in industry and in the economy as a whole. But special dissatisfaction was aroused by the hasty reorganisation of regional organisations and the creation of separate and independent industrial and agricultural regional and regional-executive committees. Almost all regions were artificially divided up, previous area-frontiers were changed

4

and mixed up, rural area committees were in practice abolished or reorganised into Party committees of the agricultural production boards – a new agricultural management-link thought up by Krushchev.

It goes without saying that Party apparatus workers were also dissatisfied with a number of undoubtedly progressive reforms undertaken by Krushchev. Before the Twenty-second Congress several undeserved privileges were removed from specially selected workers, including the notorious 'packet' system. Many Party apparatus workers were dissatisfied and disturbed by the Twenty-second Congress decision to introduce into Party rules a series of points requiring a systematic turnover of the staffs of all Party organs. In accordance with the new rules, at every election to the Central Committee and to the Praesidium of the Central Committee the turnover had to be no less than one quarter. A minimum turnover of a third was required of the Party Central Committees in the Union republics, and of the territorial and regional committees; at least a half was required of city and area committees and of the bureaux of local Party organisations. No member of these organs could hold office for more than three terms in succession. Exceptions were allowed only in special cases, depending on the practical and political qualities of the person in question, but this would require a secret ballot and three-quarters of the votes of those present at the voting. A considerable number of Party cadres, used to regarding their *elected* posts as their jobs, saw the principle of systematic turnover as a threat to their position and privileges. Many people in the Party apparatus, in the MVD, KGB and military circles, more and more openly expressed their dissatisfaction with the 'stream' of camp literature and considered that Krushchev had gone too far in his exposure of the crimes of the Stalin epoch.

Dissatisfaction, often quite justified, was also occasioned by the various ill-thought-out actions of Krushchev in foreign affairs. Krushchev's numerous improvisations introduced into Soviet foreign policy an element of uncertainty and instability.

In such conditions, where Krushchev had lost support in the highest Party echelons, in the highest echelons of the army, the KGB and MVD, it became a matter of time before he was removed.

The October 1964 Plenum of the Central Committee
of the CPSU and the first months following the Plenum

Krushchev's fall took place at the October 1964 Plenum of the Central Committee of the CPSU. The lack in our country and Party of any normal and regular mechanism for changing higher organs of authority inevitably leads to a crisis whenever there are serious disagreements in the Central Committee, and contains an element of risk. But with Krushchev's removal there was not much risk; he had hardly any defenders in the Central Committee, not to mention the Praesidium of the Central Committee.

Among the many accusations laid at Krushchev at the October Plenum nothing was said of the line of the Twentieth and Twenty-second Congresses. On the contrary, one of the most serious accusations made was that, having denounced the cult of Stalin, Krushchev began to spread, in the country and in the Party, the cult of his own personality; that he had misused his authority, violating the principles of collective leadership and the Leninist norms of Party life. In this way, the decisions of the Twentieth and Twenty-second Congresses condemning the cult of personality were now used against Krushchev himself.

Krushchev's removal from the posts of head of Party and state and from the political arena did not give rise to any difficulties or disturbances inside the country. The decision of the October Plenum was received very quietly, in many cases with relief. Naturally, no one was going to be satisfied with the announcement that N. S. Krushchev had been relieved of his posts 'for reasons of age and health'. People wanted more information about what had happened in the Kremlin and many sought the information in foreign radio broadcasts. But, in general, this was a feeling of simple curiosity rather than indignation. Members of the Central Committee Praesidium were even a little surprised, when several days after the October Plenum V. Semichastny, chairman of the KGB, reported at the next regular meeting of the Praesidium on the reaction to the recent Plenum decisions among the population and the collectives in enterprises and institutions. The huge propaganda machine, which for several years had been busy lauding N.S. Krushchev, suddenly ran idle. M.A. Suslov was clearly wrong (admittedly, only in the given, concrete case) when in his report to the October Plenum he said that 'it was more difficult to fight a living cult than a dead one'.

Many of the reorganisations implemented during the 'great decade' were abolished in the very first months following the October Plenum. The abolition or revision of some of the other reforms and reorganisations required more time. However, many of Krushchev's innovations were kept; to abolish them was considered either inopportune or no longer feasible. It was easy, for example, to bring back to Moscow the Ministry of Agriculture of the USSR and the RSFSR, to restore the Timiryazev Agricultural Academy or to remove the restrictions on keeping cattle for personal use. It was much more difficult to restore the MTSs, even in a number of regions and areas.

As we know, the question of Stalin or 'the lines of the Twentieth and Twenty-second Party Congress' was basically not raised in the months following the October Plenum. The publication of 'camp' literature had already ceased under Krushchev, the stream of exposures in 1962-3 had begun to frighten his immediate entourage and by the end of 1963 journals had stopped printing the prison memoirs and stories sent to them. In the spring of 1964 the censorship had received still stricter instructions on this score, and even Galina Serebryakova was unable to publish her memoirs, which had already been set up in print. Nevertheless, a steady number of books criticising Stalin continued to come out after the October Plenum. For example, immediately after October 1964 there appeared quite a number of hard-hitting articles and documents exposing Lysenko and his group. Many facts and documents were made public concerning the grave consequences of the Stalin cult in the field of biological and medical science. Dozens of names of outstanding Soviet scientists, who had perished and been disgraced in the thirties and forties, were received back into Soviet science. In the summer of 1965 A.M. Nekrich's book *22nd June, 1941* was published, which speaks in detail about Stalin's personal responsibility for the USSR's unpreparedness at the commencement of war. This book came out in the Academy of Science's popular series, getting through both the general censorship as well as that of the Ministry of Defence and the Ministry of Foreign Affairs. Many facts about the crimes of Stalin and his entourage appeared in the following books published in 1965-6: Y. Trifonov's *The Bonfire's Glow*, A. Mil'chakov's *The First Decade*, Ts. Agayan's *Memories of Demyan Bedny, Essays in the History of the Moscow Organisation of the CPSU* and *N. Stapanyan*, B. Dyakov's *From Experience*, P.K. Oshchepkov's *Life and Dream*, I. Maisky's *Bernard Shaw and Others* and *Essays in the History of the Ivanovsk Party Organisation* and many others.

However, by the beginning of 1965 two lines on Stalin were already visible among the Party leadership.

A group of leading ideologists, prominent military men and some writers had gone into action, demanding a review of the decisions of the Twentieth and Twenty-second Party Congress, but in fact wanting the rehabilitation of Stalin. This group was strongest in the middle ranks of Party and state organisation and in the main relied on various word-of-mouth channels to spread its views. The majority on the Praesidium of the Central Committee occupied a more cautious and moderate position, preferring to say nothing at all about Stalin or Krushchev and to avoid making public statements about any of the thorny problems of Soviet history. But it was well known that some members of the CC Praesidium clearly sympathised with supporters of Stalin's rehabilitation, only they wanted to take things more slowly. For this reason various, often very provocative statements by active Stalinists were never properly repudiated.

During the preparations for the twentieth anniversary of the victory over Fascist Germany there appeared a number of educational documents (by A.A. Epishev, Head of the Political Department of the Soviet Army, and S.P. Trapeznikov, Head of the Party Central Committee Section for Education, Schools and Institutions of Higher Learning) containing a quantity of praise for Stalin and accusing Krushchev of having distorted Stalin's role in the preparation of the war and the leadership of the armed forces. At the end of April 1965 lengthy theses on the twentieth anniversary of victory were submitted to the Praesidium of the Central Committee, prepared under the supervision of P. N. Pospelov, director of the Institute of Marxism-Leninism and in the recent past a prominent ideological *aide* of Stalin, one of the chief authors of the *Short Biography of J. V. Stalin.* The theses contained positions which signified a *de facto,* if partial, rehabilitation of Stalin. Pospelov's theses were not accepted, however, because the more moderate point of view predominated at their discussion in the Praesidium. Brezhnev in his Jubilee report mentioned Stalin's name as Head of the State Committee for Defence, but refrained from any judgements on his activity. But the mere mention of Stalin's name in the report was sufficient to set off applause from a considerable section of the participants at the grand session.

When the Jubilee festivities were over, Stalin's name began to disappear from the pages of newspapers and magazines. But little changed in word-of-mouth propaganda. The new Head of the Social Science Section of the Ministry of Middle and Higher Special Education, I. Murashev, demanded in almost every speech the reintroduction of the study of Stalin's main works in Institutes of Higher Education. 'Krushchev's subjectivism', declared Murashev in one such speech, 'brought us more harm than the cult of Stalin.' The new Head of the Central Committee Section for Education, Schools and Institutes of Higher Education, S.P. Trapeznikov, was particularly rabid in his demand for Stalin's rehabilitation. This 'man of science' likewise called for the reintroduction of the study of 'Comrade Stalin's creative heritage' in Higher Institutes and schools. Referring to obituaries of Government and Party activists who had perished under Stalin, Trapeznikov in one of his reports exclaimed: 'It's time we stopped resurrecting the dead. We can't turn our newspapers into memorial-halls.' Encouraged by similar calls some speakers at ideological conferences went still further. Demanding the restoration of Stalin's 'political reputation', they declared that under Krushchev such prominent figures as A. Bubnov, M. Pokrovsky, F. Raskolnikov and others had been 'incorrectly rehabilitated', that they could not be called 'true Leninists' because at some point in the twenties they had joined one or another of the oppositions. One speaker even exclaimed that we had been wrong to discard the concept of 'enemy of the people'. The insistent attempts to revise the line of the Twentieth and Twenty-second Party Congresses caused disquiet among the leaders of a number of Communist Parties in Eastern and Western Europe. The First Secretary of the Polish Workers' Party, V. Gomulka, remarked in conversations with Soviet leaders that Polish Communists were disturbed by the increasing attempts to whitewash Stalin. Gomulka warned that if this line continued the Central Committee of the Polish Party would be forced to make a special statement. A similar warning was given by the leader of the Italian Communist Party, Luigi Longo, during his stay in the USSR in 1965.

The activity of the Stalinists and their closeness to the new Central Committee leadership caused worry to large sections of the intelligentsia, who had been pleased by the decisions of the Twentieth and Twenty-second Congresses.

This disquiet expressed itself in a series of articles, letters and documents passed around in typewritten copies or copied out by hand. 'F.F. Raskolnikov's Letter to Stalin', for example, written in 1939, had a wide circulation. The 'Letter to I.G. Erenburg' by the Soviet publicist Ernst Henry (S.N. Rostovsky) got even a larger circulation. Ernst Henry's letter was an argued and convincing answer to all attempts to find a good word for Stalin's 'wartime services'. Adducing many facts, he showed that it was precisely Stalin's miscalculations, entirely unforgivable in a leading statesman, which caused the country to be unprepared for the war not merely in a military and strategic way, but operationally, tactically, diplomatically and morally. The fact that this letter was circulated in thousands of copies throughout the country was testimony to the protest against attempts to rehabilitate Stalin. A similar circulation was accorded G. Pomerantsev's small, but brilliant, pamphlet 'The Moral Physiognomy of Historical Personality'. The second half of 1965 saw the beginning of *samizdat*, testifying to the serious differences between the attitudes of the 'leaders' and the opinion of wide circles of the Soviet intelligentsia. At the same time the writers A. Sinyavsky and Yu. Daniel were arrested in Moscow and accused of writing and publishing abroad 'slanderous works, discrediting the Soviet social and political order'.

The question of Stalin in 1966 and 1967

At the commencement of 1966 discussion began of material for the forthcoming Twenty-third Congress of the CPSU. There were many signs that some of the influential groups in the Party and Government apparatus were aiming to use the Congress as a means of rehabilitating Stalin, partially or indirectly. Of particular note in this respect was the article of E. Zhukov, V. Trukhanovsky and V. Shunkov, 'The High Responsibility of Historians', published in *Pravda* for 30 January 1966. The authors of the article sought to deny altogether the rightness of the concept 'period of cult of personality', although this was the concept used in the Resolution of the Twenty-second Congress to remove Stalin's coffin from the Lenin Mausoleum. Rumours circulated that a large group of generals and marshals had sent a letter to the Central Committee demanding Stalin's rehabilitation. Many prominent leaders of the Georgian Republic began moving in the same direction. And the 'open' trial of Sinyavsky and Daniel begun in February 1966 had essentially the same aim. Despite numerous protests from public figures in the Soviet Union and abroad they were sentenced to seven and five years, respectively, in strict-regime corrective labour camps.

All these facts increased the disquiet among the intelligentsia. Numerous letters from old Bolsheviks, from many groups among the intelligentsia, even from individual workers and employees were sent in to the Central Committee, the Praesidium of the forthcoming Congress and to Brezhnev's office, protesting against what appeared to be Stalin's rehabilitation. A long letter from twenty-five very prominent Soviet intellectuals, well known in the Soviet Union and abroad, caused a special stir. These included academicians P.L. Kapitsa, L.A. Artsimovich, M.A. Leontovich, A.D.

11

Sakharov, I. E. Tamm, I. M. Maisky; the well-known writers
V. P. Kataev, V. P. Nekrassov, K. G. Paustovsky, K. I.
Chukovsky, V. F. Tendryakov; artistic figures like M. M.
Plisetskaya, O. N. Efremov, P. D. Korin, V. M. Nemensky,
Yu. I. Pimenov, M. I. Romm, I. M. Smoktunovsky, G. A.
Tovstonogov and several others. In a few days these twenty-
five signatories were joined by academicians A. Kolmogorov,
A. Alikhanov, M. Knunyants, B. Astaurov, P. Zradovsky, the
writers I. Erenburg, V. Dudintsev, the artistic figures G.
Chukhrai, V. Muradeli, I. Il'insky and several others. By the
time of the Congress this letter achieved the widest circulation in the whole country. I recall that I myself prepared no
less than one hundred typewritten copies of this letter for the
benefit of friends and acquaintances.

This campaign must have had some effect. In any case,
Stalin's name did not appear once in any of the reports or
speeches at the Twenty-third Congress. The Congress Resolution upheld the line of the Twentieth and Twenty-second
Congresses, but in such general terms as to give room for
manoeuvre both for those who insisted on taking further the
criticism of the Stalin cult and those who wanted his political
rehabilitation. It is not surprising, therefore, that a sharp, but
in most cases not overt, struggle over the question of Stalin
continued after the Twenty-third Congress. We shall mention
just a few episodes.

In February 1966, for example, a discussion took place at
the Institute of Marxism-Leninism on A. M. Nekrich's book
22nd June, 1941. The discussion took a different turn from
what its organisers wanted. Many old Bolsheviks, historians,
members of the General Staff, former diplomats (A. V.
Snegov, L. P. Petrovsky, E. A. Gnedin, Anfilov and others)
came out strongly in support of Nekrich's book and attacked
Stalin. A short recording of the session was widely circulated
in copies and soon published abroad. Nekrich's opponents
were afraid to criticise the book at the session itself. But they
used their connections inside the Central Committee to bring
about the Nekrich 'affair', which occurred soon after. Despite
the absurdity of the accusations brought against him, Nekrich
was expelled from the Party and his book taken out of the
libraries.

The Stalin question occupied the centre of attention at another conference, which took place soon after the Twenty-third Party Congress. We refer to the discussion of the Third Volume of the *History of the CPSU* by the editorial committee responsible for the Volume together with old Bolsheviks who had participated in the October Revolution and the Civil War. Some of the old Bolsheviks (A. V. Snegov, D. U. Zorin, A. M. Durmashkin) took the opportunity to condemn in strong terms both the crimes of Stalin and attempts to rehabilitate him.

Open Stalinists did not remain silent. The Secretary of the Central Committee of the Georgian Communist Party, D. G. Stura, declared provocatively at an ideological conference in Moscow in October 1966 that not only did he consider himself a Stalinist, but that he was proud of it, for it was under Stalin's leadership that the Soviet people had built Socialism and won victory in the Patriotic War. Stura's words were met with applause from the majority of those present – the attitude of ideological workers in the 'middle echelons' was quite different from that of the old Bolsheviks. In November-December 1966 Moscow television celebrated the twenty-fifth anniversary of the battle of Moscow by showing war newsreels for the first time in five years, including a speech by Stalin. And at the same time *Novy Mir* was forbidden to publish Konstantin Simonov's wartime diaries relating to the early period of the war. 80,000 copies of the journal, already passed by the censor, were destroyed. A small article by Simonov 'Lessons from History and the Writer's Conscience' was removed from the journal *Problems of History*. Simonov had demonstrated Stalin's culpability for the heavy defeats of the early period of the war, including the tragic catastrophe which overtook the Red Army in the summer of 1942 on the Kerch peninsula.

1967 was, as we know, Jubilee Year. At the end of the year we celebrated the fiftieth anniversary of the October Revolution. Central Committee theses for the anniversary, published right at the beginning of the year, mentioned neither Stalin nor Krushchev. And there was not one official document concerned with the Jubilee which did not carefully skirt round any difficult question in our history. This did not, however, stop the battle of ideas going on in and out of print. Among the many Stalinist sallies we may name the various publications in the journal *October,* which continued to express the attitudes and views of the most reactionary circles in our society (V. Zakrutin's novel *The Creation of the World,* V. Kochetov's *Angle of Fall,* K. Voroshilov's *Tales about Life* and others). The journal *Moskva* made its contribution to this campaign, publishing S.V. Smirnov's long poem 'I Testify Myself', full of obsequy to Stalin – 'man of rock', 'captain', 'thunderer', 'father of the people'. *Novy Mir* took up the contrary position, leaving scarcely a single Stalinist publication without a convincing answer. But even more documentation and literary production, containing criticism of Stalin and the crimes of the Stalin epoch, circulated through *samizdat.* 1966-7 was the period of the real flowering of *samizdat.* In Moscow alone hundreds, perhaps thousands, of people were engaged in copying and circulating various kinds of material. It was at this time that the texts of Solzhenitsyn's novels *Cancer Ward* and *The First Circle* received wide circulation through typescript copies, and likewise some of his stories and recorded speeches in various scientific institutes in Moscow. And Solzhenitsyn's famous letter to the Fourth Congress of Soviet Writers became a major event, having an immediate impact both in our country and abroad. A crop of diverse documents appeared in *samizdat* in connection with the 'Nekrich affair'. The most important was General Grigorenko's letter to the journal *Problems of the History of the CPSU.* Well informed on the subject, Grigorenko showed in this letter what really went on at the Soviet-German front during the first months of the war and who should take the responsibility for it. Many camp memoirs circulated amongst the intelligentsia (S.O. Gazaryan's *This Must Not Happen Again,* E.S. Ginsburg's *Into the Whirlwind,* M.D. Baikal'sky's *Notebooks for Grandchildren,* E. Olitskaya's *Memories,* V. Shalamov's *Kolymsk Tales* and several others).

The Stalinist attack 1968-9

1968 was in many ways a crisis year. From the very beginning of the year everybody's attention was drawn to the events in Czechoslovakia, where Novotny had been removed from the Secretaryship of the Communist Party and a new leadership elected, headed by Dubcek, and where a stormy process of democratisation was under way demanding socialism 'with a human face'. The further the process went and the more successful it was, the more the Politburo of the Central Committee of the Soviet Communist Party began to show acute signs of nervousness and the more the most reactionary elements in the Soviet leadership began to busy themselves. The new year began in the USSR, as we know, with the trial of A. Ginzburg, Y. Galanskov, V. Lashkovaya and A. Dobrovol'sky. This trial aroused many collective protests, several obtaining tens and hundreds of signatures. This demonstration of public initiative caught the Soviet 'authorities' by surprise, causing not only displeasure but a reinforcement of Party and administrative repression and, in some cases, fresh legal charges against 'heterodox thinkers' and 'professional signatories'. In the summer of 1968 the *Literary Gazette* began an open public campaign against Solzhenitsyn. Simultaneously, various attempts continued to rehabilitate Stalin (publication of F. Chuev's poetry, the second part of Admiral N.G. Kuznetsov's memoirs, K.A. Meretskov's book *Serving the People* and *Studies in the History of the CPSU* under the general editorship of S.P. Trapeznikov and other material). The state prize was given to V. Firsov for her poem, 'The Republic of Immortality', which contained lines like:

> The war, it seemed, gave no hope. But Stalin dictated freedom. Even Churchill, inveterate foe of the Land of Soviets, recognised this and stood up in salutation ... He is no longer, whom once the country trusted boundlessly. The Motherland needs *unconditional trust* today. Do not trust the abstract humanists. When the people suffer, take revenge. Go. You see, the Communists have taken two steps ahead. Follow them. *Our case is higher than any rightness.* And let who likes say afterwards that you have been inflexible!

The entry of Soviet troops into Czechoslovakia was an undoubted victory for the reactionary section of the Soviet leadership, although it was unable to achieve all the results it had counted on. The democratic movement in Czechoslovakia was not crushed immediately: the process dragged on until the spring of 1969. Nor in the USSR did the Stalinists succeed in all the aims they set themselves. While many people, subjected to one or another form of repression, preferred to go silent and withdraw, many new names filled the ranks of active fighters against Stalinism. The most notable and important of them was, of course, that of Academician Sakharov, one of the inventors of the Soviet hydrogen bomb, who in June 1968 issued his essay *Thoughts about Progress, Peaceful Coexistence and Intellectual Freedom,* which immediately achieved wide publicity.

1969 was the year of open Stalinist attack on the ideological front. At the outset of the year the question of the ninetieth anniversary of Stalin's birth was put by the policy-making bodies. Although this Jubilee did not arrive until the end of the year, preparation began much earlier. The new tear-off calendar for 1969, printed in ten million copies, not only recorded 21 December as the ninetieth anniversary of Stalin's birth, but provided (on the reverse side) a short article about Stalin, which gave prominence to his 'services' in the struggle for socialism and only very vaguely referred to the 'cult of Stalin's personality, alien to Marxism-Leninism'. At the commencement of 1969 a decision was taken, apparently at Secretariat level of the Party Central Committee, about certain measures in connection with Stalin's ninetieth anniversary. The decision was not published, but was no secret for members of the Party ideological apparatus. One of the ideas, for example, was to put up a monument on Stalin's grave and to call a meeting of Moscow workers and war veterans for the unveiling. The Institute of Marxism-Leninism planned a special session for December, devoted to Stalin's memory. It was also decided to prepare a long editorial article for *Pravda.* One Moscow print-shop received an order for a large number of portraits of Stalin, and some art studios began work on Stalin busts. The portraits and busts were designated for sale in the second half of December. A big gala meeting was also planned in Georgia. Back in 1966-7 the Marxism-Leninism Institute had prepared an edition of 'Selected Works' of Stalin for publication. But publication had been postponed because neither S. Murashev nor S. Trapeznikov had been able to include these works in school and college programmes. It was hoped to bring out the edition in 1969. The idea of setting up a memorial museum in one of Stalin's Moscow *dachas* was also raised. An integral part of the plan was the carrying-through of certain organisational and repressive measures. So, for example, in the spring of 1969 it had already been decided to disband the editorial committee of *Novy Mir* and dismiss Tvardovsky as editor-in-chief. In the summer the tendentious campaign against *Novy Mir* and Tvardovsky was stepped up to fulfil the decision, both verbally and in the press (especially in the journal *Ogonyok*). The decision was also taken in advance to expel Solzhenitsyn from the Union of Writers. Even stricter measures were decided on for certain well-known opponents and critics of Stalinism. In 1968 P. Litvinov, L. Bogoraz and several of their friends had been arrested for protesting publicly against the intervention in Czechoslovakia. Now it was decided to arrest P. G. Grigorenko, and this happened in May 1969. I learnt later that it had also been decided in 1969 to put both my brother Zhores Medvedev and myself into some sort of 'isolation'. But this decision was not entirely successful. The planned rehabilitation of Stalin began very cautiously, but by the spring of 1969 it was well under way. In February the journal *Kommunist* included a long review of memoirs by various generals and marshals published in 1967-8. The principal aim of the review was to use a policy-making journal to stress Stalin's 'wartime services' as Supreme Commander, and to disavow Krushchev's declarations at the Twenty-third Party Congress. *Kommunist* No. 3 for 1969 contained a long article entitled 'For Leninist Partisanship in Interpreting the History of the USSR' written by various hands, one of whom was also a leading member of the Central Committee's Agitation and Propaganda Section (I. Chikvishvili) and another Brezhnev's adviser on questions of ideology and culture (V. Golikov). In the Party press this article was the most open attempt to revise the line of the Twentieth and Twenty-second Party Congresses. It called forth considerable protest which was confined, however, to *samizdat*. The publication of this article proved that the plan for Stalin's rehabilitation was now being realised. This circumstance made me change my former position in those months. Earlier I had avoided making public statements and turned down all such proposals. But in March 1969 I sent a long Open Letter to *Kommunist*. The letter was also sent to all members of the Politburo, and at the same time I gave permission for it to be published in France as a pamphlet under the title *Is It Possible to Rehabilitate Stalin?*, which appeared in September 1969. If earlier I had refrained from letting my large manuscript *History Will Judge* pass even into the free circuit of *samizdat* and allowed only a few friends to read it, in April 1969 I let a copy go abroad and in October my friend Zhores David Zhuravsky had concluded an agreement with the New York firm Knopf to translate and publish the book.

In September 1969 the journal *October* began publication of the most scandalous novel of its chief editor, V. Kochetov, *What Is It You Want?* Lacking in artistic talent, this novel not only constituted a special manifestation by the Stalinists, but contained the fullest expression of the programme of neo-Stalinist reaction. Kochetov's novel included not only a call for the complete rehabilitation of Stalin, but also for the restoration of all the arrangements that existed in the country and in the Party in the Stalin years. The author attacked openly all the changes that had occurred in our life in the post-Stalin epoch

It is fair to point out that the Stalinist attack found support not only among the notorious 'middle echelons of government'. Attempts to rehabilitate Stalin met with support among a considerable section of workers and employees. Irritated by the growing difficulties of everyday life and the increasing power of local bureaucrats, many ordinary people began to idealise the Stalin epoch, just as in the twenties many petty bourgeois idealised the Tzarist times. In the summer or autumn of 1969 Moscow cinemas began to show the first part of the film *Liberation*, a colourful, agitational spectacular produced with the assistance of the writer Yu. Bondarev. At the first appearance of Stalin on the screen the dark interiors would almost unfailingly flash out their applause.

And the audience did not consist of Central Committee officials or distinguished military leaders. Such reactions on the part of wide sections of 'ordinary' people cannot be explained just by the strength of the 'cult' driven into them in the thirties and forties. They constituted a special kind of opposition to the present day, unconsciously taking the form of nostalgia for the recent past. I have a number of letters in my archive from ordinary workers, relating to the 1969-70 period. One of them, in particular, says:

Greetings from the Far East! I received your letter for which I heartily thank you ... Let's meet again. So much time has passed, so much water flowed under the bridge, so many changes have occurred both in our own lives and in the rest of the country. The last time we met there was forest where I am living, not one house, no town, no workers' settlements. Now there is a town with an industrial centre, there's a glass factory, a factory for making reinforced concrete, docks, a bread factory and many small workshops, not to mention cultural institutions. There are coal deposits in the town which feed not only local factories, but the entire Far East. Trains pass by our house day and night loaded with coal. The town is building its own shoe factory to produce 1.5 million pairs of shoes a year. There's too much to write about. Why not come and we can talk ... As I wrote, our food isn't up to much, you rarely get any meat, sausages, etc., in the shops. We live in a fishing region, but never see any fish, not even plaice, only herring – and that's not always very good. Our lousy government keeps on feeding its friends, but gives its own people just anything. They raise prices on the quiet and they've cut wages; try and make a living, especially if you've got a large family! I know how the Russian Ivan gets by. Be patient and fight for somebody. *But they haven't got Stalin now.* Sometimes you think the plans are being over-fulfilled everywhere and there's nothing to show for it ...

Another of my correspondents, also an ordinary worker, wrote to me about conversations with fellow workers during

breaks: 'Unfortunately, people still think that life was easier
for working people under Stalin. Prices went down and there
were products in plenty. And repression was almost only for
the higher-ups. And the people weren't exactly enamoured of
them ... '

By the middle of December 1969 the question of Stalin's
Jubilee was almost practically decided. A long article entitled
The Ninetieth Anniversary of Stalin's Birth had been prepared
and approved. This article, which carried a portrait of Stalin
and took up two sides of *Pravda,* was already set up and copies
of it not only lay in the safe of the chief editor of *Pravda,* but
had been distributed to the central newspapers of all the
Union Republics and translated into the local languages.
And it had been sent to the chief Party newspapers of the
socialist countries. 21 December was the date planned for the
appearance of the article in *Pravda* and the following day for
other newspapers. However, the question of Stalin was
discussed not only by the Central Committee of the Soviet
Party, but by the leading organs of other Communist Parties.
The Polish and Hungarian Central Committees came out
decisively against the publication of the article. I learned in
December 1969 that Gomulka and Kadar had gone straight
to Moscow on unofficial visits to try and prevent the Soviet
Central Committee from rehabilitating Stalin. They warned
that in the event of publication their Parties would be
compelled to dissociate themselves from this mistaken step.
No one doubted that this too would be the position of the
Yugoslav Party and of a number of Western Communist
Parties. This was too serious. If in 1956 the denunciation of
Stalin took the international Communist movement by
surprise and was to some extent the starting-point of the
ideological conflict with Stalin, in 1969 even the partial
rehabilitation of Stalin could start a conflict with many
Western Communist Parties and some Parties in Eastern
Europe. And although the more zealous Stalinists appealed
against 'being led by the Western Parties', the threat of a new
split made some of the Central Committee leaders think
again seriously. Only two to three days before the Jubilee the
question of Stalin was once more put up for discussion in the
Politburo. As I was later told by someone in the know, the

Politburo meeting was pretty stormy. Nevertheless, it was almost unanimously decided to cancel a large number of the proposed 'Jubilee' measures. The bust was set up on Stalin's grave without a meeting. The special session at the Marxism-Leninism Institute was cancelled as were the sessions in Georgia. It was decided not to publish the big article for *Pravda* and to make do with a small notice with no photograph and a completely different content. The Republic capitals were immediately informed of the decision. Only D. Sturua, Secretary of the Central Committee of the Georgian Party, raised an objection. He forbade publication in Tiflis newspapers of the new article on Stalin. The Soviet Central Committee removed him instantly from his post and later appointed him Director of the Georgian branch of the Institute of Marxism-Leninism. The capitals of the socialist countries were informed of the new decision by telephone. However, the operator at the Central Committee must have forgotten to ring Ulan-Bator. In any case Mongolian time is seven to eight hours ahead of Moscow time. So the big article on Stalin together with the portrait appeared in the newspaper *Unen* in Mongolian.

But the article was not in *Pravda,* which published a small notice headed 'Ninetieth Anniversary of Stalin's Birth' in which the main emphasis was given to 'the mistakes and distortions arising out of the cult of personality', and not to Stalin's services at all. Whatever its shortcomings this notice at least formally upheld the line of the Twentieth and Twenty-second Party Congresses. Tvardovsky cut this notice out of the paper and ordered a special glass frame for it. Like the most expensive photograph, this framed article from *Pravda* stood on Tvardovsky's desk almost to his last day at *Novy Mir.* The decision to disband the editorial staff of our best journal remained in force and was simply postponed for several months.

The question of Stalin 1970-75. Will the centenary
of Stalin's birth be celebrated in our country?

For all those who tried hard to rehabilitate Stalin, the events of December 1969 constituted a major defeat from which they were unable to recover later. Of course, attempts to rehabilitate Stalin continued to appear in print after 1969. One may recall I. Shevtsov's novels *In the Name of the Father and the Son* and *Love and Hate,* published in 1970. However, these pro-Stalin and anti-Semitic novels were met not only with negative reviews, but even with *feuilletons,* although the newspaper *Soviet Russia* tried to support them. Nor did anyone pay serious attention to V. Mdzhavanadze's article in the second number of *Kommunist* for 1970 where, among the 'courageous leaders of the Bolsheviks in Transcaucasia', whose 'names were close and dear to millions of people of different nationalities' and whose deeds 'serve as an inspiring example to new generations', he included Stalin. *October* likewise continued its previous line. It suffices to mention I. Stadnyuk's novel *War,* which appeared in its pages. S.P. Trapeznikov continued his line, retaining his post after 1969. In 1971 he published his book *At the Sharp Turning-points of History,* which is striking not only for its ignorance of politics and history, but also of elementary Russian style. This uniquely illiterate publication became the object of a series of satirical *feuilletons,* circulated by *samizdat.* Praise for Stalin may also be found in the memoirs of some military commanders, for example in S. Shtemenko's second book on the work of the General Staff during the war. However, these were essentially rearguard actions which attracted little attention either in the Soviet Union or abroad. Quite the opposite: the years 1970-75 saw the publication of many books abroad, large and small, which until then had only circulated through *samizdat* – novels, memoirs, scholarly and artistic studies, which taken together struck at the 'cult' and myth of Stalin as forcefully as Krushchev's famous secret report at the Twentieth Congress. The flow of exposures of Stalin's crimes grew so wide that for the overwhelming majority of Western Communists any rehabilitation of Stalin was now out of the question. And in the USSR the question of Stalin was in practice taken off the agenda. After December 1969 this question was not once discussed, neither in the Politburo nor in the Secretariat of the Central Committee. Nor was the question raised either at the Twenty-fourth or

the recent Twenty-fifth Party Congress. So one may say with
confidence that in 1979 there will be no official celebration of
the centenary of Stalin's birth. But the decision not to
rehabilitate Stalin is by no means the same as the re-
establishment of historical truth. Soviet history is simply
silent about Stalin, Krushchev and many other historical
figures, starting with Molotov or Kaganovich and ending
with Trotsky or Bukharin. Many pages of our history
textbooks have acquired a strange shade of anonymity,
mentioning congresses, decisions and successes, but no, or
scarcely any names. However, historical science cannot exist
or develop by silence. This 'figure of silence' is the main
obstacle before the development of all our social sciences. It is
impossible to go on like that for long.

The twenty years that have elapsed since the Twentieth
Congress clearly show that the Congress and all the questions
associated with it retain their actuality. The danger of an
open and direct rehabilitation of Stalin in the present time
has in effect disappeared and in recent years not even the
Chinese Communist Party has called for his rehabilitation.
But the other danger retains its force – the danger of the
restoration and recrudescence of Stalinism under whatever
name. Many elements of the system of pseudo-socialism
created by Stalin continue to exist even after the Twentieth
and Twenty-second Party Congresses and have not disappeared in the seventies; in some respects they have perfected
themselves. Therefore, the struggle against Stalinism and
neo-Stalinism in all its forms and manifestations, open and
hidden, remains one of the most important problems of the
world Communist movement.

Problems of Democracy
East and West

ROY MEDVEDEV

The chief lack of Soviet society

A. D. Sakharov is wrong to make the absence of free emigration the major fault of our public life. The main problem of the socialist countries is the guarantee to their citizens of freedom of speech and press, freedom of scientific and artistic work. It is the total restriction of freedom of speech and press which stops the Soviet Union from overcoming all its other shortcomings. For the first condition of solving any social problem is the right to study and judge it freely.

The restrictions put on freedom of speech and press inflict irreparable damage not only on the whole of society, but on the development of each separate individual. For the all-round development of the individual has been the main demand of socialism. The provision of material requirements has never been regarded by Marxism as an end-in-itself, but as the most important premise for the spiritual development of man. Lenin criticised the draft programme of the RSDWP (Russian Social-Democratic Workers' Party) at the beginning of the century for limiting socialism to the satisfaction of the material needs of society and its individual members. This, Lenin pointed out, the trusts were capable of doing. The Party programme, therefore, should not only talk about welfare, but about 'the free, all-round development of all members of society' (*Complete Works,* vol. 6, p. 232). Lenin's formulation, which he took from the *Communist Manifesto,* was

24

put into the RSDWP's programme at its First Congress. 'The point of our socialist labour', wrote A. V. Lunacharsky after October, 'lies in the construction of the kind of life which would make it possible for all the potentialities hidden in a person to unfold, which would make a person ten times wiser, happier and richer than at present' (A. Lunacharsky, *Articles on Soviet Literature*, Moscow, 1958, p. 185).

But it is obvious that without freedom of speech and the press, without the freedom of creation, without the struggle of opinions the all-round development of the individual remains a pious hope.

Karl Kautsky on the freedom of spiritual life under socialism

During 1917-18 the Bolsheviks brought out a number of editions of a little book by Karl Kautsky entitled *The Day After the Social Revolution* and written in 1902, when Kautsky was the acknowledged leader and theoretician not only of German social democracy, but of the entire First International. Kautsky at the time firmly supported the dictatorship of the proletariat, the socialisation of all the main means of production, the centralisation and planning of the economy. But he also wrote in his book:

> Doesn't the state centralisation of so wide and important a section of spiritual life threaten the worst consequences, i.e., monotony and stagnation? State power may cease to be the organ of one class, but it will remain the organ of the majority. And can one let spiritual life depend on the decision of the majority? Hasn't any new truth, any new outlook or artistic feeling always begun as the property of an insignificant minority fighting with tradition? Won't the new order contain the danger that the best and boldest fighters for the spiritual development of society will come into constant conflict with the proletarian regime?

Kautsky was sure this would not happen. According to him the various institutions responsible for intellectual work under socialism would depend not only on the state, but on local communes, which would prevent the regimentation of spiritual life. In addition, those engaged in intellectual labour could create free associations, independent of the state and having the right freely to put on theatrical productions, to publish newspapers and literary works, to organise scientific expeditions. 'In this sphere, therefore,' Kautsky declared, 'the proletarian regime leads not to the increase of constraint, but to the extension of freedom.' In his opinion the anarchist ideal, while reactionary in the sphere of material production, is progressive in the sphere of intellectual, spiritual production. 'Communism in material production, anarchism in intellectual,' pronounced Kautsky, 'that is the type of social production to which the proletarian leads by the force of logic of economic facts' (Karl Kautsky, *The Day After the Social Revolution*, Prague, 1918, pp. 50-1, 53).

The main wealth of society

Socialists in the past often remarked that the wealth of society at any given moment depended more on the level of knowledge and culture, on the character and quantity of spiritual values, than on the amount of things destined for material consumption. The same point is repeated today. For example, to the question why it is that the standard of living of large sections of the population in the West is considerably higher than in the USSR one lecturer on the staff of the Central Committee pointed out with irritation: 'Don't concentrate on the material benefits which the Soviet system gives its workers. The main thing is that it provides for the inner, spiritual development of the individual.' It is a fact, however, that the spiritual fare provided for Soviet people today remains a carefully selected and pre-digested diet. This fact contains many dangers for the development and vitality of society. In his book *Neither Marx nor Christ*, though some of the principal theses are questionable, Jean-François Revel has many right things to say. He writes:

An oligarchic society is doomed to perish because statistically four or five people will have fewer new ideas

26

than one hundred million. When a citizen is unable to criticise a useless political or economic regime without the risk of imprisonment, then the whole of society is endangered, and not only because one of its members has become the object of 'intolerable violation of human rights', but because a practical, useful alternative may have been lost forever.

[Paris, 1972, p. 122.]

Various writers on the use of free discussion,
tolerance and intolerance

The English nineteenth-century philosopher and sociologist, John Stuart Mill, wrote in 1859 in his book *On Freedom:*

I deny that a people has the right to exercise authority over the freedom of speech, either of its own accord or through its government, for such an authority is illegitimate. The best government has as little right to impose such a violation as a bad one. Such restriction of the freedom of speech is baneful even when applied with the general agreement of public opinion. It is even more baneful, when applied by a government in the face of public opinion.

Princess Zinaida Shakhovskaya, editor of *Russian Thought*, an *emigré* journal much reviled in the Soviet Union wrote:

Even a worthless person may have a useful thought, and the most honest say something stupid. Even wise people can lose their sanity ... Truth does not belong to anybody, only God possesses it completely, and all we have on earth are its grains. It is impermissible pride to consider oneself not the servant of truth, but its indisputable mouthpiece. The world does not consist of black and white, but of all colours and all shades ... Each person in accordance with his intelligence, temperament, knowledge, intuition and, above all, his conscience makes judgements about morality and politics. Even intolerance, which is so coarsely

27

expressed in the contemporary world, where a bomb often takes the place of argument, should encourage us to learn tolerance.'

[Russian Thought, 8 August 1974.]

And here is I. Pomelov writing on the same subject in the journal *Kommunist:*

> Sometimes certain foreign spokesmen ask: why do Soviet Communists show 'ideological intolerance' and prevent the spread of views and theories that run counter to Marxism-Leninism? Surely they don't fear that such ideas will weaken the mighty Soviet state. Of course, it's not a question of fear. Our Party takes a responsible approach and considers in a fully reasoned way that bourgeois and revisionist ideas are harmful to the interests and attitudes of the workers. To permit the spread of such ideas would not only be to insult Soviet people, but to openly allow our enemies to undermine the efforts of the Communist Party to educate the workers in a communist way.

[1972, No. 12, p. 27.]

The real insult, however, is the attempt by such 'ideologists' to rob us all of our freedom of choice and appraisal. And what kind of Communist education is it that does not encourage one to look at different theoretical and political positions independently and to be able to defend one's own views? The real disrespect for the intelligence of the masses and the Party is shown by the Pomelovs and Trapeznikovs, who decide in advance on behalf of us all what is 'revisionism' and what 'true' Marxism. An ideology which exists in such artificial conditions comes inevitably to require a strict political censorship and direct coercion.

Freedom of information

The freedom of creative discussion naturally presupposes the freedom of information, which we do not have, even in the most elementary spheres. Here are only some typical examples.

In 1921 the RSFSR had a bad harvest and there was famine. All the newspapers talked about it. They also reported the purchase of grain abroad and of the free help given by the West. 1975 saw a recurrent bad harvest. Again we had to buy grain abroad, 20 or 30 million tons worth, for the third time in ten years. But did our press say anything about it, either in the form of an article or a report? Shouldn't a failure of this kind be reason for some serious analysis and discussion? Of course, there are very many causes hindering the development of Soviet agriculture. But one of the main ones is the impossibility of freely discussing all aspects and problems of our agricultural production.

*   *   *   *

In the early autumn of 1975, not far from Moscow, there was a bad railway accident. A goods train carrying sand collided with a suburban electric train packed with people. About a hundred people were killed, several hundreds injured and crippled. The railway track was damaged over a distance of several kilometres, supports were knocked down, cables torn away. The catastrophe was caused by negligence on the part of the railway services. Not long before the accident a new system of signals and communications had been set up on the line. Work had been completed on the Saturday. The trying-out of the new system was left until Monday. In the meantime one of the railway chiefs decided to use the previous system of automatic points, which had not been properly tested. Something went wrong in the previous system, both trains saw a green light and travelled towards each other at top speed. There was much talk in Moscow about the accident, it was common knowledge to hundreds of thousands of people. After preliminary investigations six engineers and employees of the railway were arrested. Army units soon restored the line, even planting new trees where the old ones had suffered as a result of the accident. But not a word about the disaster got into the press, either central or regional; nothing was said of the investigation or of the punishment of the offenders. And yet on the 14 September 1975 *Pravda* and some other Moscow newspapers found room to inform their readers that as a result of a collision between a passenger train and a heavy lorry at a railway crossing in Spain three people lost their lives and more than thirty received injuries.

What clearer example of our 'freedom of information'! One does not have to have to print terrible photographs of the scene of the disaster as in Western newspapers. But everyone using the railways should know who is responsible for what happened and what measures have been taken to prevent similar accidents. Our Government expresses condolences to families in the GDR and Yugoslavia, who have lost members in accidents. It appears that Soviet citizens can do without such public expressions of sympathy.

How on earth did that get through?

Our public is so used to the censorship and to the greyness of 'permitted' literature and art that when a good, honest book or a good, honest film or play appears, it not only gets talked and argued about, but people will almost always exclaim: 'How on earth did that get through?'

Vladimir Mayakovsky and freedom of creation

Sharing the prejudices of his time, Mayakovsky reacted negatively to the demand for freedom of creativity. 'I tamed myself, standing on the throat of my own song,' he declared in a poem looking back on his work. But he did not consider it sufficient for a writer or poet to make do with an 'inner censor'. In an outburst of self-denial he exclaimed: 'I want a commissar with a command to watch over the thought of the times ... I want a factory committee to put a lock on my mouth when I have finished my work.' There would be few today who would share such a perspective.

How interesting our paper could be!

'How interesting our paper could be', a leading contributor to the *Teacher's Newspaper* once said to me, 'if only we could print even a part of all these letters and articles!' And he showed me a large sheaf of papers, many already in print, but then held up by the censor, the chief editor or the Ministry of Education. The same thing happens in all other central and local newspapers: the most interesting and challenging reports and letters get stuck in the editorial archives.

Jean Kanapa is completely satisfied with freedom of speech in the Soviet Union

In a critical review of my book *Socialism and Democracy*, published in French in 1972, Jean Kanapa, Central Committee member of the French Communist Party, wrote in *L'Humanité:*

> Those who discourse on books of this kind exclaim: 'At last Soviet people are beginning to be critical. This hasn't happened before in the Soviet Union!' What a colossal deception! EVERY DAY the Soviet press responds to criticism in a multiplicity of ways. How many of us know that apart from this daily, one might call it mass, criticism the most widely read newspaper, *Pravda*, publishes a double page entitled 'Under the Control of the Masses', where workers, citizens and their organisations criticise deficiencies, shortcomings, mistakes in a concrete fashion, naming names? But this is of no interest to our 'Sovietologists', because it spoils their thesis about Soviet 'totalitarianism'. And especially because it is a question of CRITICISM, and our Sovietologists are not interested in criticism, but in slander.

> [*L'Humanité*, 24 November 1972.]

Jean Kanapa worked and lived in the USSR for almost ten

31

years as correspondent of *L'Humanité.* He knows very well how
the Soviet ideological kitchen functions. Therefore he is fully
aware of what he is doing in defending our press, he is
deliberately misleading his readers. The French Communist
Party has often declared that when it comes to power it will
guarantee complete freedom of the press in France. One may
well doubt this, if the frontiers of this freedom are determined
by people like Jean Kanapa.

Censorship of academic publications

The Academy of Sciences in Russia has always had its own
typography and bookshop and has always been able to
publish books and papers by its members and contributors, as
well as translations of important foreign publications. In a
country like Russia the question naturally arose: what to do
about the censorship of academic publications? In the
Regulations of the Academy of Sciences, ratified by Alexander I in 1803, Section 114 says:

> The Academy must have its own censor, drawn from its
> own ranks. His duty will consist in examining all manu-
> scripts submitted to the Governing Committee for publica-
> tion by the Academy; in ensuring that they do not contain
> anything contrary to the Government or the law. The
> salary for this special work should come from the economic
> budget.

The sole privilege in this case was that the academic censor
did not belong to the general system of censorship and, as
may be inferred from the *Regulations,* was responsible only to
the President and the Permanent Secretary of the Academy.

The new *Statutes of the St Petersburg Academy,* accepted and
passed by Nicholas I, extended many of the rights of the
Academy and removed the censorship from its publications.

Section 19 of the *Statutes* reads:

> Scholarly works, approved by the Academy for publica-
> tion, are not subject to censorship and merely require the

signature of the Permanent Secretary to confirm that they are being published with the Academy's approval.

The 1836 *Statutes* remained in force with minor changes until the October Revolution. After the Revolution, when the new Soviet censorship was introduced, the Russian Academy retained its right, at Lenin's suggestion, to publish its own works and collections without preliminary censorship.

Ten years later, in 1927, when the SNK finally passed the new 'Soviet' *Statutes of the USSR Academy of Sciences,* the Academy retained its right to do without the censorship.

Section 66 of the *Statutes* reads:

Publications and works printed by the Academy of Sciences, which have the signature of the Permanent Secretary of the Academy, are not subject to censorship.

And in the following Section 67 we read:

The USSR Academy of Sciences has the right to send all its publications abroad without censorship; similarly, all books and publications received by the USSR Academy of Sciences from abroad are free of censorship.

The special rights of the Academy of Sciences were retained in the 1935 *Statutes* (see Sections 53 and 54).

In 1937 the post of Permanent Secretary of the Academy was abolished and Section 53 was amended by decision of the SNK as follows:

Publications and works printed by the USSR Academy of Sciences, which have the signature of the President of the Academy, are not subject to censorship.

We believe that even then this privilege of the Academy was a pure fiction, and that all Academy publications passed through the censorship, i.e., the so-called *Glavlit.* In the subsequent revision of the Academy *Statutes,* however, it was decided to remove even this formal point. At least, in Section XI, 'Special Rights of the USSR Academy of Sciences', there is no point which permits the Academy to publish its works without censorship. We have in mind the *Statutes* passed in 1959. Only four years later, in 1963, new Statutes were agreed which are in force up to the present day. These *Statutes,* too, contain nothing about the Academy's right to publish its works and papers without censorship. (Cf. *Statutes of the USSR Academy of Sciences,* 1724-1974, Moscow, 1975, pp. 85, 96, 148, 197.)

The journal 'Annals'

The decision to free all Academy of Science publications from censorship was neither formal nor false in the 1920s. For example, in the first half of the twenties the Russian Academy of Sciences published a journal of general history entitled *Annals.* It was not a Marxist journal. It explained its credo in its first number in an article 'From the Editors', which said, among other things: 'The editors accept as obligatory a wide measure of tolerance towards all views and viewpoints put forward in the field of scholarship.' Like other publications of the Academy of Sciences, *Annals* was not subject to censorship. Reviewing the early issues of *Annals,* the Marxist philosophical journal *Under the Banner of Marxism* pointed out that its contributors 'are far from taking Marxist, and certainly not revolutionary, positions in the field of scholarship', but it did not demand the suppression of the journal. This journal, the review said, 'has united around it all the important forces of bourgeois historical science in Russia. Apart from E. Tarle, there is F.I. Uspensky, N. Kareyev, V. Buseskul, F.F. Zelinsky, N. Grevs, L. Savin, S. Zhebelev, S. Oldenburg and others. The fact that the journal has been able to gather together such important forces is sufficient to draw the attention of Russian Marxists to it' (1923, Nos. 8-9, p. 281).

So-called 'modernists'

For the first years after the Revolution different currents of modernism were dominant in our art. It was thought that these tendencies were the ones most suitable to expressing the moods of the revolutionary masses. Then everything changed. Today the canvases of the classics of world art, Kandinsky and Malevich, are kept in storerooms, seen neither at permanent nor temporary exhibitions. 'Modernist' artists and sculptors cannot join the Union of Artists. Their best work is bought up by foreigners. Yielding to international public opinion our Government allowed 'modernists' to hold unofficial exhibitions in various places, but then resorted to new pressures which they combined with permission to emigrate. Several scores of artists of different calibre have now left the USSR. At this moment a world-famous sculptor and artist, known for his monumental sculptures, an outstanding contemporary artist, is preparing to leave.

Two years ago the American industrialist and art-collector, Hammer, presented the Soviet Union with a painting by Goya costing 30,000 dollars (some art historians question whether the painting is by Goya, and this is reflected in the price). Furtseva, accepting the present, asked what Hammer would like in return. Requesting something of Malevich and Kandinsky, he soon received a Kandinsky and Malevich from the Ministry of Culture commanding a much higher price on the world market.

Choosing leaders for society

In the present one-Party system, where there is no opposition nor genuine freedom of speech or press, the choosing of cadres for all the echelons of the Party and state machine takes place according to many criteria, of which personal talent, knowledge, intellectual ability, high moral qualities and other human qualifications are less important than personal ties and personal devotion to one or another leading figure. The opinion of the workers in a region or district plays a much smaller role in determining a person's promotion than the opinion of the authorities. This is the main reason why the Soviet government includes so many more mediocre (in all respects) than able people. Many Soviet leaders resemble the driver of a heavy truck who can manage the steering-wheel and read the roadsigns, but has no idea how the motor works. Their reaction to events, therefore, is very often inadequate and corresponds little with the complex situations that arise. While the major problems of Soviet society are ignored, a huge amount of attention is paid to trivia. A bad driver, hearing a strange noise in his vehicle, will be unable to determine its cause or how dangerous it is. Maybe the noise is caused by a loose screw in the bodywork and is of no importance. But the driver stops his vehicle, gets agitated, calls up help and so wastes valuable time. At the same time, he may not notice that there is rust in the engine, that an important shaft is worn out, that some essential parts need changing. These defects may not be noticeable on the outside, they do not make a noise, but at the next turning-point they may unexpectedly lead to disaster. And with the number of vehicles on the road today even a steering-wheel requires more skill. Otherwise our heavy truck may find itself rampaging across an entire country, as happened in 1968.

Separation of Church and State

The Decree separating Church and State was composed by Lenin himself and belonged to a system of democratic changes. The Orthodox Church ceased to be a State church. Freedom to practise any or no religion was introduced into the RSFSR. School was also separated from Church and compulsory religious teaching ended. But the Decree also contained the following point: 'Citizens may study religion and receive religious instruction privately' *(Decree of Soviet Power,* 1959, vol. 1, p. 374). In practice, however, this right was subsequently abolished. If priests organise private groups to study religion, they risk legal harassment. All of which violates the elementary norms of a democratic society.

From history

At one of Lunacharsky's seminars the conversation turned to

Faddei Bulgarin, a journalist who lived under Nicholas I and was notorious as an informer and favourite of the *gendarmerie*. The critic, G. Lelevich, one of the editors of the journal *On Guard,* suddenly remarked: 'I should like to be a proletarian Bulgarin.' 'What do you mean? asked Lunacharsky. 'I should like to be as devoted to the cause of the proletariat as Bulgarin was to his class,' replied Lelevich. 'But Bulgarin was not devoted to his class,' answered Lunacharsky, 'he was devoted to the Third Section.'

Democracy and force

Before October 1917 Lenin said repeatedly that under socialism violence would disappear. 'In our ideal', he wrote, 'there is no place for violence' *(Complete Works,* vol. 30, p. 122). 'We are convinced', Lenin remarked several years later, 'that socialism will grow into communism and when this happens the necessity for force will disappear' *(Complete Works,* vol. 33, p. 83).

Thomas Jefferson was convinced that democracy had to support itself with the help of its citizens. 'God save us', he wrote, 'from spending twenty years without a revolt ... What country could defend its freedoms, if its rulers did not feel that the nation retained a spirit of resistance? Let this nation remember how to use its weapons ... What are several human lives in the scale of one or two centuries? The tree of freedom has to be sprinkled from time to time with the blood of patriots and tyrants.'

One-party system

In Libya in 1972 the Council of the Revolutionary Command of the LAR issued a decree banning all party-political activity outside the framework of the Arab Socialist Union, which was to be the only lawful political organisation. By party the decree understood 'any association or grouping, whatever its organisational forms or number of participants, who propagated a political ideology in opposition to the principles of the Libyan revolution'.

Infringement of the decree in any way would be punished by execution.

'Bourgeois' democracy

The concept 'bourgeois' democracy is very inexact. Of course, many of our democratic rights and freedoms were won by the 'third estate' from the aristocracy. But very many were wrested from the bourgeoisie by the working class. R. Hilferding wrote:

> Historically, democracy was always the affair of the proletariat. I have always been surprised by the assertion that democracy was the affair of the bourgeoisie. To maintain this means to ignore the real history of democracy and to come to know it in a thin, academic manner through a few theoretical books. In fact, there has been no fiercer political struggle than the struggle for democracy between proletariat and bourgeoisie. To disregard this struggle, not to see it as one of the major aspects of the proletarian class struggle, not to see that it is historically inaccurate to talk of 'bourgeois democracy' – means to deny the whole history of socialism, starting from the moment when Marx uttered his famous words that it was necessary to turn the working class into a political party. Democracy was *our* affair. We had to wrest it from the bourgeoisie in bitter struggle. Remember the fight for the vote. How much proletarian blood had to be shed for the right to an equal vote!

> [R. Hilferding, *Capitalism, Socialism and Social-Democracy*, pp. 137-8.]

The formula USSR

Article 13 of the Constitution of the USSR declares that our state is founded 'on the basis of *voluntary* association by Soviet Socialist Republics enjoying equal rights'. Article 17 of the

Constitution states: 'Each Union Republic has the right to leave the USSR.' Nevertheless, in books, pamphlets and articles on the national question we often come across phrases about the *'indissoluble* union' of socialist nations, about their *'inseparable unity'* and so on. The Address of the Central Committee of the Communist Party, the Council of Ministers and the Praesidium of the Supreme Soviet *To the Soviet People, To the Workers of All the Nationalities of the USSR* contains the following phrase: 'We are an *inseparable* Soviet people and there are no forces able to stop our triumphal march ahead' *(Kommunist,* 1973, No. 5, p. 1).

Lenin wrote before the October Revolution:

> To get rid of the national yoke one foundation is necessary – socialist production. But this foundation requires a democratic state ... By transforming capitalism into socialism, the proletariat makes it possible to do away entirely with national oppression; but this possibility only becomes a reality – only! – when democracy is carried fully into every sphere, including the complete freedom to secede. And on this basis, in turn, all national frictions, all national distrust can disappear, it will be easier for nations to get together and merge, which will happen once the state dies away. That is the theory of Marxism.
>
> [*Complete Works,* vol. 30, p. 22.]

National problems

21 May is the anniversary of the transfer of Shevchenko's ashes from St Petersburg to the Ukraine. For many years the Ukrainian public have observed this day by placing wreaths at Shevchenko's monument, by songs and dances. The Kiev authorities have for a long time tried to give these manifestations an official character. A stage was set up round the monument, entertainment brigades were brought in, concerts were organised. Nevertheless, amateur concerts and dances went on. In 1972 it was decided to put a stop to all 'amateur'

attempts to honour the poet's memory. On 21 May the Shevchenko Park was surrounded by militia and *druzhinniki* ('homeguards'). Almost everyone who wanted to get to the monument, who sang Ukrainian songs, who wore a Ukrainian national shirt or an insignia in honour of Shevchenko was stopped. Over fifty people were arrested in this manner and some put in jail for ten to fifteen days for 'resisting the authorities'. Obviously, such methods are not conducive to the disappearance of 'all national frictions, all national distrust'. 'National friction' has occurred in almost all the Union Republics in recent years, taking different forms in different areas. Latvia was the scene for particularly dramatic events in 1972, including *autos-da-fé* and public disorders; hundreds of people were picked up and arrested. Students and schoolchildren would regularly remain seated during the performance of the national anthem at sports events.

The well-known Tartar writer T. speaks of KAMAZ with hostility: 'Neither in this building nor on the Boats Embankment do you hear Tartar spoken.'

The well-known Russian poet F., carried away by criticism of China at the RSFSR Congress of Writers, exclaimed: 'Anyway I hate all those yellow faces and slant-eyes.' At which the delegation from Buryat-Mongolia left the hall and could only with difficulty be persuaded to remain for the rest of the Congress.

Anyone openly campaigning for the secession of his Republic from the USSR is very often convicted under Article 70 of the UK RSFSR (or analogous Articles in the Republic codes) for 'anti-Soviet agitation and propaganda', although this clearly violates the Constitution of the USSR. On the other hand, can a single person be found in our camps who has been sent there under Article 74?

Propaganda or agitation aimed at inciting racial or national enmity or discord, and similarly the direct or indirect restriction of rights or the procuring of advantages, direct or indirect, for citizens on the basis of their racial or national origin are punishable by deprivation of freedom for a period from six months to three years or exile for a period of two to five years.

Bureaucracy

F. Dzerzhinsky, criticising bureaucracy in many sectors of Soviet and Government machinery, remarked at the Twelfth Congress of the RKP(b):

> These machines are constructed according the principle of least initiative on the part of individual workers. They are so unwieldy that those in charge cannot control them, on the contrary they are subordinate to the machine. As a result, we have a horrendous bureaucracy and red tape, and this is common knowledge. In no Western European country will you find such mind-boggling bureaucracy. It was there under the Tzars, has been handed down to us and unfortunately not yet disappeared ... Our machinery has become an end-in-itself for those wishing to avoid jobs that involve physical labour ... Their main and fundamental concern is personal enrichment ... What we witness is the unbelievable pillage of the hard-won gains of the proletariat.

[Stenographic report of the Twelfth Congress of the RKP(b) Moscow 1972, pp. 760-1, 762.]

Don't have anything to do with fools

S.P. Trapeznikov, Chief of the Central Committee Department for Science, Schools and Institutes of Higher Learning, has for some time shown himself to be a dyed-in-the-wool reactionary and Stalinist. But he has also given many proofs of his elementary ignorance, not merely in the field of history and Marxism, but in the simple grammar and style of the Russian language. Most scholars who have had anything to do with Trapeznikov simply smile. Nevertheless, he has held his post as Chief of the Central Committee Department for Science, etc., for twelve years and is also a member of the

41

Central Committee. Even his failure to get elected to Corresponding Membership of the Academy of Sciences, after two successive votes, did not lead to his removal. Nor, it appears, is V. F. Shauro, Chief of the Culture Section of the Central Committee, a man of the highest qualities. When, for example, People's Artist R. complained to P. Demichev, Secretary of the Central Committee, about Shauro's extreme vulgarity and lack of tact (Shauro was directly responsible to Demichev), Demichev retorted angrily: 'Don't have anything to do with fools!'

Mikhail Agursky's new theory

An article appeared recently in the 5th issue of *Kontinent* entitled 'Liberalism and Radicalism as Manifestations of Social Activity by the Intelligentsia in Democratic Societies'. *Kontinent* is a literary, socio-political and religious journal founded two years ago by a group of well-known writers and publicists, *emigrés* from the USSR and Eastern Europe.

Agursky's article is primarily an examination of the social role of the Western intelligentsia. But it begins by criticising the incompetence and fantasising of the Bolsheviks after their accession to power in 1917. Agursky cites as a particularly glaring example of such incompetence the activity of Yu. Larin. Larin was a former Menshevik who joined the Bolsheviks in 1917. He was author of many books, especially on economics and national construction. In 1918 Larin headed the Commission for Legislative Proposals and took part in the preparation of many of the laws of the young Soviet regime. He testifies in his autobiography (published in the Encyclopaedic Dictionary *Granat*) how he personally formulated many laws relating to the most diverse areas of the economic life of the Russian Republic and that on publication they appeared mostly over his signature, although sometimes those of Lenin and other leading Bolsheviks were added with their permission. In the subsequent period of 'war communism' (until summer 1921) Larin's work embraced all the main domains of the economy, starting with finances and distribution and ending with agriculture, transport and external economic relations, not to mention industry and labour legislation. It was Larin who in the autumn of 1920 proposed the idea of a State Plan and was one of its organisers. With the coming of NEP, Larin participated in the formulation of many laws and projects, and worked in various commissions of the Central Committee, the Central Executive Committee, the SNK, the STO. But an incurable illness brought a halt to his tempestuous activity and he confined himself more and more to literary work. Shortly before his death in 1932, Larin headed the Society for Struggle against Alcoholism.

Mikhail Agursky makes no attempt to analyse Larin's laws and resolutions. Noting merely that Larin had only completed secondary school studies and listing the various spheres in which he worked after the October Revolution, Agursky exclaims: 'It is not surprising that such reformist zeal should meet with complete failure' (p. 161).

Such a dismissive evaluation of Yu. Larin's career is unjust. The activity of the economic and planning organs which he led was by no means mistaken and fruitless. Nor does it become Agursky to ridicule the fact that Yu. Larin should have initiated so many reforms and laws without a higher education.

Agursky does not have a 'humanities' education. Engineer by profession, Mikhail Agursky has in recent years turned to problems of history, economics, religion, sociology, literature and politics. True, Agursky does not, like Larin, publish laws and enforceable resolutions. He has, however, in the past years put together a host of theories, conceptions and projects with no less energy than Yu. Larin and with considerably less competence. Paradoxical in appearance, these theories are not particularly original, they merely assemble bits and pieces of other theories and conceptions in a fanciful manner. The way they are put together is not very difficult. Agursky, as a rule, applies his attention to just one side of reality, to one aspect – and often not the most essential – of a real process. This aspect is then absolutised and pronounced the principal side of reality, its universal law. It is according to this scheme that all the major positions of his article 'Contemporary Socio-Economic Systems and Their Perspectives' (collection *From Under the Rubble,* Paris-Moscow, 1974) are constructed, as it is with his article 'New Dimensions of Stalinism' *(Times Literary Supplement,* 30 June 1972). The same method is used in the article under discussion.

Which does not mean that everything Agursky argues should be dismissed as unscientific. You can always find at least one grain of truth in what he writes and he is able sometimes to catch reality from a quite unexpected side. At the same time, he is much too quick in his judgements and conclusions, unwilling to spend time on a full study of difficult phenomena and processes. If facts don't fit into Agursky's scheme, they are simply ignored.

Agursky's new theory is primarily an examination of the role of the intelligentsia in Western society. Where many Western ideologues (John Galbraith, for example) would see the intelligentsia as the main progressive section of the advanced industrial countries, M. Agursky considers it the most destructive element in society. 'The intelligentsia,' he writes, 'a social group primarily interested in the growth of consumption, is one of the major destructive forces in contemporary society. It would be more exact to say that it is the section constituting the social phenomenon of liberalism which is the destructive force' (p. 152). It is the liberalism of the intelligentsia, according to Agursky, which is undermining the moral foundations of Western society, its former sense of self-discipline and responsibility and, as a consequence, its parliamentary system. More significant, however, is the emergence of a radical intelligentsia from within the liberal intelligentsia, which is even more destructive. The liberals have neither the desire nor the capacity to fight the radicals, the two sections of the intelligentsia are inseparable from each other. The radical intelligentsia, born of liberalism, allies itself with all the discontents (industrial workers in the nineteenth century and beginning of twentieth, the youth and national minorities in the present) and seeks to destroy democracy by revolutionary means, to set up a totalitarian regime which will have no place for liberalism. However, every totalitarian society produces in time a new bureaucracy which destroys the radical intelligentsia, while retaining the totalitarian ideology to strengthen its regime.

Summarising his article, M. Agursky writes:

Liberalism and radicalism turn the intelligentsia, by virtue of the dialectical peculiarities of its position, into a serious opponent of real social justice, peace and democracy. The intelligentsia is one of the main forces destructive of present-day parliamentary systems. It has become a social stratum which professionally exploits the ills of the consumer society for its own ends and aggravates them. As historical experience shows, the liberal intelligentsia opens the way to the radical intelligentsia and destroys itself as the latter comes to power. In turn the radical intelligentsia is unable to retain power because of its incompetence and unrealistic, ideocratic approach to social and economic problems. It too is destroyed, this time by the bureaucracy which inherits the totalitarian regime installed by the radical intelligentsia.

[p. 170.]

Such is M. Agursky's schema. Obviously it contains some elements, which reflect individual aspects of reality. The radical intelligentsia does, wherever possible, try to use the democratic structures which have liberal support, it does cash in on the dissatisfaction of workers, peasants or youth with existing social conditions. It is also well-known that many radical social turn-abouts had led to a renascence of bureaucracy and to new forms of social injustice. However, these processes are not forever fixed. On the contrary, the less democracy there is, the fewer the democratic traditions in a given country, the less liberal influence there is, the more influential will the currents of radicalism be in such a country. The fact that the most radical wing of international social democracy should have acquired such strength, and then power, in Russia is connected in the first place not with Russian liberalism, but with the rule of the autocracy. Bolshevism developed in Russia through bitter struggle with liberalism and the less radical sections of the socialist intelligentsia. The 'purges' of 1936-8 were not at all the result of a struggle between the bureaucrats and the radicals, since most of the radicals had by the mid-thirties turned into bureaucrats. The purges had a much more complex character.

45

The so-called 'cultural revolution' in China had a different, but no less complex character: 'radicals' and 'revolutionaries' *versus* bureaucrats. In the 1918-23 period in Western Europe liberals and social-democrats took up a decidedly anti-Communist position and succeeded in ousting the Communists and crushing their initiative. Today, in such liberal countries as the German Federal Republic or England, left radicalism is much weaker than in Portugal, Spain or Italy. In Chile Salvador Allende was by no means the radical that M. Agursky has in mind. In many countries of Western Europe the programme of the Communist Parties resembles more the programme of the Social-Democrats in the twenties than that of the parties of the Communist International. Agursky not only ignores the extremely complex nature of the Western world, he consciously disregards the fact that the communist and socialist movement arose in the first place out of the protest of the masses against social injustice, against the restriction of democratic rights and the freedom of the popular masses. And should the victory of radical movements in one or another country lead to the recrudescence of social injustice in other forms, this gives no right to blame the revolutionaries and liberals of previous generations for their battle against injustice and arbitrary rule. Honest people in every generation must wage battle against the forces of evil, against the misdeeds both of individuals and of society as a whole. And each person should in the first instance fight the ills of his own society and only then the shortcomings and ills of other, more distant countries. How is one to understand, therefore, M. Agursky's indignation when he blames Western intellectuals for paying much more attention to arbitrariness and illegality in South Africa or Chile than in the GDR or the USSR? I won't mention Agursky's attempts to suggest to his Western readers that the regime in Chile is 'softer' than in the GDR or that the national minorities are treated more harshly in the USSR than in South Africa.

What, actually, does M. Agursky propose for the West? What is his positive programme? He does not come out into the open. From the odd phrase or hint in the article we may draw the conclusion that M. Agursky is as hostile to right radicalism as to left, i.e., he is against the various fascist and neo-fascist movements. He proposes, however, the transformation of Western societies 'by means of moral rearmament' on the basis of 'universally recognised moral values'. From his disquisitions about the 'high level of self-discipline of the population, based on the strict ethical character of Protestantism' which has receded into the past, about the evils of unlimited consumption, about the exaggerated influence of writers, philosophers and scholars on society – one may draw the conclusion that M. Agursky's ideal is a society in which religion and the church would play the dominant role and where democratic freedoms ('liberalism') would be restricted. Such a society would require a political and moral censorship 'reflecting the accepted values of society' (p. 148). And such a censorship would put an end not only to 'ideological capitalism' which feeds on the surplus from 'sexually oriented commodities' and the propaganda of 'sexual revolution'. It would restrict generally the influence of the intelligentsia in society and also the increasing autonomy and influence of the many information media which promote the ceaseless change in ideologies, styles, tastes and fashion. In Western society, according to Agursky, it is not only the wasteful consumption of material values that needs cutting down, so too does the production of creative work. 'In the conditions of a consumer society,' writes Agursky,

> a special form of capitalism emerges – *ideological* capitalism, which takes its profit from creative work, so making the latter a commodity. This form of capitalism cannot by its nature be conservative ... Ideological capitalism exerts a mass psychological effect upon the consumer, compelling him to follow all the demands of the mass information industry. The intelligentsia as the social basis of ideological capitalism appropriates his interests, in particular his constant interest in changing styles and, therefore, his extreme hostility to conservatism ... Ideological capitalism and the intelligentsia wish to clear from their path all obstacles blocking, or that might possibly block, the increase of cultural production. Such obstacles are in the first instance restrictions of a social, religious or moral

47

character ... which does not mean, of course, that ideological capitalism is not ready to satisfy any needs, religious ones included, but that in the long term considers it advisable to keep down the number of conservative consumers in order to encourage those who opt for the ever-changing ideological commodity. Ideological capitalism is the main base for political liberalism, differing sharply from industrial-mercantile capitalism which enjoys greater security under conservative regimes. One of the main aims of political liberalism is the abolition of censorship ... A censorship causes ideological capitalism serious material losses ...

Such a situation, according to Agursky, 'increasingly threatens democratic society with political collapse. It is pregnant with total catastrophe' (pp. 146-52). From all these arguments it is clear that M. Agursky's programme for the West is a conservative and autocratic society based on the rule of religion, in which material and spiritual consumption will be kept down to a 'necessary' minimum. It is quite clear, however, that such proposals will find as few followers, East or West, as Solzhenitsyn's similar suggestions contained in his *Letter to the Soviet Leaders* and in the collection *From Under the Rubble*.

Centralisation and decentralisation in the economy

National centralisation of the means of production and national planning have always been one of the programmatic demands of Marxism as distinct, say, from certain currents of anarchism and petty-bourgeois socialism. However, Marxists have never demanded total and complete nationalisation. In his book *The Day after the Social Revolution* (Prague, 1918) Karl Kautsky wrote:

There is nothing more erroneous than to imagine a socialist society as some kind of simple, crude mechanism whose wheels are set into motion once and for all and go on working with deadening monotony. In a socialist society all sorts of forms of ownership of the means of production can exist side by side: state, communal, cooperative (property of productive and consumer associations), private; the most diverse forms of enterprise: bureaucratic, trade-union, cooperative, personal; the most diverse forms of remuneration ... [p. 44.]

Kautsky's statements were shared by all Social-Democrats at the time, including the Bolsheviks.

Responsibility and rights of a Party member

Soon after Krushchev's removal a leader in *Pravda* remarked: 'The Party considers it its duty to ensure that everywhere, in all sectors of our society, the conditions are created which will foster the maximum development of a sense of responsibility on the part of each Communist for the state of the Party and the country, the spread of comradely criticism and self-criticism and a genuine implacability towards any violation of the Leninist norms of Party life.' (*Pravda*, 11 November 1964). The newspaper admits that such conditions did not obtain either during the period of 'subjectivism', i.e., under Krushchev, nor during 'the cult of personality', i.e., in Stalin's time. But neither have such conditions been created during the last ten to twelve years. S. P. Rashidov, First Secretary of the Central Committee of the Uzbekistan Communist Party, hazarded at the Twenty-second Congress of the CPSU: 'A marvellous situation has been created in the Party and the country and now prevails: an atmosphere of mutual trust, of mutual respect and support, of mutual expectation, comradeship, an atmosphere of Leninist principle. This beautiful atmosphere, this healthy political climate pervades every Party organisation ... ' (*Pravda*, 27 February 1976.)

But Rashidov's raptures are no more than empty political rhetoric.

Democracy and the majority

In their advocacy of democracy Marx and Engels paid most

attention to the fact that the bourgeois state trampled on the
will of the majority of workers, that the working class did not
have the rights it might expect as the largest class of workers
in society. For Marx socialism equals democracy, since the
workers would become the majority of the population and
have it in their hands to decide the affairs of society on the
basis of the will of the majority. Even under capitalism the
workers should fight for all democratic rights in order to
alleviate the subsequent transition to socialism. The position
changes when the revolution has been successful. Here the
main effort should go towards defending the rights of political
minorities and oppositions, because, if not, a new minority
will later on gradually usurp power in the name of the
majority.

L. B. Kamenev

(Reflections on his Personality and his Role in History)

M. P. YAKUBOVICH

Translated by Tamara Deutscher

I

My concern here is not with Kamenev, the Commander-in-Chief famous for his exploits in the Civil War, mentioned often in the works of Soviet historians not because I underestimate the services he rendered the Soviet government, but with the other Kamenev, Lev Borisovich, because his merits were incomparably greater. So was his role in history. He played this role not only in the history of the Soviet state but also in the pre-revolutionary Bolshevik Party. His merits were not only unjustly forgotten and denied, but his role was also maliciously distorted and falsified. The young generation either knows nothing about L. B. Kamenev or has a completely wrong idea of him.

Lev Borisovich Kamenev committed many political mistakes for which Lenin more than once criticised him sharply. These mistakes should not, of course, be passed over in silence. But neither should one concentrate on the mistakes alone. If Lenin's and the whole Party's positive evaluation of Kamenev's activities and his personality is suppressed, one cannot comprehend why Lenin had so consistently entrusted to him leading positions in Party and state. Why did Lenin, during his grave illness when the running of the government had to be passed on to other hands, choose precisely Kamenev? As Chairman of the Council of People's Commissars

and of the Council of Labour and Defence, Lenin had two
deputies: A. I. Rykov and A. D. Tsiurupa. Obviously he was
completely satisfied with the work of both. But when later
it became clear that illness would prevent him for quite a
time from exercising his leadership, he suggested that the
Central Committee should appoint Kamenev (not nominally but in fact) as the First Deputy. Thus Lenin placed
the reins of the government in Kamenev's hands. Rykov
and Tsiurupa became Kamenev's Deputies as they had
been Lenin's before. This choice was all the more meaningful, since Lenin also passed on the leadership of the Politburo to Kamenev and not to Stalin who assumed the post
of the General Secretary of the Central Committee of the
Party.

It is quite clear that among the leading cadres of the Party
Lenin saw nobody at that time more suitable than Kamenev
to replace him in practical work and to become the factual
head of the government. Was this not a clear and unambiguous proof of the high opinion Lenin had of him? One must
fully realise the whole weight of responsibility which Lenin
placed on Kamenev in that historic period, and also of the
grave responsibility he himself assumed when he recommend-
ed Kamenev for this post. To conceal these facts means not
only disrespect for Lenin's memory, but also falsification of
Lenin's political heritage.

But perhaps Lenin did not value highly Kamenev's
performance as his Deputy at the time of his illness? An
answer to this question can be found in his last public speech
at the enlarged session of the Moscow Soviet. Lenin made it
when his health had somewhat improved and when he could,
unfortunately not for long, resume his work at the Council of
People's Commissars. He spoke about Kamenev's activities
in highly positive terms. He called him a 'distinguished
little horse' who was able to pull two carts at once – that of
the Council of People's Commissars and of the Moscow
Soviet where he acted as Chairman. At the same time
Lenin expressed a wholly negative evaluation of Stalin,
recommending his removal from the post of the General
Secretary.

II

Historical justice towards Kamenev demands an objective evaluation of his merits as well as his weaknesses and blunders. He was undoubtedly a man of great talents; his education was wide and many-sided. He was deeply committed to the idea of socialist revolution; quick to understand a complicated political situation, possessed of uncommon literary gifts. Highly appreciating Kamenev's accomplishments, Lenin often entrusted to him the chairmanship of Party congresses and conferences. He had a special ability to *formulate* ideas, to sum up objectively the content of a discussion and its conclusions.

But together with these undisputed personal merits Kamenev's character and mentality showed certain shortcomings which prevented him from following the revolutionary road with persistence and unfailing steadfastness. For these Lenin attacked him mercilessly. If one sees in this a contradiction, then it is inherent in life, certainly in Kamenev's life and in his historic activity.

Kamenev had a thorough knowledge of the works of Marx and had absorbed his ideas fully, but he accepted them formally and interpreted them in a dogmatic manner. This explains his disagreements with Lenin which occurred in the decisive, critical hours of the revolution. Kamenev, like Kautsky, Plekhanov, and Martov, could not conceive that a socialist world revolution could begin in such a backward country as the Russia of 1917. He saw the idea of a possible transition from a bourgeois democratic to a socialist revolution as a deviation from orthodox Marxism, especially in Russia torn by war and with a numerically weak proletariat.

He propounded this point of view when he returned from exile to Petrograd after the February revolution. At that time his comrades shared his view, and he became the main ideologue and leader of the Bolshevik organisation. His formulation of the tasks of the revolution in progress was accepted by the great majority of party activists (among others by Stalin) not only in Petrograd but also in the rest of the country. Kamenev's ideas were not disputed until Lenin returned from abroad. In Kamenev's interpretation, the

Bolsheviks were a Left Social Democratic Party and remained social democrats in name as well as in spirit.

In the spring of 1917 none of the Russian Bolsheviks conceived of the necessity to break with this 'spirit' – to pass over to the ideology, strategy and tactics of the 'uninterrupted' revolution which would lead from general democratic aims to socialist ones. In this respect Kamenev represented the general mood of nearly all Party workers. He could not feel the pulse of the Russian proletariat and the army and did not detect the upsurge of their revolutionary consciousness. They could not remain satisfied with the perspective of a bourgeois revolution – they longed for further revolutionary developments. To perceive this the sensitivity of a genius like Lenin was needed. Kamenev was, of course, not a genius; he was not made to be the leader of a revolution.

Lenin understood this and, placing in Kamenev's hands the practical leadership of the Soviet government, could not, however, without reservations entrust to him alone the leadership of the Party. Lenin was looking for another man who could act as a kind of counterweight to Kamenev. This was why he agreed to the appointment of Stalin to the post of the General Secretary. At that time it seemed to Lenin that Stalin might provide the necessary corrective to Kamenev's state and Party activities.

Lenin soon discovered that Stalin was not fit for the role assigned to him. But Lenin's active life was drawing to a close and in the short time left to him he did not manage either to remove Stalin or to designate a substitute. In this consisted the tragedy of the Party. However, Lenin's disappointment with the behaviour of Stalin did not affect his attitude towards Kamenev, whom Lenin continued to consider to be one of the best possible leaders of the Soviet government.

Why did he continue to think so in spite of Kamenev's excessive 'orthodoxy' which was similar to that of Kautsky? How could Lenin disregard Kamenev's 'semi-Menshevism' and recommend him for the post of the head of the government? The reason for Lenin's decision can be found in this: he knew that Kamenev would obey Party orders with the sense of discipline particular to all Bolsheviks. In this respect Kamenev had none of that sectarian laxity which was characteristic not only of Russian Menshevism but of international social democracy. (Incidentally, in this sense, and not only in this, 'Menshevism' was undoubtedly just as much an international phenomenon as was 'Bolshevism'.)

III

To my mind there is no contradiction between this view of Kamenev and the fact, often recalled, that on the eve of the revolution he, together with Zinoviev, came out publicly in the semi-Menshevik paper *Novaya Zhizn* against the decision to pass over to armed uprising. One has to be well aware in what circumstances they came out with their statement. It was at the time of a very sharp political struggle inside the Party centre about the question on which the destiny of Party and revolution depended. The tension was unbearable. Nerves were near breaking point. The conclusion reached after the discussion in the home of the editor of *Novaya Zhizn*, Sukhanov (who however did not take part in the meeting) seemed to Kamenev, and to Zinoviev who joined him, catastrophic for the revolution. On the spot he wrote a letter to the editorial offices of *Novaya Zhizn* and handed it to Sukhanov. Still in the fever of the tense debate the two men did not fully realise the political meaning of their anti-Party statement. Lenin saw it as an anti-Party act. Furthermore, in the heat of the struggle, he qualified it as 'treachery' and demanded that the Central Committee should expel Kamenev and Zinoviev from the Party. The Central Committee desisted. Very soon afterwards Lenin recognised that the Central Committee was right and he himself withdrew his demand.

On the very first day of the proclamation of the Soviet Republic Lenin proposed no other than Kamenev as Chairman of the All-Russian Central Executive Committee of the Soviet of Workers' and Soldiers' Deputies, that is, of the highest organ of the revolution. (At the time he also proposed Zinoviev not Trotsky as head of the Petrograd Soviet.) Trotsky became a member of the Council of People's Commissars.[2] Would Lenin have come out with such a proposal if he had continued to regard Kamenev as 'traitor'?

What considerations made Lenin change his view? Both Kamenev and Zinoviev acknowledged that they had been wrong in coming out with their factional statement; they submitted to the decisions of the Central Committee and took their place side by side with the supporters of the armed rising regardless of their disagreement and private reservations. Lenin valued this 'practical Bolshevism' of Kamenev, abandoned his own harshness and considered it to be in the interest of the revolution to take advantage of Kamenev's abilities at the head of the Central Executive Committee. Lenin's opinion of Kamenev had not even changed when the latter decided to resign from his post at the time when some Commissars (Rykov, Nogin, Miliutin, Skvortsev, Stepanov, Teodorovich and others) were dismissed from their jobs. These were Bolsheviks who did not agree with the Central Committee's decision not to enter into negotiations with the Mensheviks about the setting up of a coalition government. Kamenev's resignation (he was replaced by Y.M. Sverdlov) was a consequence, of course, of his general attitude, of his doubts about the possibility and expedience of Russia's transition to socialism. Resigning as Chairman of the Central Executive Committee, Kamenev continued to take part in all Party work, and after the transfer of the government to Moscow, in the spring of 1918, he was, at Lenin's recommendation, appointed Chairman of the Moscow Soviet. It should also be recalled that during Lenin's lifetime Kamenev was also a member of the Politburo. It was precisely this experience of team work in the Politburo which apparently confirmed Lenin in his evaluation of Kamenev as one of his best collaborators and his most suitable deputy.

IV

Kamenev was neither ambitious nor greedy for power. In this respect he was the exact opposite of Stalin. Lack of ambition sometimes led him into passivity and an undue conciliatoriness, characteristics which in a number of cases turned out to be detrimental to the Party and state. This weakness of character was less noticeable while Lenin was alive. It was precisely his readiness to compromise that during Lenin's illness allowed Stalin to concentrate 'immense power' in his hands. Lenin took note, and with anxiety warned the Party Congress about this.

It would have been logical, after Lenin's death, to confirm Kamenev in his post as head of the Soviet government. However, Stalin, with Zinoviev's support, managed to persuade his colleagues to separate the post of the Chairman of the Council of People's Commissars from that of the Chairman of the Soviet of Labour and Defence, although under Lenin these posts constituted one single unit. The argument that it would be awkward in our 'muzhik' country to have a man of Jewish origin as head of the Sovnarkom, served as a pretext. Kamenev's father was a Jew and in his Tzarist passport his name was given as Rosenfeld. And yet for a number of years the Jew Sverdlov as Chairman of the All-Russian Executive Committee was formally the head of the Soviet Government! And even before Sverdlov, Kamenev was the first Chairman of the Executive Committee after October. It is quite possible that this consideration would not have swayed the majority of the Central Committee if Kamenev himself had not immediately agreed with it. Precisely because of his complete lack of ambition, he withdrew his candidature.

But the Central Committee did not go as far as removing him from leadership entirely. It was then that the harmful decision was taken to establish 'dual power' – to appoint Rykov as Chairman of the Sovnarkom and Kamenev as his Deputy and Chairman of the Council of Labour and Defence. The decision was all the more harmful because it allowed Rykov to engage in all sorts of intrigues against Kamenev which contributed to the confusion and disorganisation of the work of the central state apparatus; it also made Rykov Stalin's instrument in the struggle for total removal of Kamenev from political activity.

Here the lamentably compliant nature of Kamenev fully manifested itself. He did not oppose in good time Rykov's demand supported by Stalin, nor did he put the question openly before the Politburo. He allowed difficulties to mount until the point of crisis and then let the direction of state slip out of his hands. This mistake produced a situation which pushed him towards Zinoviev and then towards Trotsky and prepared his accession to the so-called 'united' opposition. Politically, Stalin prepared this *rapprochement* by supporting Bukharin and his follower Rykov. At that time both men opposed the policy of intensive industrialisation which, in their view, would endanger the 'harmony' ('smychka') between town and country. Neither Stalin nor anybody else thought then in terms of forced collectivisation. The road towards that large-scale industrialisation on which the country was to embark was not yet clearly charted. But Kamenev recognised that industrialisation constituted an important stage in the development of the USSR and that it could be accomplished only by the strength and resources of the Soviet people.

Bukharin and Rykov were the only two leaders who opposed this view. It would have seemed that Stalin, the future 'great industrialiser', would have given Kamenev his support. But Stalin was at that time motivated only by his struggle for personal power and supported Bukharin, or 'Bukharchik' as he was then affectionately called, 'the favourite of the Party' whom, as he said, 'we shall not allow to be insulted'. Such an alignment in the Party leadership pushed Kamenev towards Zinoviev and into the 'united' opposition; this, in turn became Kamenev's major political blunder. Kamenev's report to the Fourteenth Party Congress was suppressed. He was demoted to the position of a candidate member of the Politburo, removed from the post of the Chairman of the Soviet of Labour and Defence, and from that of Deputy Chairman of the Council of People's Commissars.

V

Here I would like to deal with the question of Kamenev's participation in the 'united' opposition headed by Trotsky. The 'unity' was rather precarious. Indeed, Trotsky had great disagreements with the Party leadership already in Lenin's time. He had little belief in the staying power of the Russian revolution and saw it only as a torch which would set alight the flame of world revolution, in the first instance in Europe. He maintained that the seizure of power by the Russian proletariat was not sufficient in itself, though it was of tremendous importance as a 'revolutionary example', whether it would be followed by victory or by defeat. What mattered to him foremost was the 'purity' of this example in which he saw the main strength of revolutionary influence on the consciousness of the European proletariat. Starting from such a premise, Trotsky rejected any compromise with capitalist governments. In his mind even a temporary and purely political opportunistic accommodation with the German or any other government would automatically lead to the weakening of the revolutionary influence of the Russian October and to diminishing of the chances of world 'permanent revolution'. This led Trotsky to deny the necessity and expediency of the Brest Litovsk Peace and, immediately after October, to political disagreements with Lenin.[3]

Trotsky's conception was contrary to that of Lenin, for whom the conquest of power was most important in itself; this power should on no account and in no circumstances be relinquished, he maintained. The correctness of Lenin's position in this fundamental disagreement with Trotsky was fully confirmed first in connection with the Brest Litovsk Peace, and later by the whole course of Soviet history.

In this Kamenev was no doubt on the side of Lenin. His differences with Lenin were concerned not with the question of the necessity of preserving power but that of the means to preserve it.

What was it that years later brought Kamenev into an alliance with Trotsky? Remaining after Lenin's death not so much the formal head of the Soviet government as its unquestionable practical and ideological leader, Kamenev was conscious of the whole extent and weight of his responsibility for further direction of economic policy. The awareness of this responsibility and the fear of repeating the pre-October blunder due to lack of confidence in the strength of proletarian revolution induced Kamenev to pose the problem of the timeliness of the industrialisation of the country. As an eminent economist, Kamenev knew full well that industrialisation could be pursued only by means of internal resources of the Soviet state, and that part of the cost would have to be borne by the countryside: it was from the private hands of the well-to-do kulaks that the means to industrialise would have to come. Kamenev did not count on loans from abroad or on economic concessions given to foreign capital.

In this conception he came into conflict with Bukharin who denied the possibility of internal redistribution of the national income and maintained that any attempt at such a redistribution would inevitably result in the break-up of the *smychka* between the proletariat and the peasantry, which would then be followed by the disintegration of the proletarian regime.[4]

In this period of Kamenev's political isolation Trotsky, his co-thinker and ally, extended to him a helping hand. Although he approached the industrialisation programme from a different view on the historic role of the revolution, at the moment practical issues brought the two men nearer to each other. In this way came into being a 'united opposition' of two party leaders who differed so much in their ideas and intentions. A very active role in bringing about this alliance was played by Zinoviev, who was moved not only by idealistic motives, but also by narrow egoism, by frustrated hopes of occupying the first place in the leadership. He firmly expected to gain such a position after the Thirteenth Congress at which he made the main report and at which, with self-denial, he did much to maintain Stalin as the General Secretary. Zinoviev felt that Stalin 'betrayed' him by gradually pushing him out, between the Thirteenth and the Fourteenth Congresses, from the leadership of the Party. With his characteristic modesty and lack of ambition, Kamenev accepted in the 'united opposition' the position of the third man, leaving the two main roles to Trotsky and Zinoviev. His alliance with Trotsky could not be very solid because their premises were so dissimilar, and the 'united opposition' would have probably disintegrated soon by itself. But events moved swiftly and in a somewhat different direction.

VI

In the end Kamenev shared the common fate of the leaders of the opposition. But he evolved more slowly and stubbornly and for a long time tried to remain within the general Party line.

Assuming the post of the Commissar of Trade assigned to him after he had been dismissed as chairman of the Soviet of Labour and Defence, Kamenev in a speech to the Collegium of the Commissars pledged to pursue the policy of the Party defined by the Fourteenth Congress and stressed that he expected the same from his comrades and collaborators. Then, looking around the gathering, he added in a jovial tone: 'Eh, well, I shall have to learn to trade.' Turning towards the Deputy Commissar Frumkin who sat next to him, he smilingly said: 'Under your enlightened leadership, Monsieur Ilyich.' Frumkin was at that time one of the most faithful followers of Rykov and Bukharin and turned out to be quite an original 'Commissar'.

Later on in the debate, Kamenev spoke about his well-known reasonableness and warned the audience against underestimating the Party's general opinion. In the work at the Commissariat of Trade he constantly sought to be in touch with Dzerzhinsky as the Chairman of the Supreme Soviet of the National Economy, whose views on the immediate tasks were much closer to those of Bukharin than to his own.

On coming into the Commissariat of Trade, Kamenev did not bring with him any of his co-thinkers; neither I. I. Khloplyanik, who had previously been in the Soviet of Labour and Defence, nor Muzyko, his private secretary, could have been considered as such; they were no more than conscientious clerks who followed Kamenev's instructions without discussing the merits of his policy. On the other hand, together with the appointment of Kamenev, Sh. M. Dvolaytsky was introduced into the Commissariat. The latter was one of the Party's eminent economists, a member of the Praesidium of the Communist Academy and a man of great erudition and brilliance, a close friend of Bukharin whose views he shared. He was the only one who could intellectually and ideologically counter Kamenev's influence. This was the precise reason why he was directed to work at the commisariat, and Kamenev understood this better than anybody else. But he welcomed Dvolaytsky in a friendly manner, without mistrust and ready to cooperate with him. Dvolaytsky became the head of the economic department of the Commissariat and there was no friction between the two men. One cannot deny that Dvolaytsky was tactful and generous and that he always greatly respected Kamenev both for his intellectual stature and his services to the Party and revolution.

Scrupulously following the Party line, Kamenev cut short the polemics between the members of the Commissariat of Trade and of the Soviet of National Economy about the methods to be employed in the regulation of trade. As I was at that time the *de facto* head of the journal *Trade News* (A. M. Kaktyn was only nominally the editor), Kamenev called me in and said: 'You must stop this literary quarrel; after the Fourteenth Congress it is out of place. We must find a common language with the people of the Council of National Economy and the collaborators of Dzerzhinsky. And you must help me in this.'

Kamenev pursued this line firmly as long as he remained the Commissar for Trade. But it was not for long. The snowball of inner-Party struggle kept rolling on and the fatal 'softness' of Kamenev *vis-à-vis* his comrades in the 'united opposition' just organising itself, led him away from all-party work. Kamenev was never a traitor to the Party. Moreover, unlike Stalin, he never engaged in an unprincipled struggle for power – he never craved for it. And, of course, he was never implicated in any deeds like the assassination of Kirov. In prison, in the Verkhneuralsk political isolator he loudly proclaimed that he was a victim of false charges, and of a frame-up, in which, he said, Zinoviev played an indirect role.

In July 1936, at the time when the NKVD was busy preparing the 'public trial of Zinoviev and Kamenev', I was in the hospital of the Butyrki prison. Through an open window I heard a desperate cry coming from the next cell. I recognised the familiar voice of Lev Borisovich whom I had known so well for so many years. 'Leave me alone! At least here, leave me alone!' he shouted. I heard nothing more as, obviously, someone closed the window. Maybe his 'conciliatory nature' at this time made him yield to his interrogators who also resorted to terrible tortures. The outcome? Kamenev's depositions at the trial ...

VII

It is unjust that Kamenev's literary works should be consigned to oblivion. He was a brilliant writer and much of what he wrote deserved attention, as for example his paper on Herzen, written in the last year of his life, when he was at the head of the *Academia* publishing institute. It is one of the best historical-literary essays devoted to Herzen.

Kamenev was also an excellent speaker, lucid, convincing and not at all verbose. He was not an emotional orator and addressed himself to the mind rather than to the emotions of his audience: in this he was obviously Lenin's disciple.

Kamenev committed many political mistakes and had many grave personal shortcomings. But among the Bolshevik old guard, exceptionally rich in talented and outstanding people, he was nevertheless remarkable for his gifts and capacity for political work. Among the Bolsheviks, Kamenev was an exceptional figure, and this was certainly acknowledged by Lenin.

NOTES

1 Editor's Note. This essay was written in October-November 1966. It is based on personal recollections, not on documentation and research. In this, in our opinion, lies its value. This opinion was at the time shared even by Solzhenitsyn, who after having met Yakubovich and having read his work, wrote: 'I am writing briefly and under the fresh impression ... The personality of Kamenev is presented by you very clearly and convincingly; and so are the important events in his life. The factual material is extremely important and interesting for the contemporary reader.' (See *Politicheskii Dnevnik,* Amsterdam, 1972, p. 276.) The essay has not, however, been published until now.

2 Translator's note. According to Sukhanov, Lenin apparently proposed that Trotsky should become the head of the government. See N.N. Sukhanov, *Zapiski of Revolutsii,* vol. VII, p. 266; L. Trotsky, *My Life,* p. 291.

3 Translator's note. Trotsky's formula at Brest Litovsk was 'neither peace nor war'; it was Bukharin who headed the faction of 'Left Communists' strongly opposed to the conclusion of peace.

4 Editor's note. Yakubovich sums up the views of Kamenev as well as Bukharin from memory, incorrectly and schematically. Bukharin was in fact not against industrialisation and a partial redistribution of national income. The problem consisted in the scale of such a redistribution. In the light of further developments Bukharin's point of view proved better founded.

G. Zinoviev

(Written in the first days of October 1971)

M.P. YAKUBOVICH

I

Until Lenin and Zinoviev returned from abroad, the ideological and political leadership of the Party was in the hands of L. B. Kamenev. He was one of those who viewed the revolution in progress as a bourgeois-democratic one. On this there was no disagreement in the Party. This point of view was also shared by J. V. Stalin. At that time Stalin was the actual editor of *Pravda* and Kamenev a member of its editorial board. Had Stalin wanted to pursue a different line, Kamenev, in his softness, would probably not have prevented him from doing so. But if that had been the case, there would have been other people to oppose Stalin and either to remove him from his post or to impose on him the line favoured by Kamenev. But this never arose because there was not a trace of any disagreement between Stalin and Kamenev.

* The opening pages of this essay were published in the journal *Politischeskii Dnevnik* (see *Political Diary*, Amsterdam, 1972, no. 63, December 1969, pp. 618-30). At that time the author was dictating his memoirs using a tape recorder. In October 1971, after his return to Moscow, he continued the text begun two years previously. Without sharing some of his views and opinions, we consider that his memoirs constitute an interesting document which undoubtedly merits publication. M. P. Yakubovich had spent twenty-six years in prisons and concentration camps (1930-56); he was rehabilitated in 1957. He now lives in an old people's home in Karaganda, Kazakhstan. (Editors.)

The policy of the Bolshevik Party was much more clearly defined than that of the Menshevik and Social-Revolutionary leadership of the Petrograd Soviet. In the understanding of the fundamental ideological meaning of the revolutionary events there were, generally speaking, no disagreements. The question of how the bourgeois-democratic revolution would develop and what the role of the proletariat should be was often debated, but there was no difference of views on the *nature* of this revolution. On this, I repeat, there was no disagreement.

When Lenin returned to Russia together with Zinoviev, he immediately put forward his 'April Theses'. To the Petrograd leadership of the Bolshevik Party and to the activists of the local organisation these 'Theses' were entirely unexpected. Lenin's mere questioning of the nature of the revolution was something new and startling.

What was Zinoviev's position with regard to this? He was well acquainted with Lenin's views, and at the time when Lenin presented his 'Theses', Zinoviev was in full agreement with him. It was later said that Zinoviev did not share Lenin's opinions and that this showed itself subsequently in his stand in October 1917 when he opposed the uprising. This is simply not true. How he changed his position, how his decision to act together with Kamenev matured, I shall relate later. I will only state here that at the time of his return with Lenin there were no disagreements between the two men. (It is not worth re-telling how it came about that the majority of the members of the Petrograd Bolshevik organisation and other party members were swayed by Lenin. All of them, or at least an overwhelming majority, finally adopted Lenin's position. This fact is by now well known and well attested.)

I should like to repeat that Zinoviev returned to Russia as a faithful adherent of Lenin, convinced that the revolution could not remain in its bourgeois-democratic phase but that it would have to transform itself into a socialist one.

Trotsky was not correct when later on, after Lenin's death, he maintained that it was not he who 'came over' to Lenin's view, but that Lenin adopted his, Trotsky's, stand. Lenin did not accept the theory of permanent revolution as it had been formulated by Parvus and Trotsky in 1905. Moreover,

Trotsky himself in 1917 was not an adherent of this theory. In the interval between 1905 and 1917, Trotsky, if he had not forgotten about permanent revolution, had certainly pushed it into the background. In these years Trotsky's policy consisted mostly of the attempt to form the August Bloc; this was a line of thought quite distant from the concept according to which a 'permanent revolution' was to follow the pioneering initiative of the Russian proletariat. After the defeat of 1905, Trotsky thought that a socialist revolution on a world scale had become considerably delayed and that Russia would not play the role he and Parvus had assigned to her – that of the initiator, the prime mover of the world socialist revolution. On the contrary, it seemed to Trotsky that for a long time to come a great deal of preliminary, preparatory work would have to be done and that this should consist in the integration and unification of all socialist and workers' parties, regardless of the different shades of opinion between them. Such was the idea behind the August Bloc. Trotsky was not against the participation of the Bolsheviks in the August Bloc, but he was *for* the participation of *all* socialist and workers' parties, from the Bolsheviks to the Mensheviks-Liquidators. Trotsky, as we can see, had then worked for an integrationist policy and in no way for the 'permanent revolution'; and this was the reason why Lenin could not have 'come over' to him.

In the spring of 1917, after Lenin 'converted' the majority of the Bolsheviks to his point of view, it was precisely Zinoviev who was his closest assistant, collaborator and comrade. Kamenev's position was different: he neither opposed Lenin actively, nor did he abandon his own convictions. He submitted to the Party discipline, but continued to consider that the revolution in progress was bourgeois-democratic, and that it would not necessarily become a socialist one.

Such was the alignment in the Bolshevik Party after Lenin's return. A great majority of the members of the Party, among them Stalin, adopted Lenin's line. From an adherent, a disciple, and a follower of Kamenev who had been the ideological leader of the Party before Lenin's arrival, Stalin became a follower of Lenin. Kamenev stuck to his opinions, without, however, actively opposing the line of the Party. True, at the April conference he tried to put forward his reservations, but without much determination. In this we should seek the reasons for his attitude in October 1917. Zinoviev's stand in October was not directly connected with his state of mind in April. His evolution will be described further.

As events were unfolding, it was becoming more and more obvious that the Petrograd proletariat was following the Bolsheviks and the political line advocated by Lenin, strikingly so during the June demonstration. To start with this was conceived as a demonstration organised by the Bolshevik Party and planned for the first days of the First Congress of the Council of Workers' and Soldiers' Deputies. The Bolshevik initiative provoked the indignation of the Mensheviks and the SRs, especially of the Mensheviks who played quite a considerable role in the Petrograd Soviet as they had traditionally more links with the Petrograd proletariat (though the SRs also had many adherents). The Mensheviks and the SRs still laboured under the illusion that if in the name of the Congress they proposed to postpone the demonstration, the Petrograd proletariat would obey the directives of the Congress representatives. (In the Petrograd Soviet the Mensheviks and the SRs were in a majority.) That this was only an illusion became clear during the preparations for the demonstration. The preliminaries were characterised by various phases. Right from the beginning there was an open clash between the Mensheviks and the SRs on the one hand, and the Bolsheviks on the other: should the demonstration take place at all? Here Lenin showed his tactical subtlety. He agreed to postpone it and to organise it later not as the initiative of the Bolshevik Party but at the call of the All-Russian Congress of the Soviets. In this way it would appear that all parties agreed to hold a peaceful demonstration, so to speak, in honour of the First Congress. But disagreements came again to the surface when in the course of the demonstration it became clear whom the Petrograd proletariat was following. This could be seen from the slogans carried by the demonstrators. Those of the Mensheviks and the SRs were: 'Support the Provisional Government', 'Peace without Annexations and Indemnities', and 'For a Constituent Assembly'. These were the political demands which the Mensheviks and the SRs tried to debate at public meetings, in factories and in soldiers' barracks. But the crowds did not want to listen to them and chased them off the platforms.

When the procession formed itself, and on the Mars Fields the demonstrators were filing past the tribunes on which stood the leaders of the First Congress, it could be seen that an overwhelming majoity of slogans were those of the Bolsheviks: 'All Power to the Soviets', 'Down with the Provisional Government', 'Down with the Ministers – Representatives of the Bourgeoisie'. This was a striking picture of the complete unity of the Petrograd workers and soldiers with the Bolsheviks. For the SR-Menshevik leadership of the Petrograd Soviet this was quite unexpected. They had to admit that although they still preserved their majority at the Congress and in the Petrograd Soviet, although they still officially led the whole movement of the Soviets, in Petrograd they had in fact no following. Their slogans could be seen only among the printing workers and small groups of functionaries and office workers. The soldiers marched under Bolshevik banners only.

This was the moment when Petrograd established its link with Russia and the military front. Delegates from other cities streamed into Petrograd incessantly, from factories and plants, and especially from various sectors of the front. They all passed through the White Hall of the Tauride Palace, once the seat of the State Duma. Endless meetings, unending contingents of delegates, were now filling the Hall to overflowing. From the platform spoke representatives of all the parties of the Petrograd Soviet. The Bolshevik speakers were received with the greatest emotion; and they conveyed to the delegates the mood of the Petrograd soldiers and workers. Zinoviev was on the platform almost all the time. He was greeted warmly and listened to with attention.

There were many other speakers. Victor M. Chernov was one of the best orators among the SRs. Avksentiev too spoke on behalf of the SRs – though only rarely as he was busy organising the All-Russian Soviet of Peasant Deputies. So did Bunakov-Fundaminsky – but they did not attract many people. Tseretelli and Liber had more success than Chernov and Fundaminsky, but even they could not compete with the Bolsheviks. Lenin appeared rarely, so did Trotsky. The most effective speakers were Zinoviev and Alexandra Kollontai, most popular with workers and soldiers. But undoubtedly the past master was Zinoviev in spite of his high-pitched voice which was a great handicap for an orator. But he was capable of dominating the audience, and nobody was listened to with more attention. In Zinoviev the Bolshevik Party had a propagandist of ideas; he also expressed the feelings of the Petrograd garrison and the Petrograd proletariat.

I do not remember whether Zinoviev spoke at the First Congress. Maybe he did, but his role there was unimportant. There is no need to describe the tremendous impression which Lenin's speech made on the Congress, and indeed on the whole of Russia – this has been well known. But one should perhaps mention Trotsky's position in order to give an exact picture of the balance of ideological forces at the time of the Congress, because this balance differed considerably from that which existed on the eve of the October revolution.

Trotsky spoke at the Congress a few days before Lenin. The platform was given to the important revolutionary Narodniks, to Social-Democrats, and to the SRs so that they could express their views on the progress of the revolution. It was in this context that Georgi Plekhanov made his contribution.

Trotsky advocated the establishment of a coalition government of socialist parties. Clearly, he did not put forward the idea of the permanent revolution. Nor did he speak about a socialist revolution or about the dictatorship of the proletariat. Trotsky, in fact, remained a partisan of the August Bloc and repeated what he had said in 1912 in his speech at the Congress. He stressed that all the democratic forces of the country were represented at the First Congress of the Soviets – the whole proletariat and the whole army, and the army stood for the peasantry or for its most active element. And that was why the First Congress represented the whole Russian nation, with the exception of the possessing classes and part of the intelligentsia which remained outside the Soviets. Therefore the Congress was entitled to decide all political questions and to form a government from among its members and according to its wishes. True, Trotsky did not carry his argument to the end and did not propose that the Congress should follow the example of the French revolutionaries and proclaim itself as the Constituent Assembly. This would have been more consistent and more attractive. It might have produced a split in the ranks of the Mensheviks and the SRs where some supporters of such an idea could be found. But Trotsky did not go so far. He proposed only to exclude representatives of the bourgeoisie, the Cadets, and to form a socialist coalition government. He summed up his views in a sentence which became popular at the time: 'We need a government of twelve Peshekhonovs.' He said so because just before him spoke the Minister of Trade Peshekhonov, representative of one of the most right-wing socialist parties, the National-Socialists. Peshekhonov behaved with exemplary loyalty towards the Congress. He stressed that in the government he considered himself to be a representative of the Soviets and that he came to report to the Congress on his work. He spoke to the point and avoided anything which would exacerbate the relations between his party and those which stood more to the left. He made a very good impression on the delegates. This was why Trotsky used the phrase: 'We need a government of twelve Peshekhonovs.'

It is obvious that Trotsky's stand was quite far from that expressed a few days later by Lenin, who declared that none of the socialist parties, with the exception of the Bolsheviks, was in a position to solve the tasks facing the Russian revolution. Trotsky did not understand as well as Lenin did that all the other parties were in fact serving the bourgeoisie and were politically bankrupt.

The Congress came to a close. The delegates had witnessed the demonstrators carrying Bolshevik slogans demanding peace and the end of the Provisional Government. At the last session a Central Executive Committee was elected, in which all socialist parties were represented according to the number of votes their candidates received. The Petrograd garrison and the Petrograd proletariat expected that the Central Executive Committee would fulfil all the demands put forward at the demonstration. But the Executive in no way intended to be bound by these demands. It intended to continue its indecisive and vacillating line, incomprehensible to the masses. In this way there grew a gulf between the hopes of the garrison and the workers on the one hand and the Central Executive Committee on the other. And this led to the crisis of the July days. I shall not dwell on this in detail as I had already described the problem elsewhere. I would like, however, to say something briefly about the demonstration, in order to trace the way in which it influenced Zinoviev and Trotsky and in order to show how under this influence they evolved ideologically in differing directions.

The demonstration was a spontaneous affair. The leadership of the Bolshevik Party did not quite approve of it. Lenin had considered it to be premature: in his view the masses were not yet mature enough to understand the necessity of a socialist revolution. But workers and soldiers expected their demands, which they had put forward in June, to be met. One month had passed. Now, they thought, the time had come to put new pressure on the Executive so that it should carry out the decisions of the masses and not merely the formal resolutions of the First Congress. The meaning of the demonstration lay therefore in its restatement of popular demands, this time not before the Congress but before the Central Executive Committee.

Only when the demonstration was already forming and crowds gathering in the streets, did the Bolsheviks give it their blessing. Lenin appeared on the balcony of the Kshesinskaya Palace and spoke precisely as the masses wanted and expected him to speak. But the Bolshevik support for the demonstration in no way amounted to an attempt to seize power, as the Mensheviks and the Social-Revolutionaries maintained. Such an attempt would have been, in Lenin's eyes, quite premature. This demonstration was a reminder of previous demands and not a bid for power. But spontaneously it acquired a different character. While in June, workers and peasants, called out into the streets by the First Congress, marched in orderly fashion carrying banners and slogans, this time there was much more excitement. The soldiers were irritable and nervous and many of them carried arms. They had no intention of occupying the Tauride Palace. They could have done this easily as it had hardly any defences.

Chernov and Tseretelli came out to address the demonstrators, but they were constantly interrupted and could not make themselves heard. They were not in any way manhandled or apprehended, though such a possibility had existed. The Central Executive Committee was not swept away because this was not the aim of the demonstrators, although the Mensheviks and the SRs expected it and feared that the whole upheaval would end in the seizure of power. And at that moment the Executive Committee made a blunder similar to that committed by the Tzarist regime on 9 January 1905, during the procession led by the priest Gapon. Those who had marched behind Gapon had no intention of attacking the Tzar, his family or the government, yet the Tzar, trembling at the mere thought of such a possibility, called out the troops and ordered the shooting of the demonstrators.

Now the leaders of the Mensheviks and the SRs viewed the crowds with similar feelings and were anxious to seek protection from possible violence. On whom could they rely to protect them? The soldiers of the Petrograd garrison were milling around with the crowd. Except for the Cossacks there was nobody. And so the Mensheviks and the SRs called in the Cossacks, who came out fully armed, the same Cossacks who not so long ago were used to disperse these same Mensheviks, the SRs and the Bolsheviks during their common demonstrations. This appeal to the Cossacks was the greatest error the Menshevik and the SR leadership had ever committed. They thus destroyed any chance they had ever had to lead a Soviet democracy of workers and soldiers. Both sides were armed, and so it was inevitable that there should be clashes. Who started shooting first? Individual soldiers who marched under Bolshevik banners? But in this they did not act according to the directives of the Party, but according to the logic of the situation created by the confrontation with mounted and armed Cossacks. Under provocation a few soldiers might have fired ... and that was how shooting began. There were many victims on both sides.

After the shooting died down, the Cossacks were recalled and the crowd moved towards the Tauride Palace. If the Bolsheviks had wanted it the demonstrators could have taken over the Palace and proclaimed a new government. But there was no such plan. The multitudes stood around the Palace, shouted and made a lot of noise. Tseretelli, Chernov and other speakers tried to address them, but felt quite helpless. Then the Mensheviks and the SRs took another step which, from their point of view, was more astute and better thought out. They recalled from the front those detachments which, they felt, would support them, those which had not adopted the Bolshevik watchwords and did not identify themselves with the Petrograders.

These troops entered Petrograd ostensibly in order to defend the Soviet and its Central Executive Committee from 'putchists' (the actual word was not yet in use then), from a band of scoundrels disrupting the work of the Soviets. The notion that the Petrograd soldiers were shirking service at the front was then being widely spread among the soldiers in the firing line. The troops called into Petrograd were of great military value to the Provisional Government, which had more links with the General Staff than with the Central Executive and yet benefited from the authority and prestige of the latter. Kerensky was completely under the influence of the General Staff and the Ministry of War.

The arrival of the troops seemed to have frightened the Petrograd garrison, impressed by the new watchword of 'law and order'. The soldiers became subdued, and less noisy on the streets of the capital – at least at first, until the newcomers became infected by its revolutionary mood. The proletariat also seemed to become somewhat overawed by the marching troops. Not only the supporters of the Mensheviks and the SRs but also the bourgeois elements, the middle classes of the 'city who until recently had watched with alarm the unfolding of revolutionary events, now raised their heads. For a time the whole mass of the reactionary petty bourgeoisie began to dominate the city. Individual soldiers and workers continuing to carry Bolshevik slogans were beaten up and had to run for safety, away from the new crowd now spilling onto the streets.

There was no doubt at that time that Lenin might have been killed; one might even say that everything was being prepared for such an assassination. Rumours were being spread that he was in the pay of the German government, that he carried on Bolshevik propaganda with German money. Such stories were eagerly repeated in the bourgeois circles in Petrograd. It was also assiduously maintained that Lenin and the Bolsheviks had 'sold themselves to the Kaiser', that their aim was not at all the achievement of socialism but the victory of Imperial Germany. Lenin's life was in jeopardy. And not only his life but also that of his close collaborators, in the first instance, of Zinoviev.

In this anti-Lenin agitation one of the most popular and authoritative figures was Grigori A. Alexinsky. His popularity and authority was enhanced by the fact that he had, in the past, been regarded as a Bolshevik. As a young man, after graduating from the University, he was elected in 1907 to the Second State Duma as a representative of the Petrograd workers. At that time there was no separate workers' list in the elections to the Duma; but the Cadets, who were then the leading political force, assigned one seat to the representative of the working class. Because, in 1907, the majority of the workers followed the Bolsheviks, this seat fell to Alexinsky. Thus he had appeared as a Bolshevik leader, while Irakli Tseretelli was the head of the whole Social-Democratic faction which comprised both Bolsheviks and Mensheviks. However, on certain questions there were shades of difference between them. Alexinsky, in all his utterances, was expressing Bolshevik moods and slogans, demonstrating his Bolshevik determination. But after the dispersal of the Second Duma, when the whole faction, with Tseretelli at its head, was arrested and accused of treason against the state (June 1907), Alexinsky managed to escape abroad. There was nothing reprehensible in this: any Social Democrat would try to escape, but only a few succeeded and these caught were sentenced to penal servitude. Abroad, Alexinsky was slowly changing his views. He did not keep up any close contact with the Bolshevik emigrés and though he did not formally break with them, ideologically he gradually drifted away and became more involved with those emigrés whose political positions were less clearly defined. At the outbreak of the war, when Lenin came out with his defeatist slogans, Alexinsky, like many other Bolsheviks, became an adherent of Plekhanov who was an uncompromising and determined 'defensist'.

75

In 1917, together with other Bolsheviks, Alexinsky joined Plekhanov's group 'Unity', which stood to the right of the Mensheviks who in Plekhanov's eyes were semi-Leninists. Alexinsky shared Plekhanov's view on the need for *national* unity in time of war, but while Plekhanov never sought any contact with the Russian General Staff or war commanders, Alexinsky, from the moment of his return to Russia (he came as a patriot and democrat not in a sealed train) tried to establish such relations with them. After July he became the chief representative of those who accused the Bolsheviks of treason and of being in the pay of the German General Staff. Alexinsky, however, never advanced these accusations in a straightforward manner, but through innuendo and hints which were all too clear. This propaganda had its effect, and Lenin and Zinoviev had to go into hiding to save themselves.

Lenin took his escape calmly. A great realist in politics, he had reckoned with a temporary change in the general mood, with a temporary ebb in the revolutionary temper of the Petrograd workers and soldiers. But he viewed this as a passing phenomenon and foresaw that a new revolutionary wave would follow. He understood that he was in great danger, but he was ready to face the court. He was prepared to clear himself before the court of the charges levelled at him. Only under the pressure of the leadership of his party did he agree to go underground.

The campaign against Lenin and Zinoviev threw many of the Party leaders into confusion. Some thought that Lenin should give himself up to the Provisional Government and face the court. Among those was Stalin. But most of them were convinced that it would never come to a trial as Lenin would have been murdered well before such an eventuality. The search for legal justice would end in catastrophe they maintained, and insisted that Lenin should go into hiding.

Lenin followed their advice. He remained calm, while Zinoviev reacted much more nervously. He had none of that stamina, composure, self-control, and readiness to risk his life which characterised Lenin. Zinoviev grew panicky. He did not share Lenin's view as to the transient nature of the prevailing political atmosphere; he saw it as something deep and lasting and maintained that within the foreseeable future there would be no insurrection, that the revolution would take a different, much slower course and, consequently, the programme of Lenin's April Theses would remain unattainable.

Zinoviev's close political association with Kamenev began at this time, an association which led to their declaration against the October insurrection and their disbelief in the chances of victory. Zinoviev moved away from Lenin's position after the July events thus showing a meanness of spirit of which Stalin later took full advantage. Kamenev had no reason to seek security in Finland. No accusations were directed against him: he had been in exile, had not come back in the 'sealed train' and, as he had occupied a much less exposed position, his name did not provoke so much hostility and anger. In spite of all this, the Provisional Government, under the pressure from the right and influenced by the campaign about the treachery of the whole Bolshevik leadership, instructed the Ministry of Justice to issue a warrant for Kamenev's arrest. He was detained, in spite of the fact that he was a member of the Praesidium of the All-Russian Central Executive Committee of the Soviets.

The arrest of Kamenev marked a further degradation of the Executive, which in July had called out the Cossacks and then gave its tacit agreement to the imprisonment of a member of its own Praesidium.

I was at the time working in the offices of the Central Executive and for this reason I was allowed to maintain almost daily contact with Kamenev in the Kresty prison.

To give a full picture of the political situation, something also should be said about Trotsky's position. While Zinoviev, having lost belief in the revolution's chances opposed the idea of the rising, Trotsky abandoned his slogan of 'the government of twelve Peshekhonovs'. How could there be a united socialist government if one faction of socialists called out the Cossacks against the other? One could not expect that the Mensheviks and the Social-Revolutionaries would really break with the bourgeoisie, and Trotsky soon realised how illusory was the idea of the integration of all socialist and workers' parties in the August Bloc. He concluded that the task now was to unmask all the corrupt parties and counter their influence on the masses. This led him to take a clear decision: to join the only truly revolutionary party – the Bolshevik Party – able to serve the cause of the working classes. His mind returned to the theory of permanent revolution, according to which the Russian upheaval, in order to achieve socialism, would open a revolutionary epoch on a world scale. He was not correct in maintaining, after Lenin's death, that Lenin had adopted his views. No, in 1905 Lenin did not consider 'permanent revolution' a valid theory. Trotsky returned to the idea after July 1917, while Lenin had spoken of it in April. Lenin did not use the expression 'permanent' but 'uninterrupted' which, however, comes to the same thing. Trotsky now had before his eyes the example of the Paris Commune.

Thus Zinoviev and Trotsky had moved in two opposite directions. After July Zinoviev abandoned socialist revolution while Trotsky fought for the unification of the whole proletariat under the banners of the Bolshevik Party, the only party faithful to the revolutionary cause.

II

This low ebb in the mood of the Petrograd proletariat and the garrison brought about the events of July and by the arrival of fighting units from outside which regarded the capital's soldiers with hostility as faint-hearted cowards, did not last long. The first sign of a great change could be seen in the growing contacts between the local garrison and the soldiers brought from the front. The newly arrived units were put under the command of a member of the Central Executive Committee Lieutenant Yuri Petrovich Mazurenko.

Mazurenko was not a counter-revolutionary. He was in no way connected with the General Staff or with the circle of Kornilov or other generals. He acted on instructions of the Executive and was a member of the Menshevik Party. Finding himself at the head of fighting units marching into Petrograd, Mazurenko felt like a hero in whose hands was placed the destiny of the revolution. Carried away by his own role, addressing public meetings, Mazurenko did not notice how he had become a commander without an army. Fraternisation between the men from the garrison and the newcomers soon convinced the latter that they were in no way different from their Petrograd comrades; they shared the same views, the same aspirations and the same hopes. First of all, they wanted peace and then they wanted to go back to their homesteads and get some land. Discussions with local soldiers and workers made it clear to them that their expectations would not be fulfilled under the existing government. In effect the newly arrived troops very soon became 'Bolshevised'. They were influenced not only by their fellow soldiers but also by the Bolshevik agitation carried on in the press and at meetings, especially those at the Cirque Moderne where every day prominent Bolshevik speakers addressed the crowds. Outstanding among the orators was Trotsky who by far surpassed all others. People were coming especially to hear his speeches; after the meetings he was carried shoulder high by his audience.

Trotsky never dissociated himself from Lenin, whose name resounded during every meeting. Nobody could forget that Lenin was indeed the chief leader. Lenin's name was coupled with that of Trotsky. Zinoviev was not mentioned, though everybody knew that he was in hiding together with Lenin. But his name was not a symbol like that of Lenin's in the first place and Trotsky's in the second.

The 'Bolshevisation' of the troops and a gradual return to the previous revolutionary atmosphere went on right through July and August, when the Sixth Congress of the Bolshevik Party was in session. At this Congress it was decided that Trotsky and a group of other Social Democrats, internationalists of long standing, who until now belonged to the so-called Inter-Borough Organisation, would join the Bolshevik Party. Among them were Lunacharsky, Volodarsky, Uritsky, and others.

When the revolutionary mood of the masses in the capital reached a high point the time had come for Lenin and Zinoviev to return from Finland.

*   *   *   *

The process of consolidation of the Bolshevik influence was

considerably speeded up by Kornilov's attempted *coup*. Kornilov's openly counter-revolutionary attempt gave a powerful stimulus to a new burst of revolutionary activity not only in Petrograd but also in the provinces. The proletariat understood that from behind the temporising Central Executive Committee there crept up open counter-revolution: the military junta. The revolutionary process in the whole of Russia had accelerated, nowhere more than in the capital.

Lenin arrived in Petrograd, at first illegally, for a conference of the Central Committee of his party, which was to decide whether the time had come for open action, for issuing a call for insurrection.

Another important development, apart from the Kornilov revolt, occurred also at that time: workers and soldiers began to recall their Menshevik and Social-Revolutionary deputies to the Soviet and replace them by Bolsheviks. In this way the Soviets were being gradually 'Bolshevised', until in the end the Petrograd Soviet was in the hands of the Bolsheviks. The leadership of the Soviet had therefore to be changed and Trotsky replaced Chkheidze as President. Chkheidze had been elected in the first days of the February revolution. In the eyes of the majority of the workers and soldiers, he personified the February revolution. Now there was no better candidate than Trotsky. He had already become the main representative of the Bolshevik Party; his audiences at the Cirque Moderne noticed not a shade of difference between him and Lenin and their names were linked together. From the moment of Trotsky's election a new centre came into existence, a centre of a growing revolutionary wave, opposed to the official All-Russian Central Executive Committee. The Petrograd Soviet had already played a similar role up to the time of the First All-Russian Congress of the Soviets. After the Congress, however, its role became insignificant as the Executive took over its functions. Now again it resumed its leadership over the revolutionary movement in the country.

Following the Petrograd Soviet, the majority of other Soviets at the front and in the provinces passed into Bolshevik hands. The Petrograd Soviet became, of course, a centre of all other Soviets, those with the Bolshevik majority as well as those where the Bolsheviks formed a strong opposition. The authority of the executive became undermined and it lost most of its previous influence.

The question of the seizure of power rested with the Central Committee of the Bolshevik Party, which could not take any decision in Lenin's absence. Where should the Central Committee meet? It made no sense to travel out of Petrograd; in the city Lenin and Zinoviev were still endangered. There began a search for a safe place, and it was found in the flat of Nikolai Nikolayevich Sukhanov.

It is customary now to say that the flat was put at the disposal of the Bolsheviks without Sukhanov's knowledge by his wife Galina Konstantinovna, who was a member of the Bolshevik Party. This is not so. Sukhanov's agreement was essential for the safety of those meeting there. And this agreement was not difficult to obtain. True, Sukhanov at that time was close to the Mensheviks. (I do not remember whether he was officially a member of their party; after February he belonged to no party and before he was a Social-Revolutionary. Even then he considered himself to be a Marxist.) Together with another old social democrat Bazarov he became the editor of the social-democratic party *Novaya Zhizn*. In the autumn of 1917 he became in fact the sole editor, while Bazarov, Gorky and some other ex-Bolsheviks were members of the editorial board. It seems to me that at the time Sukhanov was already in the Menshevik Party though he did not share their policy of a witch-hunt against the Bolsheviks neither did he approve of the imprisonment of Kamenev nor of the order to arrest Lenin and Zinoviev. He belonged to that group of Mensheviks who considered that such measures and the calling out of the Cossacks dishonoured the leadership of their party. In the past Sukhanov was often a 'dissident', that is, a politician who allowed himself to deviate from the Party line and sometimes to take an anti-Party stand. Opposing the Menshevik leadership in the matter of arrests, Sukhanov now saw the service he rendered to the Bolsheviks as a repayment of a political debt he owed to the persecuted party. In his opinion, no true socialist could connive at the persecution of any socialist party regardless of his disagreements with it. This is why he put his flat at the disposal of the Bolsheviks and provided a safe place for their meeting with Lenin and Zinoviev while they were banned from Russia.

While the meeting was in progress, Sukhanov remained outside, in the corridor. I would not like to say that he was eavesdropping, but in one way or another he was naturally *au courant* of what went on and he knew what decisions were taken. I have spoken here about Sukhanov's role, because this sheds some light on the positions adopted by Zinoviev and Kamenev later on, and helps to explain how I evaluate future events.

Lenin, who consistently took a revolutionary stand and waited – with tenacity and without any hesitations – for the moment when it would be possible to give the signal for open insurrectionary action, expressed at the meeting his firm belief in the chances of victory. He put forward a plan for a revolution in Petrograd in the name, so to say, of a revolution in the whole of Russia. The great majority of the Central Committee supported Lenin. ('Great' is perhaps not the most suitable word as at that time the Central Committee was not yet the large body it has become in our time: as far as I remember at that meeting there were perhaps a dozen people.) Only Kamenev and Zinoviev disagreed with Lenin's views.

Kamenev was consistent in regarding the revolution in progress as a bourgeois-democratic one. From such a point of view he had guided the Bolshevik Central Committee until Lenin's return from Switzerland; he followed this line in his intervention at the April conference and after, and the July débâcle only strengthened him in his conviction. He himself had been imprisoned when Lenin and Zinoviev went into hiding and was released only just before the meeting. His stay in gaol may have also, to a certain extent, confirmed him in his views: surely Lenin was overestimating the revolutionary possibilities if even he, Kamenev, a member of the Praesidium of the All-Russian Executive Committee, found himself behind bars at the time when the Executive played such an enormous political role and without whose sanction nobody could be arrested. Thus Kamenev's attitude was fully consistent right from February 1917.

Zinoviev's position was quite different. As I have said

before, at the time of the April conference he agreed with Lenin's view that Russia's bourgeois-democratic revolution would inevitably transform itself into a socialist one. But Zinoviev was particularly affected by the shock of the July days so painfully felt by everybody. He was not the only one to become confused. I well remember the reaction of Yuri Steklov who, though not threatened with imprisonment, was seized with panic. Every night he sought shelter at the Tauride Palace asking Chkheidze to let him sleep in his office. He was reluctant to return home fearing that, even if he were not arrested, some counter-revolutionaries, so numerous at that time in the city, might subject him to torture or even kill him. Zinoviev, in Finland, was also gripped by fear which was not allayed even by Lenin's presence.

At the Central Committee meeting Zinoviev came closer to Kamenev's view; they both were opposed to the open insurrection, warning that it would end in a defeat similar to that of the July days. When, however, the decision was taken, they hesitated as to what their next step should be. They did not immediately come out with their famous letter, about which so much has already been written and for which, quite rightly, they have been blamed. They remained hesitant for nearly a week. I would venture a suggestion for which in truth I have no precise evidence: that they were influenced by Sukhanov. It was in his home that they had debated the problem; they stayed on after the meeting was over and it was while the participants were gradually leaving, I imagine, that they must have had a talk with Sukhanov. They were deeply convinced that in the interests of the Party the insurrection should not take place, and this view was rejected at the meeting. I think that they must have shared their apprehension with Sukhanov, who straightaway suggested that they should express their *votum separatum* in *Novaya Zhizn*, because the official organ of the Bolshevik Party could not possibly publish their statement. They were still vacillating. But when five or six days later the problem of insurrection was again discussed at a conference and they were outvoted (though some Bolsheviks supported them), they accepted Sukhanov's proposal to publish their statement in *Novaya Zhizn*.

Kamenev and Zinoviev remained isolated not only in the

Bolshevik Party but also among the soldiers, workers and sailors of Petrograd. When they took the decision to publish their warning, they had expected that it would make a great impression and provoke expressions of support not only within the Party but also outside it. This, they thought, would make the Central Committee reconsider its plans. But very soon they realised the degree of indignation their action caused. They realised that nobody supported them, except the intelligentsia which until quite recently tended to stand behind the Menshevik–SR Executive, which had approved the order to arrest Lenin and Zinoviev and which had put Kamenev himself behind the bars. They saw that there was only a handful of people who like Sukhanov were both against the arrests and against the insurrection. They understood that there was nobody behind them and that they had committed a serious breach of discipline not only in respect of the Bolshevik Party but also of the revolutionary proletariat.

There was great indignation in the Party and outside it while the Central Committee discussed their case. Lenin was, of course, exasperated all the more as in their Finnish retreat he must have often talked with Zinoviev about the July events and about the prospects of revolution. He was certainly led to believe that Zinoviev shared his opinion. He could have hardly expected that now, at the decisive moment, Zinoviev would side with Sukhanov against him, his old comrade and teacher, and would denounce, in a quasi-Menshevik paper, the decision of his own party's Central Committee.

I reckon that it was then that Lenin, *in the heat of the debate*, demanded the expulsion of Kamenev and Zinoviev from the Party. I repeat 'in the heat of the debate' because very soon he withdrew this demand. It is only now, half a century after the event, that the present leadership maintains that Kamenev and Zinoviev should have been ostracised and expelled. If Lenin had been of this opinion, he would have adopted quite a different attitude towards the two men during the actual uprising.

In spite of Lenin's greatness, his self-control, his judiciousness and his tremendous stamina, he was only human and could act on impulse. Obviously, the majority of the members of the Central Committee also thought that Lenin was just roused by anger, because they rejected his proposal. Incidentally, Stalin also belonged to that majority and voted against the expulsion. Thus the two men remained in the Party although their action was unanimously condemned.

So the moment came when the insurrection, long awaited by the Petrograd masses and decided upon by the Central Committee, was to occur. But the exact date still had to be fixed, and here some differences arose between Lenin and Trotsky who otherwise were in complete agreement about the imminence of the open uprising.

About that time, under the pressure of the Bolshevik Party and the Petrograd Soviet already in Bolshevik hands, the Central Executive, after long hesitations, doubts and delays, resolved at last to convene the Second All-Russian Congress of the Soviets. It is quite possible that it would have procrastinated even longer, if it could have foreseen that the Second Congress would follow the Bolsheviks. But among the members of the Executive the illusion persisted that the Bolshevisation of the Soviets had not yet gone so far and that the majority of the delegates would still remain faithful to the Menshevik-SR leadership.

Trotsky, who had recently been appointed the President of the Petrograd Soviet, reckoned that it would be wise to delay the uprising by a few days and obtain from the All-Russian Congress in session an overwhelming support for the decisions of the Petrograd Soviet. He reasoned that the chances of success would be considerably increased if the action were sanctioned by the Second All-Russian Congress; the revolution would thus be carried out in the name not only of the Bolshevik Central Committee and on behalf of the Petrograd Soviet but also on behalf and in the name of all the Soviets of Russia. This would invest it with an undisputed authority in the eyes of the whole country and all the Soviets, as well as in the eyes of the whole proletariat, the whole army and the whole navy (not only of the Baltic Fleet). For this reason Trotsky was opposed to the plan of giving the signal for revolution before the Congress had assembled. On this point there was disagreement between Trotsky and Lenin, disagreement which had not shown itself before, at the session of the

Central Committee. Trotsky considered that it would be risky to start the uprising before the Congress, while Lenin thought that, on the contrary, a delay would be more dangerous as it would give the bourgeois government time to prepare a riposte. This was not a fundamental conflict between the two leaders, but one based on different general impressions. Trotsky was influenced by the huge meetings at the Cirque Moderne, by stormy demonstrations in the Petrograd Soviet; he had grown accustomed to his triumphs in the Cirque Moderne which used to end with the enthusiastic mass audience carrying him shoulder high and shouting: 'Long Live the Revolution!', 'Long Live Lenin and Trotsky'. He was under the spell of the turbulent crowds of the Soviet over which he was holding sway, and it seemed to him absolutely certain that the Second Congress would follow the Bolshevik Party.

Lenin was much more sceptical. He considered it already a great victory that the Petrograd Soviet followed the Bolsheviks and he was not at all convinced that the provincial Soviets had been 'Bolshevised' and revolutionised to the same degree. He envisaged the possibility that the Petrograd Soviet would take the lead and that the uprising would be limited for the time being to the capital. He was afraid too that the government would manage to mount a counter-offensive, which seemed to Trotsky quite unreal. Being in Petrograd, in the centre of events, and not in Finland, he felt the pulse of life; he witnessed the disintegration of the governmental milieu and rated its ability very low – especially the ability of Kerensky himself – to organise any serious opposition. This disagreement between Lenin and Trotsky was by no means as great and important as it was made to appear later, when we were told about 'a deep breach' between the two leaders. It is complete nonsense, of course, to say that Trotsky was 'consciously betraying the revolution'.

As far as Kamenev and Zinoviev were concerned, they very soon realised that they had committed a mistake, even an offence. This was brought home to them when they heard Lenin demanding their expulsion from the Party. We have to assume that they understood then that once the uprising took place, even if in their view the time for it was wrongly chosen, and once the Party had decided on such a course of action in which the masses were to be involved, the duty of every true revolutionary was to join the ranks. Once the proletariat was rising as it had done in the days of the Commune, the genuine revolutionary marched with it.

How to decide on the actual date of the uprising? Well, it was set for 24 October – the eve of the Second All-Russian Congress. Power had to be seized on the morning of 25 October, as in the evening of the same day the Congress was to have its inaugural session. The taking over of power by the proletariat was to be completed during the day and sanctioned in the evening by the Congress. The revolutionary government would then be set up, representing not only the Petrograd proletariat and the capital's garrison, but the whole of Russia's working class and the whole of the Russian army. Thus the disagreement between Trotsky and Lenin resolved itself: though the uprising actually started before the opening of the Congress, Trotsky's plan to legalise the seizure of power was successful, as that same evening the Congress did indeed give it its sanction.

The uprising began by the setting up, at the directive of the party, of the Military Revolutionary Committee of the Petrograd Soviet. In fact, it is beside the point to debate who was actually the head of the Military Revolutionary Committee. Some historians later insisted that it was Podvoisky. This is not correct. Only the President of the Petrograd Soviet could also preside over the Committee. But he did not have to spend all his time at the headquarters of the Committee to deal with the current problems. Podvoisky was indeed one of the most active leaders of the Committee and later, after the formation of the Council of Commissars, was in fact an acting chairman of the Revolutionary Committee. But on the very day when the masses came out into the streets and when the actual revolution took place the Military Revolutionary Committee could not but act in unison with the Petrograd Soviet and a man like Podvoisky could not play the role of the main standard bearer. The standard bearer, the symbol of the revolution, was Lenin who came out of hiding; so too was Trotsky, the leader who gained tremendous admiration and popularity by his speeches at the Cirque Moderne, which earned him the post of the President of the Petrograd Soviet; this in turn made him the actual head of the Revolutionary Committee and as such he became the head of the first revolutionary government. And no one else but Trotsky could play this role. This 'government' existed only for half a day, because already that same evening the Congress of the Soviets took over power in the country and set up the Revolutionary Council of People's Commissars, headed by Lenin and of which Trotsky became a member. But for the day which preceded the inaugural session of the Soviets, it was Trotsky who led both the Petrograd Soviet and its Military Revolutionary Committee. It is absolutely futile and useless to question this historical reality.

III

The Second Congress proclaimed the rule of the Soviets and set up the Council of People's Commissars. Lenin proposed that Trotsky should become the Commissar for Foreign Affairs. His work in the Revolutionary Committee was over, said Lenin, and he would be much more effective in this new post.

What was to be the business of the Commissariat for Foreign Affairs? Diplomacy, to which Trotsky was not inclined? At that time there could be no question of any diplomatic activity. The business of the Commissariat was, in fact, *agitation*. The Commissariat was then viewed as an organ which had to address itself to all nations of the world and to the world proletariat with a call to revolution, with an appeal for solidarity with the revolution in Russia. The task of transforming the Russian revolution into a world revolution was the first task of Trotsky's Commissariat. From the Cirque Moderne the agitation had now to be transferred to the tribunes of the world. For this job Trotsky was the best-equipped leader.

Who was now to head the Petrograd Soviet? Yes, the revolutionary power was in the hands of the Council of People's Commissars under Lenin, but the Petrograd Soviet was still playing a considerable historic role and its work could only gradually be taken over by the Council of People's Commissars and by the new All-Russian Central Executive which was to replace the previous one dominated by the Mensheviks and the Social Revolutionaries. The new President of the Petrograd Soviet had to uphold the banner under which revolutionary workers and soldiers took power.

Lenin, who three weeks earlier had proposed that Zinoviev should be expelled from the Party, now put forward Zinoviev's candidature for the post of the President of the Petrograd Soviet. This should convince any impartial student of history that the expulsion demand had been made in the heat of the debate. The importance of the Petrograd Soviet was still considerable. It was regarded as the heroic pioneer of the revolution and only a true revolutionary could preside over it. Zinoviev's previous vacillations were thus forgotten. A new page of history was turned: Zinoviev was now to play a leading role in the Party and the revolution. The same can be said of Kamenev, whose opposition had been even more consistent. He refused to view the revolution as a socialist one and was against the October insurrection. If one can say that Zinoviev became confused under the impact of the July events, Kamenev remained clear-minded and convinced of the correctness of his line. But as soon as he realised that by breaking the discipline of the Party he had been in the wrong, Lenin again regarded him as a Bolshevik whose place was in the Party and even among its prominent leaders.

The All-Russian Central Executive Committee was the highest organ of the revolution to which the Council of People's Commissars, as an executive body, was responsible. Lenin proposed Kamenev as the President of the Central Executive Committee. And in this way both men who had so recently been regarded by Lenin as traitors, came to occupy two of the most responsible official positions.

Zinoviev was never a member of the Council of People's Commissars, but in Petrograd his role was quite considerable; it increased even more after the government was transferred to Moscow after the March crisis when peace negotiations at Brest Litovsk broke down.

Without going into details of Zinoviev's activity, one has to stress that his behaviour earned him great authority and the confidence of the Petrograd proletariat, though not of the garrison which in that period ceased to play the historical role it played during October. After the insurrection the weight of the Petrograd garrison diminished so rapidly that not much can be said about it. Soldiers' representatives sat on the Soviet where, however, to an ever greater degree workers' deputies predominated. The Soviet was becoming an organ of proletarian dictatorship. It was in this sense that the attitude of the garrison towards Zinoviev was less important. Here I cannot be more precise because these processes were hardly noticeable.

Within a short period of time the Petrograd workers accepted Zinoviev as the leader of their Soviet, although before October they had hardly any contact with him and he had played no active part in their lives. He had been one of the many speakers at meetings in the Tauride Palace, but there he had addressed mainly soldiers coming to the capital from other parts of Russia. He also spoke at the Central Committee of the Party, but in the factories he was not as popular as, say, Trotsky, who roused great crowds while Zinoviev was in hiding in Finland. But very soon he managed not only to gain the confidence of the workers, but one can even say their affection. Of course, he committed many mistakes as any man would in such a difficult period of rapid transformation of all social and political relations. But, on the whole, Zinoviev pursued a correct and consistent policy. In dealing with complex and difficult problems he gave proof not only of positive, but even of exceptionally valuable sides of his character.

He often had to battle against the determined hostility of the bourgeoisie. This hostility made itself felt in the whole of Russia, but nowhere to such a degree as in Petersburg which was the centre of financial and industrial capital. He was in favour of severe repressive measures. But right from the beginning others beside him had a say in these matters and there were people who restrained those among the revolutionary young workers, soldiers and even intelligentsia who demanded even more ruthlessness towards the class enemy. I knew of cases when even the Petrograd Cheka (Extraordinary Commission for Struggle against Counter-revolution) was trying to curb such demands. This is a fact which may now seem odd. The head of the Cheka was at that time M.S. Uritsky, a highly cultured man of a mild disposition. He took this task upon himself as a revolutionary duty, which had to be fulfilled, if need be, with the utmost severity. But the exercise of power as such had no attraction for him.

In the Petrograd department of the Cheka there were many young, devoted and fiery revolutionaries who, faced with the opposition of the bourgeoisie, were at first inclined to resort to ruthless and even bloody repressions. Uritsky used his authority to restrain them. I knew of instances when young activists in the Cheka reproached Uritsky for hindering them. They were trying to persuade him that no one should refrain from bloodshed if this was necessary, that heads should roll if that was needed for the victory of the revolution. After listening to them, Uritsky used to answer: 'You are bloodthirsty boys. I shall not put power into your hands. You do not understand that precisely such methods may harm the revolution.'

Zinoviev accused Uritsky of weakness. There were cases when even Lenin did not approve of Uritsky's 'softness' and thought that he was carrying his humanitarianism too far. At the same time the bourgeois and Social-Revolutionary youth hated Uritsky. They considered him responsible for all the repressive measures and knew nothing of the humane and conciliatory role he played behind the scenes.

And so the murder of Uritsky followed that of Volodarsky and occurred more or less at the time of the attempt on Lenin's life in Moscow. Uritsky's restraining influence had gone. But even this might not have been effective in the heated atmosphere created by the attack on Lenin. Whoever stood at the head of the Cheka, in fact it was Zinoviev who became responsible for the whole administrative and political machinery of the Soviet power in Petrograd, who had to deal in the harshest possible way with counter-revolutionary activity. Strict measures were taken in Moscow and other cities, but nowhere were they as rigorous as in Petrograd. Zinoviev introduced terror on a mass scale. Many people who knowingly would not have taken part in counter-revolutionary action were denounced and perished only because they had belonged to the former ruling classes or had contact with the Tzarist regime. In fact many more people were destroyed in Petrograd than in other cities.

It seems to me that Zinoviev's aggressive attitude was not the result of a calm analysis of the situation, nor a conviction that there was no other way. Trotsky and Dzerzhinsky too sometimes applied rigorous methods which, whether correct or not, were dictated not only by emotions (unavoidable at the time), but essentially by an evaluation of historic circumstances demanding, in their opinion, the utmost severity. Both Trotsky and Dzerzhinsky were capable of annihilating suspected opponents of the Soviet regime, but only when they were convinced that the safety of the revolution demanded such action. Only then would they assume responsibility for mass terror. Zinoviev's attitude was, I think, somewhat different. His whole evolution was marked, now and again, by some degree of cowardice. In July 1917, when Petrograd was occupied by Mazurenko's troops, Zinoviev became faint-hearted and repudiated the views he had held on his return to Russia in April. He persisted in his new attitude even in Finland where he stayed with Lenin, sharing with him the log cabin or sleeping in the same haystack. He could not bear defeat and the whole weight of danger which came to threaten them both. He lost his bearings and gave up the idea of socialist revolution which was just beginning in Petrograd and consequently he opposed the October insurrection.

It seems to me that he was in a similar frame of mind after the assassination of Uritsky and the attempt on Lenin's life. Danger was again looming ahead, the danger that Lenin might be killed, the danger that he himself might be murdered. He was seized with panic. To my mind this panicky mood was responsible for the extreme harshness of his reaction and for the fact that the terror unleashed in Petrograd was so much greater than the security measures introduced in Moscow under Dzerzhinsky. Zinoviev's was a counsel of despair because he thought that the revolution was being defeated. He was as frightened as he had been in July; and this lack of courage would again manifest itself later in his life.

As President of the Petrograd Soviet Zinoviev was active in

many spheres of the city's life. He was very interested, among
other problems, in cultural activities; he was also involved in
the reorganisation of education and in propaganda work.
There are still traces of his influence. It was on his initiative
that some of the city's streets were re-named in memory of old
revolutionaries. Nowhere else have the Decembrists been thus
honoured. Kammenostrovskyi Prospect owes its name to the
poem by Emile Verhaeren 'The Red Dawn'. Zinoviev also
made the valedictory speech at the grave of Plekhanov.

While great events were taking place, while Petrograd was
threatened by the German army and the government moved
to Moscow, while the revolution was in danger, nobody
remembered Plekhanov dying of tuberculosis of the throat in
Tsarskoye Selo. He himself had withdrawn from the process
of the revolution and the masses had forgotten him so
completely that when a group of sailors broke into his home,
his name was quite unknown to them. They had no notion
who he was and what role he had once played as a great
revolutionary teacher of the Bolsheviks. They dragged him off
his bed, poked the mattress with their bayonets searching for
hidden arms. But it was not the roughness of the sailors that
killed him, but his most terrible disease. After his death nobody recalled him in the way Zinoviev did. He spoke at his
funeral and paid due tribute to his historical role. Only after
Zinoviev's tribute did others speak and write about Plekhanov's
past services. By now his place in history is generally acknowledged and his monument stands in front of the Polytechnic
Institute. But at the time of his death he was either forgotten, or
despised, as a man of the counter-revolutionary bourgeoisie. It
was, of course, wrong to see him in this light, and yet this was
the opinion of the majority of people. Zinoviev was perhaps the
first among the communist leaders who recalled Plekhanov's
role with respect and reverence.

Zinoviev was active in Petrograd, but Petrograd was
becoming more and more provincial and Lenin recognised
that for a man of Zinoviev's talents there was not enough
scope there. As orator and agitator he was somewhat inferior
to Trotsky, but he had given proof of his uncommon
organisational talent at the Longjumeau School and in the
Petrograd Soviet.

The time came when Lenin saw fit to separate the functions of Narkomindel (National Commissariat for Foreign Affairs) from those of a propaganda agency. After the failure of the Brest Litovsk negotiations it became clear that Narkomindel's role was not to address itself 'to the nations of the world and to international proletariat' but to engage in diplomatic activity on behalf of the *State*. Another non-State but party-political organisation was needed for propaganda activity. Such an organisation was the Comintern, which took over the tasks assigned to the Narkomindel in the first festive days of the victorious revolution.

At the head of the Commissariat for Foreign Affairs stood the diplomat Chicherin. From now on it was the Comintern's task to call upon the world proletariat to rise. The roles were divided, but in one way the Comintern was a direct successor of the Narkomindel as at first conceived.

Lenin placed Zinoviev at the head of the Comintern. The overall direction was, of course, assumed by Lenin, who was concerned not only with the general idea of world revolution but also with the problems of particular countries. But practical day-to-day work, all the details and all the decisions of the moment were dealt with by the Executive Committee of the Comintern under Zinoviev. In this Zinoviev's cooperation with Lenin proved most effective. Thanks to his organisational ability, Zinoviev gathered around him the most eminent foreign communists and directed their work through the Comintern's Executive.

From time to time Zinoviev also appeared on the scene as a propagandist. I should like to end this sketch with a description of an event during which Zinoviev reached the peak of his revolutionary-propagandist career and had shown himself to be an agitator *par excellence*. This was at the Party Day celebration of the German Social Democracy in Halle.

At that time the crucial discussions centred on the direction in which the German Social Democracy, a party where revolutionary feelings ran high, was going. Previously these feelings had characterised the Spartacus group which shared the Zimmerwald internationalism, but which also included such people as Edward Bernstein. Right from the beginning of the war Bernstein did not follow the majority of the

94

German Social Democrats who adopted a patriotic and chauvinistic line. He remained in opposition, left the official party and joined the Independents. In the Independent Social Democratic Party far from all the members were revolutionaries; but all were in opposition to the war. In this they were truer socialists than the official party, but in theory and practice they were also 'revisionists', that is they envisaged the way to socialism not through a socialist uprising but through gradual reforms. But at that particular period of time in the essentially non-revolutionary Independent Socialist Party there appeared some revolutionary elements far removed from 'Bernsteinism'. Incidentally, some such elements also appeared in the official Social Democratic Party. The Halle Congress was decisive for the future course of the whole German democracy: Would it turn towards a revolutionary solution or was it going to remain with the opportunistic positions adopted during the war?

All shades of opinion were represented at the Halle Congress. On the eve of the meeting an exhaustive discussion took place and the resolutions decided upon were to be adopted next day. Fraternal delegates of the Bolshevik and Menshevik Parties were also invited. Martov, who had shortly before, with Lenin's agreement, left the Soviet Union and settled abroad, represented the Mensheviks. Zinoviev was there on behalf of the Comintern. The famous 'duel' between Zinoviev and Martov turned out to be the central and high point of the Halle gathering. There was a variety of tendencies among those in the audience, and although some delegates were in a revolutionary mood, the majority viewed the Russian October Revolution with scepticism. This majority was inclined to pay most attention to Martov's speech.

I have earlier considered in detail Zinoviev's role in the revolutionary terror in Petersburg precisely because I wanted to return to this question in connection with the Halle Congress.

Martov denounced the repressions in Petersburg in the sharpest terms. He declared that the socialist revolution under the Bolsheviks was a bloody upheaval, therefore it had become a denial of socialist humanism and socialist ideals. As an example he recalled events in Petrograd, stressing their odious character. Zinoviev was scheduled to speak after Martov.

Martov was not a great orator. He spoke indistinctly, in a low and dull voice, and his listeners tended to move forward in their seats to be as near the podium as possible so as to catch his words. Although technically he was at a disadvantage, once the hall became completely quiet, his audience was often under his spell. His manner of speech was simple; he would sometimes repeat or contradict himself; he would digress, then return to the point, but he spoke with great sincerity, with much conviction and it seemed that he was not delivering a previously prepared text, but that he was just thinking aloud in front of his audience. This always impressed his listeners, especially the more knowledgeable. At a mass meeting he would simply not have been heard and his listeners would not have been capable of appreciating the finer points of his eloquence. But at the Party Day in Halle he had an educated audience which he impressed immensely by stating *his own* view, his own assessment of the revolutionary methods which he characterised as bloody and inhuman.

When after Martov Zinoviev mounted the rostrum, his reception was not auspicious. He was greeted with catcalls like 'Zinoviev – the bloody dog.' Of course, with a great part of the audience in such a mood, it is not easy to address it and not every speaker could keep his bearings or find the words and the approach which would enable him to get the attention of the hall and make himself heard. Zinoviev was at an additional disadvantage because when his nerves were strained, his high-pitched voice would break into a jarring falsetto. This is a great handicap for an orator and does not endear him to the public. And yet, in spite of this drawback, the public listened to Zinoviev intently. At the beginning hecklers interrupted him with cries of indignation; but gradually the whole audience was captured by his speech.

He did not try to cover up the mistakes committed. He spoke openly about blunders and even misdeeds for which even he might have been responsible. Yes, he said before the Congress, perhaps we have made terrible mistakes which may have disgraced our socialist movement. But, comrades, who is to be blamed? In the whole of history there was never a situation in which the proletariat had seized power. The precedent of the Paris Commune was on an infinitely smaller scale in comparison with events in Russia. And the example of the Commune showed precisely that the Paris proletariat had not shown enough determination, persistence, and ruthlessness in defending its power. Perhaps that was why it was so quickly defeated. Perhaps the Paris Commune was doomed to be vanquished because, surrounded by enemies, no force came to its rescue. It would, however, have lasted longer had it shown more tenacity and more harshness towards its foes. This was the lesson we, Bolsheviks, and with us the proletariat of Petrograd had learned from the Paris Commune ...

[Here the text breaks off.]

Components of Socialism

M. BOGIN

Socialism is one of the most popular words in the world. It is popular not only in Eastern Europe, in the 'Communist' countries, but in the West too, in the developed countries of capitalism, and in the so-called 'Third World' – in short, everywhere. And the main reason for this is the meaning attached to the word. To the majority of those who use it, it means: a new, perfect and just order replacing or promising to replace the old, imperfect and unjust order.

But this general and necessarily brief definition still says little. Supplementary questions arise, like: what is socialism precisely? what is its essential character? what are its components? what are the ways and means for constructing a socialist, i.e., just, society?

These questions have in the course of many decades (if not centuries) received contradictory answers, not only from opponents of socialism, but from individuals, currents and parties inside the socialist movement. There are many of them, and they all (Narodniks, Marxist social-democrats, socialist-revolutionaries, Labourites, syndicalists, anarchists of various shades, communists of different persuasions – Bolshevik-Leninists, Trotskyists, Stalinists, Maoists, Titoites, communist-democrats of the Dubĉek type, Arab socialists of the Baas type and others) answer these questions differently.

In order to cope with this complex and confused labyrinth of ideas and programmes, in order to establish what socialism is (without reducing the answer to absurdity), it is necessary, I believe, to relate the above mentioned tendencies and parties (and one's own) to two fundamental, root problems of every society – the problems of property and power. All the rest flows from the solution of these two problems.

Of course, this task requires a major historical study. In the following essay I shall try simply to analyse how these questions are approached first by the official ideologues of the CPSU and then by myself, whom I consider to be a communist-democrat.

The many and often confused definitions of the specifics of a socialist society given by our official ideologists, if one peels away the empty phrases, boil down to two positions: socialism is state ownership of the means of production under the political leadership of the Communist Party.

Let me begin with this formula.

Socialism and property

There are three kinds of property: private, social and state. In the USSR and other 'Communist' countries a system of state property prevails (it is no secret that the collective farms created by Stalinist methods are only a variant of state property). State property, therefore, according to the above-quoted formula, constitutes the chief economic basis of socialism. And in maintaining this the proponents of *state* property usually refer to the *Communist Manifesto* and declare themselves authentic socialists, Marxist-Leninists.

Is this the case?

Neither the *Communist Manifesto* nor any other work of Marx and Engels suggests that state ownership is socialist. The *Communist Manifesto* says something different. It characterises private property as an ill which should be replaced by *social* ownership. This idea is based on Marx's prediction that capital will inevitably concentrate into the hands of the industrial and finance magnates, so eliminating the peasantry in the countryside and the middle classes in the towns and leaving two polarised classes – the rich property-owners and the propertyless proletariat, i.e., the entire working population.

Marx conceived the proletarian revolution, which would destroy private property, classes and the state and set up a classless, socialist society on the basis of social ownership, as an action undertaken by the overwhelming majority of the people *vis-à-vis* a tiny handful of rich men who had appropriated social wealth from the people. The basic components of socialism according to Marx are: *social ownership; self-management by the working people; a fair distribution of material wealth (first according to work, then to needs); abolition of the gap between mental and physical labour, between town and country.*

Is there anything in common between these ideas of Marx and our system of state property based on super-centralisation, on the concentration of power in the hands of the bureaucracy and technocracy, on the vast privileges of the *élite* and the total lack of participation of the masses in what is called 'decision-taking'? The gap is enormous.

Apart from all else the gap is conditioned by that characteristic habit of bureaucrats, calling themselves socialists, to ignore the historical process, to ignore real life which doesn't always develop according to their theoretical schemes.

Marx's predictions of the polarisation of society did not, as we know, materialise. The concentration of capital, increased by the scientific-technical revolution, led to a sharp decline of the peasantry in the developed countries and to the movement of many white-collar workers into the working class. But it did not bring about the impoverishment of the lower classes nor the disappearance of the middle layers, neither in the town nor in the country. Small and medium-sized property did not disappear, but found their place within the system of capitalist relations, survived and consolidated – and for many millions of working people today they constitute not just a source of exploitation, but one of initiative, activity and well-being. The working class does not by itself make up the bulk of the population. Other working people live, act, influence and make decisions alongside it. Only *together with them* do the workers and employees constitute the majority of the population – and the interests of these middle layers are by no means opposed to those of the working class (as are the interests of the monopolies). On the contrary, they are natural allies of the working class (as is evident in the contemporary economic and political life of many countries, where middle-class parties play an active part in political life).

In the light of this development of the historical process every honest socialist-democrat should ask himself the following questions: is it any longer an absolute condition for socialism to replace all private ownership of the means of production with social ownership? Doesn't it better answer the interests of the majority of the people (workers as well as small property-owners) to combine social ownership of large-scale production with private ownership of small- and medium-scale production (this applies too – and perhaps primarily – to trade, the production of utilities and so on)? And can socialism be a just system, enjoying the support of the majority, if it is founded on the expropriation not just of a handful of magnates, but of wide layers of small property-owners?

At the present stage of the development of productive forces and with the problems posed to the organisers of production by the scientific-technical revolution, both kinds of ownership are viable and complementary. It is incomprehensible that the builders of a just socialist order, faced with the problem of providing people with all their material and moral necessities, should not profit from the opportunity given them by the productive forces of society to combine these two kinds of ownership in a flexible way. Why for the sake of dogma should they range wide sections of small property-owners against socialism instead of drawing them into the construction of a socialist society via the natural course of things?

Of course, as the productive forces develop, in particular as production and control are automatised, the relationship of large, socialised to small and medium private property will change in favour of the former. But if we are to construct a really fair and economically viable socialist order, then it is extremely important that this process takes a natural course without administrative pressure and forceful expropriation, without destroying in an unnatural, senseless way such economic relations as are still operational and perform important functions for society. History may develop in the way we suggest, it may take another path, but, starting from

101

the present situation in the world, we must see that the most realistic and effective economic structure for socialism is the combination of social and private property.

But how do you turn large-scale, capitalist (monopoly) property into social property serving the interests of the people rather than those of the industrial and finance magnates? The path of proletarian revolution and forceful expropriation drawn up by Marx and Lenin seemed for some time the only possible one. And so it would have been, had Marx's scheme of historical development been realised (the universal impoverishment and proletarianisation of the over-whelming majority of the population and the total concentration of social property in the hands of a group of financial and industrial overlords – Jack London, by the way, describes the same scheme in *The Iron Heel*). But history has taken a somewhat different path and the working class has been able within capitalist conditions to increase significantly its material welfare and cultural standards. The trade unions have become a huge, influential force in the contemporary world and political parties supported by the working class participate in the governments of a number of Western countries or even head them. In such conditions nationalisation of heavy industry, for example, can avoid sudden and drastic measures dislocating production, business and daily life, and can proceed along a peaceful, democratic path, moving gradually through stages of account and control, paying out reasonable compensation to the previous owners and gradually introducing new forms of self-management.

Speaking of self-management, we must not forget that present-day, large-scale production and present-day organisation of trade and services are very different from what they were in Marx's day. Trusts, concerns and companies today embrace not merely whole areas, districts, branches, but are very often multinational. Everything has got more complicated, interconnected, interdependent. So that it is simply impossible today to limit forms of self-management to the parameters of a single factory or supermarket. We need to work out a system of management which can link the self-management of a local collective with the running of a district, zone, republic, country, based upon two principles:

1. Maximum of decentralisation and local initiative; 2. Accountability of management organs.

From everything that has been said above it follows that radical correctives must be made in Marx's socio-economic programme.

Much of what has been said here was in fact worked out by Lenin, when he formulated his programme of a new economic policy for the construction of socialism (NEP). Lenin's new economic policy was a flexible economic system corresponding to the prevailing situation in the country and its level of economic development. It envisaged the combination of social ownership in large-scale production with private ownership in small- and medium-scale production, in trade and services. The programme took account of the single peasant household as the basic supplier of foodstuffs for the country and envisaged many measures for strengthening and developing this household (the replacement of requisitions by tax, the supply of credits, the development of market relations and so on).

The NEP programme also included extending the rights of the *Sornarkhozy* (Councils of People's Management) as organs of self-management, making them more democratic by involving hundreds of advanced, active workers in their work and so gradually transforming state ownership into social and people's ownership.

Subsequently, Stalin and his myrmidons (Mikoyan and others) were at pains to prove that Lenin's new economic policy was designed only for a short period (ten years) and that Stalin brought it to an end, when it was time. This is a falsification. NEP was a new method of building socialism and, according to Lenin himself, was designed 'seriously and for a long time'. Lenin's articles written shortly before his death show that he never contemplated forcible and wholesale collectivisation. In all the documents that we have Lenin talks only of *voluntary* and very gradual cooperation among individual peasants, initially taking on the simplest forms *(Better Few, But Better)*. And insofar as Lenin understood very well that the peasants in mass would never give up their private property *voluntarily,* he doubtless envisaged the combination of various kinds of ownership as the economic basis of the construction of socialism (as we see today in Yugoslavia and to some extent in Poland).

Stalin liquidated Lenin's economic policy by terroristic means, dispersed the *Sovnarkhozy*, forcibly collectivised the countryside, concentrated the management and disposal of all material resources in the country in the hands of the state or, more exactly, in the hands of a top Party and state apparatus which was totally obedient to him. And he was certainly no dogmatist. He departed from all the basic components of Marx's socialism (self-management, abolition of privilege, fair distribution, etc.), creating a new ruling, privileged layer of bureaucracy (it was then that the maximal permitted salary for a Party official was abolished) and subordinating to himself the councils, the trade unions and the Party. Ordinary citizens were turned into obedient executants without the right of criticism or protest, unable to struggle for their rights or even express their opinions.

This sad experience testifies that the nationalisation of large-scale industry does not by itself guarantee the building of socialism, that state ownership of the means of production (i.e., the concentration of huge power and huge material resources in the hands of the government) leads only to the substitution of one form of compulsion by another, to the disenfranchisement of the working people and to the degeneration of many professional revolutionaries into professional bureaucrats.

The Stalin experience showed state ownership to be the opposite of socialism. We have to find another form of management for large-scale production, trade and the organisation of services – by creating at the centre and in the localities elected, social organs of management independent of the government. In this connection the unhappy history of the *Sovnarkhozy* in our country is not without interest.

The *Sovnarkhozy* came into being when Lenin was alive (the SCPM, Supreme Council of People's Management, at the centre and the provincial Councils of People's Management in the localities) and, as was said above, Lenin hoped to democratise them and involve workers in their activity. The *Sovnarkhozy* were not social organs, they were not elected and were entirely subordinate to the government, but even so were entirely subordinate to the government, but even so they were felt to stand in the way of Stalin's super-centralisation and were got rid of. Khrushchev resuscitated them, but, like all his reforms, this one too was a half-measure. Nevertheless, even as risible pendants to the ministries and the State Plan they did arouse some local initiative and this is obviously the reason why they were once again done away with. It made it easier to return to the Stalin system of super-centralisation in the management of the economy and super-centralisation of power.

* * * *

Summing up what has been said above, I shall try to formulate my own scheme for solving the problem of ownership in a democratic socialist society. In general terms (although with necessary corrections) I think it can be applied to both East and West.

1. Combination of social ownership in large-scale production (trade, organisation of services) with private ownership in small production (trade, services). Combination of planning and directed activity in the social sector of the economy with initiative, competition, influence of the market in the private sector. Combination of self-management by production collectives in localities with elements of general control according to the size of the country, republic, district or zone (in the social sector).

2. Cooperation by private property-owners in small and medium production, in agriculture, trade and the organisation of services should be undertaken only on a voluntary basis by the producers themselves (administrative measures are strictly forbidden in this sphere).

3. Nationalisation of large-scale production should occur gradually, without haste and arbitrariness, so that production, trade, supply of services continue to function normally, without stoppages and loss.

4. When nationalisation takes place former owners should be paid a fixed amount according to laws of compensation. Shares owned by workers, peasants, employees

and members of the middle classes generally should not be subject to confiscation.

5. The large enterprises, which are nationalised, the supermarket chains, the service industries are not handed over to the government, but become the social property of the workers, employees and the small and middle-scale shareholders. A workers' council (or workers' committee) is elected to run the enterprise, and to run the whole of nationalised industry a *Sovnarkhozy* is set up, again by election, independent of the government. These elected organs are set up at nation-wide level (SCPM) as well as at the levels of republic, district and zone (*Sovnarkhozy* – Councils of People's Management).

6. The workers' council (or committee) has the right to direct and control the activity of the administration (appointment and dismissal of the director and other responsible persons; approval of the roll of rank-and-file administrators; approval of plans, norms, prices, wage and bonus rates; distribution of profit, etc.). The administration is simply a responsible executive body, which has to give a systematic account of itself to general meetings, and between meetings to the elected Workers' Council.

7. Workers' Councils – zonal, district, republic and All-Union Councils of People's Management – are elected for a period of three years by secret ballot at general meetings, conferences, congresses of workers, employees, small and medium shareholders, at which an unlimited number of candidates may be put forward and discussed.

8. All privileges and ranks enjoyed by the administration are abolished. The earnings of employees should not exceed those of a qualified worker.

9. In working out pay norms, wage and bonus scales the *Sovnarkhozy* should be guided by the principle: equal rights and equal opportunities for all citizens of the country.

10. The SCPM, the republic and district Councils should collaborate in creating various competing enterprises,

trusts and companies in all branches of the economy so as to prevent monopoly and stagnation in this or that branch.

11. The Workers' Councils and Councils of People's Management will give a systematic account of themselves, as appropriate, to general meetings or conferences and congresses called by the producers. The SCPM and Councils of People's Management will besides report once yearly (or more often) to Parliament or, as the case may be, to a session of the Republic (District) Council. The Councils of People's Management are not accountable to government organs (Council of Ministers, Ministries, etc.). Workers' Councils will report regularly to zonal Councils of People's Management.

12. All resources provided by the state budget for the needs of the country's economy are put at the disposal of the SCPM, the Councils of People's Management and the Workers' Councils, who utilise them independently and are accountable only to their electors and Parliament.

Such or a similar programme would undoubtedly help the development of the productive forces of socialism more than the armour of statification and centralisation, which distorts and constrains this development in the Soviet Union and other countries of Eastern Europe. Can it be carried out in these countries? That is a matter for argument. However, the events in Poland of 1956, when the peasants instantaneously liquidated the collective farms and returned to a single-household economy, like the events in Hungary of the same year and in Czechoslovakia in 1968, show that the Stalin single-type, state-owned economy, posing as socialism, is preserved essentially by force and that a return to a varied economy and to Lenin's combination of different kinds of ownership is quite feasible in a number of countries.

The situation is more difficult in the Soviet Union, where a policy of universal statification and super-centralised control has been in force for a long time. Here it is not possible to foresee either a mass return by the peasants to a single-household economy or a broad movement to open up small, private businesses or other kinds of enterprise in the towns.

The reasons for this are many – and we will not discuss them here. However, everything should be done in the legislative, economic and material (the so-called prestigious) spheres so that individual use of land, small trade and various small, private enterprises offering a range of services may become feasible, lawful and non-prejudicial occupations and so that the citizen himself may decide whether he wishes to work in a collective farm or on his own land, in a factory or, let's say, in his own domestic workshop. There will be people who wish to experiment, if they are not persecuted for doing so, and this will be much more advantageous to a socialist society than the secret and unlawful trade and speculation in commodities of high consumption, which goes on today. And in conditions like these all the various cooperative associations and artels will become genuinely voluntary and self-managing. And more important is that our large enterprises, collective and state farms will become genuinely self-managing, the workers will finally become real masters of the wealth they produce.

Socialism and power (the problem of force)

Economics and politics are interconnected. The system of monopoly state ownership cannot exist without a super-centralisation of power, without the concentration of power in the hands of the top functionaries of the state. The single-party system and a party apparatus, which was able to penetrate everywhere, enabled Stalin to create a system of state ownership which he was able to rule autocratically for many years. The concept of socialism as state ownership plus party direction is a completely Stalinist, totalitarian concept – the opposite, it may be said, to Lenin's formula: 'Socialism is Soviet power plus the electrification of the whole country.'

A socialist society, based on the combination of social property in large-scale production and private property in small- and medium-scale production, needs neither the super-centralisation of power, a system of privileges, nor the coercion of the majority by a minority. On the contrary, the system we envisage is only conceivable in a democratic, political order, where citizens may express their will freely and where a democratic government carries out the will of the majority. Of course, every form of power, every state presupposes the presence of force. Even the most humane legislature entails the restriction of the self-will of those who infringe this legislature, which means using coercion and constraining their interests. We may judge how democratic a state is by the extent to which its laws, measures, etc., express or protect the will and interests of the majority or the minority of the population. And this can be determined only by the people themselves, not by a minority in their name.

In discussing the question of power and coercion we shall not in this article touch on Marx's and Lenin's ideas on state and revolution. The question today is not whether socialism may be achieved by a peaceful or a revolutionary path (both paths are real, possible, permissible). Nor is it whether we should preserve or abolish the state (the complexity of present-day society necessarily involves an administrative apparatus – and the question of abolishing state power recedes into infinite distance). The quintessential question of socialism today, when Stalin and his successors have so compromised the very idea of socialism, is in whose hands – the majority or the minority – is the socialist transformation (revolution, reform) and who controls the state that calls itself socialist – the majority or the minority?

In other words: how shall socialism be built – by democratic means, i.e. where the majority expresses its will, refusing the proposals of the minority (although the minority is allowed to express its will), i.e., by the majority exerting its power over the minority, or – by the minority imposing force on the majority, which is also disabled from expressing its will?

Fifty years' experience show that a one-party dictatorship does not, as the Stalinists maintain, express the will of the working class and the peasantry, i.e., the majority of the population, that the word 'vanguard', which present-day Stalinists use to cover up the uncontrolled power of the Party apparatus, is only a mask for the ruling minority, which has usurped the majority's right to think, criticise, choose a path, decide.

Asserting the Party's right to unlimited power, official ideologists once again refer to Marx's *Communist Manifesto* and his idea of the dictatorship of the proletariat. They maintain that in our country Marx's idea has been realised and even grown into the power of the whole people, the power of the majority in the interests of the majority.

Generally speaking, this is not new: during the whole course of human history dictatorial regimes have used the words 'people', 'in the interests of the people', 'the majority of the people', etc. Marx has nothing to do with it. There is nothing in common between Marx's understanding of the dictatorship of the proletariat and our dictatorship by the heads of the Party and state apparatus.

It has been pointed out above that Marx based the socialisation of private capitalist ownership on the perspective of the concentration of capital and the polarisation of classes. He looked upon the socialist revolution, therefore, as the organised coercion of a handful of rich people by the overwhelming majority of the population, as the realisation of *people's power* (which corresponds with the original meaning of the Greek word *democracy*).

One hundred and thirty years ago Marx considered that the only path to socialism was revolution by the majority and the dictatorship of the proletariat. So it was then. The capitalists refused to make concessions and the poor workers, without rights, had no alternative other than a revolutionary one. But much has changed in the ensuing hundred-odd years. We spoke about this above. In the new conditions the working class, especially in coalition with middle-range labouring sections, has become a large, influential force and it has the opportunity to bring about the transfer of economic and political power to the people by democratic means. These means, which have been used by the labour movement in Western countries, are well known: strikes, demonstrations, parliamentary struggle, collaboration with parties of the middle sectors, formation of popular coalition governments, etc. Marx and Engels stood at the head of this path: they did not insist that the revolutionary path proclaimed by the *Manifesto* was the only one, but on the contrary expended a lot of energy in helping the working class to conquer those

110

powerful economic and political positions, which it controls now.

Apart from which, Marx and Engels never considered the dictatorship of the proletariat or the exercise of power in a socialist state as the property of a single party, as the dictatorship of one party. On the contrary, they always talk of *coalition*, of the collaboration of all tendencies and all parties in the labour movement (why only labour is clear from Marx's conception according to which the concept 'working class' is in the final analysis identical with the concept 'people'). It was on behalf of such collaboration that Marx subsequently, when helping to create the First International, retreated from the programme of the *Communist Manifesto* and worked out a compromise programme acceptable to trade-unionists, Lassalleans and Proudhonists. It was on behalf of such collaboration that he was willing to forgo the adjective 'Communist' and call the First International socialist. Marx defended and supported the Paris Commune, although it was headed by Blanquists and Proudhonists, whose activity he had often and sharply criticised. He acted in this way because what mattered to him most was the unity of the working-class movement – not as a formal unity, a unity of the 'graveyard', but as a genuine unity reachable only by way of compromise and mutual concession.

According to Marx, therefore, socialist revolution or the dictatorship of the proletariat is the democratic power of the labouring majority of the people as represented by all its tendencies and parties and realised by means of coalition and collaboration amongst them. In Marx's time it was only a question of coalition between parties of the working class; the course of history has shown that this coalition needs widening to include parties of other labouring classes in the town and country who do not wish to disappear, despite the concentration of capital.

Lenin adhered to a different point of view. Starting from his characterisation of contemporary capitalism (*Imperialism, the Highest Stage of Capitalism*) as a system in a state of rapid degeneration (decay, parasitism, technical regression), Lenin stood by the positions of the *Manifesto* and refused the path which Marx and Engels finally took – the path of compromise, coalition and collaboration among all parties of the working-class movement. Setting out his party of a new type, Lenin refused genuine (not tactical) alliances and coalitions with whatever other parties, including socialist ones (Mensheviks, Social-Revolutionaries). For him the only legitimate representative of the working class (and even of the peasantry, whose specific interests he understood) was the Bolshevik Party, which had the right to act in the name of the majority of the people. Here lay the origin of the idea and reality of single-party rule.

To be sure, at the beginning Lenin held to the principle of the majority. He said, we shall take power and say to the delegates of the Second Congress of Soviets: 'Here is your power, use it.' And at this congress a majority government, which included left SRs, was created. But this coalition did not last long – and the reason was the inability or disinclination of the Bolsheviks to compromise. The events which followed are well known: the disbanding of the Constituent Assembly, the subsequent exit of the left SRs from the government, their rebellion and defeat. The government became single-party, that is, Bolshevik, and the Party leadership was convinced that since it possessed the final truth it had the moral right, in the interests of the majority, to drive out, discard, crush and even destroy its political opponents.

Many thought at the time that this path was the direct, short, just and only possible one for building socialism. We thought that all we had to do was to make a start, conquer power and consolidate ourselves for the workers in the West and the colonial peoples in the East to rise up behind us and the world revolution would be victorious. This is what Lenin counted on and hence his revolutionary, uncompromising strategy and tactics, during and after the revolution.

But the world revolution did not take place. The war in the West came to an end, but for another four years a cruel and bloody civil war continued in Russia (not without the participation of the Western powers, now free of their war commitments). The Bolsheviks acted decisively, vigorously, were ruthless and self-sacrificing at the same time – and they won. But at what price? The country lay in ruins, many millions had perished; devastation, hunger and unemployment preyed on the people. How, by what means to set the country on its feet again – these were the questions round which inner-party struggle turned. And, although the decision to accept Lenin's New Economic Policy did hold out the possibility of restoring the country and of beginning the gradual construction of socialism, the principle of single-party political rule not only remained in force, but went as far as to exclude even inner-party opposition.

In this way Lenin's decision on the question of power (the single-party system) contradicted the programme of NEP – the first stood in the way of the second. Lenin still hoped for the victory of world revolution, for the victory on a world scale of the Communist minority – to be sure, in the interests of the majority.

But as subsequent events showed the sectarian policy of the Third Communist International very much weakened the working-class movement in the West, and in a number of countries (Italy, Germany, Spain) brought the fascists to power. In the USSR the persistent application of the principle of one-party rule brought Stalin to power, who widened the sphere of coercion to a limitless degree, making punitive politics the basis of his rule. The punitive organs set up under Lenin and trained to deal with political opponents were now used to crush and destroy large sections of the working population – peasantry, working class, intelligentsia, Leninist party cadres. By a stroke of the pen the New Economic Policy was abolished, the *Sovnarkhozy* disbanded, the countryside forcibly collectivised, any independent thought forbidden and the best, most selfless and principled party activists destroyed. Stalin created his own cadres – silent, selfish and ambitious, giving them enormous rights and privileges (though not the right to think, but of this they did not stand in much need), and subordinated all social organisations in the country (party, trade unions, soviets, cultural associations, etc.) to the state which exercised power exclusively through him and his henchmen. Stalin and his apparatus became the sole managers of the country's material resources and of the fruits of labour of its citizens, who were turned into 'cogs'. Naturally, it was impossible to achieve all this without terror, the victims of which were numbered in millions. And the terror arose in the final analysis from the one-party system.

In this way Stalin, by taking Lenin's idea of a one-party system to its extreme limits, turned Lenin's revolutionary idea of socialism into its complete opposite in real political practice.

After victory in the Second World War Stalin's policy of splitting the people and imposing minority rule not only continued within the country (in particular, by the use of terror against entire populations), but was transferred to the liberated countries (which at the beginning were genuinely liberated from the fascists). When it entered the territory of these countries the Soviet army, acting on orders received, handed over power by all sorts of combinations not to the democratic majority, but to an insignificant minority of the population – the Communist Parties, who as a rule followed the Stalinist path of imposing minority domination. So instead of a world system of socialism the Stalin empire was created.

What is the balance of the Marxist idea of a classless, socialist society, which has gone through so many stages of distortion?

In place of the liquidation of the state, as dreamt of by Marx and Engels at the outset of their careers, in place of its democratisation (the position they subsequently took up), in place of a temporary, 'transitional' state, as put forward by Lenin, Stalin created an all-powerful, almighty state, armed to the teeth, in which all power resided with a tiny upper stratum, who decided everything, subordinated everyone to themselves, deadening the society which ruled.

In place of a voluntary union of free, independent republics, enjoying equal rights, which included the right to self-determination and, if necessary, secession, as Lenin wished, Stalin created a great-power empire, held together by centralised rule, but riven by internal, national contradictions.

In place of the emancipation of the working majority of the population from the yoke of capitalist exploitation and lack of political rights, in place of people's power, Stalin created a state in which the labouring masses are not only deprived of rights, but deprived of the possibility of fighting for their rights, a state in which power belongs to a group of bureaucrats.

Instead of proletarian revolution, occurring, as Lenin said, because 'those below no longer wish to live in the old way and those on top are no longer able to govern them', instead of the revolution of a vanguard followed by broad masses of workers and peasants (as Lenin planned and to some extent realised), Stalin and his successors created a 'revolution' by means of occupying bayonets and tanks.

Such are the facts. Such is the evolution – more precisely, the degeneration – of an idea.

The sad experience of history shows that any idea, even though it were the most noble and were it professed, preached and propagated for the noblest of ends, will degenerate and turn into its opposite, if it is not accepted by a majority and imposed upon that majority by force.

*   *   *   *

After Stalin's death Krushchev denounced Stalin at the Twentieth and Twenty-second Party Congresses. Krushchev released and rehabilitated the victims of Stalin's arbitrary rule – alive and dead. In his political practice he tried to depart from Stalinism, to democratise the state, to lessen tension in the world and to raise the people's standard of living.

The trouble was all these attempts were half-hearted and inconsistent. Krushchev was unable to free himself of Stalin's basic inheritance – the concentration of power in the hands of a small, privileged minority, fear of opposition of any kind or of different ways of thinking. Despite the best intentions his methods of action and manner of thought moved within the same narrow, single-party, strictly centralised system, where personally he might from time to time allow himself now a liberal (Tvardovsky), now a reactionary (Lysenko) indulgence, but where there was no place for any real democracy and freedom of thought. It was this failure to find support among the best and most thoughtful of his contemporaries, this continuation of anti-democratic traditions which facilitated Krushchev's fall and the gradual ('creeping') rehabilitation of Stalin and Stalinism (publication of sympathetic novels, verse, memoirs, issue of films, etc.). But it was more than a matter of publishing pro-Stalinist literature and forbidding anti-Stalinist. Neo-Stalinist methods of dealing with those who think differently found their way into our state practice (sacking, expulsion from the Party, mud-slinging in the press, imprisonment, camp, psychiatric hospital and – the most recent achievement – forcible exile abroad).

All these forcible methods are accompanied by a flow of phrases about the defence of workers' interests, about socialism, communism, progress, peace and so on and so forth. But real upholders of socialism and communism have no need of psychiatric prisons to prove their rightness.

We, communist-democrats, reject the path of coercion of the majority by a minority. We consider that persuasion rather than violence can teach people the viability of the socialist system.

Starting from here, I shall try to formulate briefly the political part of my programme for democratic socialism:

1. Freedom of speech, opinion, tendency, opposition. The right to organise different political parties. Abolition of censorship.
2. Release of trade unions from state control. Guarantee of workers' rights to fight for their interests (freedom to strike, of assembly and demonstration).
3. Abolition of all privileges.
4. Abolition of the secret police.
5. Government actions and organs subject to public scrutiny and criticism. Abolition of those Party organs (departments, offices) which duplicate or displace the proper economic, scientific, cultural and other organisations subject to the immediate authority either of the government and its organs or of the *Sovnarkhozy*, cultural associations, etc.
6. Really free elections to Parliament (in the USSR – the Supreme Soviet) and to local municipal organs (soviets) with the participation of all political parties, putting forward their candidates.

7. A majority government – single-party or coalition – appointed, ratified, controlled and changed by Parliament alone.

8. The minority is guaranteed the right and opportunity to criticise government measures and to discuss with the government ideological and political matters – both verbally and in print.

9. The national republics have the right to self-determination inclusive of secession; national minorities, living on their territories, have the right to cultural autonomy.

10. All citizens of the country are guaranteed the right of free movement across the country as well as the right to travel abroad and return home.

11. End to all military bases on foreign territories.

12. Complete destruction of all kinds of weapons of mass extermination (nuclear, hydrogen, rocket, chemical, bacteriological, etc.) and restriction of conventional weaponry to a minimum.

The programme of democratic socialism (including its economic and political sides) may be briefly formulated as follows: 'Socialism is the end to the exploitation of man by man plus the guaranteed access of each individual to all democratic freedoms.'

This programme differs to some extent from the ideas of Marx and Lenin, but incorporates the most vital of Marx's ideas, which corresponds to the present stage of development – the revolution of the majority and the government of the majority for the majority. It also includes the results of other socialist thinkers of the nineteenth and twentieth centuries.

From the position of this programme we criticise not only Stalinism, neo-Stalinism, Maoism, Castroism, but also the Yugoslav social system. For in Yugoslavia, where the economic programme of democratic socialism has been partially realised (combination of types of ownership, self-management), the whole of political power is concentrated, according to the Stalinist model, in the hands of the leaders of the Yugoslav League of Communists. In Yugoslavia, too, therefore, criticism, protest, opposition are forbidden and disagreement with the government lands you in prison. This combination of economic self-management and political lack of rights cannot last long. The development of the Yugoslav state and social system may take the path either of the further strengthening of the dictatorship or that of the further democratisation of society.

Upholders of single-party power declare that the system created by them in the USSR and other countries of Eastern Europe is monolithic, stable and indestructible and that all talk of rebuilding it on democratic, multi-party foundations is illusion, fantasy and unrealisable raving. In addition, they declare that upholders of such reconstruction are agents of the international bourgeoisie, aiming to destroy socialism and restore capitalism in the USSR and the countries of Eastern Europe.

This is untrue. First of all, quite apart from the subjective desires of the supporters of democratic socialism, it is impossible to destroy what does not exist and impossible to ignore the historical stage we have been through and turn history back. Secondly, we are not trying to set up a capitalist society, the defects of which are well enough known to us, but to create a society of genuine socialism, free of the defects of capitalism and pseudo-socialism.

As for stability, monolithicity and indestructibility, what is there to say? All right, this system exists today and is apparently powerful. But not everything that exists is reasonable, fair or useful to people. And powerful does not mean forever. And what do sixty years of history signify? The powerful weakens and grows feeble in the course of time. Haven't there been other powerful empires, kingdoms, regimes in history?

Everything flows, everything changes.

Very much obviously depends on how the world around us today will change.

What perspectives are there for reconstructing this world on foundations of democratic socialism? What path will this reconstruction take?

Economic and political development in the world is irregular and multi-faceted and takes various, sometimes tortuous paths. For this reason it is difficult to make concrete prognoses. We do not know – and cannot know – where, when and in what circumstances the changes will come: in the East or in the West, gradually or suddenly, in conditions of war or peace, above or below, by democratic or revolutionary means. But we know that changes are unavoidable, they mature – and one has to be ready for them when the time comes. To be able to do this one has, in particular, to take account of the mistakes of the past, so as not to repeat them.

So, for example, the events of 1969 in Czechoslovakia showed that the communist-democrats led by Dubĉek did not create the main condition for victory – the legalisation of socialist and other democratic parties and the organisation of close collaboration with them. The lack of such collaboration, doubts, vacillations, glances towards Moscow allowed internal and external enemies of the 'Prague Spring' to gather strength, strike suddenly and cause defeat.

In Chile all this was apparently taken into account. Dubĉek's errors were not repeated: Communists, socialists, social-democrats and left radicals worked together in close collaboration. But events showed that this was not enough and that the victory of socialism requires more than the collaboration of the workers' parties: it requires their coalition with parties of the middle classes without which a majority government is impossible. Allende and his supporters did not understand that such a coalition has to be permanent, not temporary; that, by alienating the Christian-Democrat Party, they were pushing small and medium property-owners to the right and into the arms of reaction, because they were sowing doubts that the government might be preparing to put an end to all private ownership, including small and medium. It was this that turned them into supporters of the junta and destroyed the work of those supporting socialism.

Unfortunately, the majority of communists of our generation are a long way from working not just with the middle classes, but in a genuine way with socialist parties. As recent events in Portugal (and to some extent France) have shown, a number of western communists still look upon such collaboration as simply a tactical means. True, the Italian and

Spanish Communists condemned the actions of the Portuguese Communist Party, separated themselves from Cunhal and declared their readiness to work not only with the socialists, but with the Christian Democrats, i.e., with the representatives of the middle classes. This is a very hopeful declaration: the Italian and Spanish Communist Parties do not, like Cunhal, look to Moscow, but choose their own, independent road to socialism. In the West, however, these declarations are treated with caution, because it is not the first time in history that proclaimed programmes of collaboration in practice turn into single-party systems. Let us hope that the declared programme of these Communist Parties will be realised, because there is no other way of building democratic socialism than through the collaboration of the political parties of the working class and the middle layers.

Whatever happens, the ideas of democratic socialism are alive and active and are making people think, despite all the draconian measures. The future lies with them.

Communism and the Soviet Union at the End of the Twentieth Century

(Article One)

N. PESTOV

In our day many people who are concerned with the fate of the world or of their own nation – or simply with the peripeties and perspectives of their personal lives will agree that the question of communism – whether communism is desirable or possible and how it may be achieved or prevented – is the chief question for humanity at the end of the twentieth century. Never before has the whole world been divided into those who consider and declare themselves supporters or opponents of communism. And with every year the number of indifferent or neutral people gets less and less. What is the reason for, and historical significance of, this truly universal phenomenon?

The law of historical progress of humanity, which defines 'the general course of world history', is the development of society through a series of socio-economic formations logically following one upon the other. This 'general line of world development'[1] has led humanity in the twentieth century to the next such change – the process of transition from the rule of the capitalist formation to the rule of the communist formation. Popular movements and grandiose social utopias have portended this change over a number of centuries and by the middle of the nineteenth century Marx and Engels were justified in declaring that 'the spectre of communism is haunting Europe'. And Marxism gave a scientific basis to the inevitable change from capitalism to communism, seeing and pointing out the social forces which would prepare and accomplish this change and foretelling its historically imminent realisation.

The transitional epoch began in the first decades of the twentieth century. The first move fell to a large, not very developed, capitalist country – Russia, which in 1917 accomplished a socialist revolution as the first step of a world revolution. Following a Marxist programme under the guidance of Lenin, Russia set about constructing the first phase of communism – socialism – in its own country on the supposition that other countries would follow its example in the more or less foreseeable future. However, the transition to socialism was not brought about by the Russian socialist revolution either in Russia or in those countries which after the Second World War overthrew capitalism and in building a new society took the path of Russia's heir, the USSR. And the reason for the failure of the Russian experiment in constructing a socialist society – the first in the world – lay in Stalinism, in the victory of Stalinism over Leninism in Russia and in all the accruing consequences in Russia and beyond its borders. True, the societies established upon the territories of victorious Stalinism have left capitalism behind them and describe themselves as 'full' or 'mature' or 'developed' or 'real' socialism, but they do not represent socialism in the sense of the first phase of communism, nor will they lead to it. And in the rest of the world this Stalinist distortion of the socialist revolution and the example of Stalinist 'socialism' have frightened people off, discredited the struggle for communism and disoriented the communist forces. Capitalism, which had already outlived itself on a large historical scale at the beginning of the century and was ripe for world socialist revolution, acquired new vital forces (economic, social, intellectual) and possibilities for manoeuvre, yes, and even new prestige – by contrast with Stalinist pseudo-socialism.

So, once the Russian experience of building socialism had failed, humanity's movement to communism broke off and shifted back a half-century. Obviously, in terms of world history a half-century is not a very large interval. In the nineteenth century, for example, when there were almost no radical social upheavals or events that embraced the whole world and when people were accustomed to thinking that such events and upheavals were impossible, a further fifty years would scarcely have brought about substantial changes in the world-historical situation. But the half-century we have experienced is not the same. It suffices to mention the terrifying barbarism of Hitlerism and Stalinism, the very possibility of which in the twentieth century put in question the content and meaning of human progress; the Second World War which carried off many millions of lives and finished up by first using and then legalising the atomic bomb – capable in one moment of destroying the human race with all its millennia of culture; the entry into the arena of historical action, independent statehood and social development of several dozens of nations hitherto politically enslaved, removed from civilisation and lacking a voice – which not only changed radically the political picture of our planet, but redefined the character and conditions of political interrelations upon it; the popular anti-capitalist revolution in the enormous area of China and the overthrow of capitalism in a dozen other countries of Europe, Asia and America ...

And if in the last quarter of the twentieth century it has at last become possible to take up again mankind's movement towards communism, which began in the first quarter of the century and broke off for a half-century (and the present article is written in the belief that it has become possible!), then *how have the conditions and ways of this movement changed* as a result of the changes which have occurred in the world during this stormy half-century?

It is generally accepted (and conforms to reality) that our contemporary human world consists of three worlds: 1. the capitalist world 2. the world which has left, and is opposed to, capitalism and which calls itself socialist, and 3. what is known as the 'Third World'. It is obvious that the paths to communism cannot be the same in these three worlds. Let us examine all three worlds from this point of view.

1. *The capitalist world.* A radical restructuring of capitalist society, and its entire world, is occurring as a result of its

extension of life. Capitalism is forced to pose, and seek solutions for, a set of problems reserved by history for socialism and which only socialism can properly solve.[2] Capitalism does this in its own way with its characteristic distortions and antagonisms. This raises anew the question of the general crisis of capitalism as a socio-economic formation, for capitalism offers new possibilities and sows new hopes. And then there is the disappointment of the peoples in capitalist and under-developed countries with Soviet socialism (and its October methods) and the failure of communists in these countries to take a critical position towards this 'socialism', to work out such a position and explain it to the masses. Now to draw the countries into socialist revolution has as a result been turned into a difficult and complex historical problem.

2. *The so-called socialist world.* These are non-capitalist societies which have formed and established themselves upon a quarter of the territory of our planet with more than a quarter of its population. State ownership of the means of production combines with authoritarian state control in the form of one or other kind of political totalitarianism. These societies had not been foreseen by the social sciences: they are characterised by having broken with capitalism, but having neither reached nor being on the way to socialism. Possibly the chief and specific difficulty of including them in the world process of socialist revolution arises from the fact that their social structure is not a necessary stage on the path to communism. On the contrary, it is no such stage at all, but a deviation from the path. In the form in which Stalinist societies exist today there are no tendencies or paths within them which might spontaneously move towards communism – or even towards its first phase, i.e., *genuine socialism.*[3]

The situation is further complicated by the presence of Maoist China in this world – with its strong appeal. The Chinese revolution was born of Russia's October and has led almost a fifth of our planet's population along the road to communism. The Chinese path differs in some notable respects from Stalinist pseudo-socialism. The

Chinese revolution developed during the period of Stalinist monopoly in what was then the first and only country
with a successful socialist revolution. It passed through
the school of Stalinism in the second quarter of the
twentieth century. The traces of that period remain and
in some important respects China is re-enacting its own
form of Stalinism. Nevertheless, during the second half of
the century China moved farther and farther away from
Stalinism and its neo-Stalinist modifications in the way it
understood and implemented the path to socialism and
socialism itself. We are not speaking here of the estrangement between the USSR and the Chinese People's
Republic and between their Communist Parties – an
estrangement which has assumed the character of rivalry,
of a more and more bitter and hostile, even irreconcilable,
kind. We have in mind the nature of Stalinist and Maoist
societies, and whether or not Maoist society constitutes a
greater or less departure from socialism, as the first phase
of communism, than Stalinist society, the following is
unquestionable: as far as the restoration of a genuine
socialist revolution, a movement to genuine socialism in
our time is concerned, China represents its own original
and independent highway and not a variant of canonical
Stalinism.[4]

3. *The so-called 'Third World'*. Historically, this world was
   formed out of the colonial system of world capitalist
   imperialism and consists of former colonies and semi-
   colonies of the latter. As early as October 1917, when the
   world socialist revolution had just begun, Lenin, its
   theoretician, inspirer, organiser and leader, was thinking
   out the next step and showed that it would take two
   different directions which would from the beginning
   interact and intertwine and finally merge. The two
   directions were: transition from completed capitalism
   into socialism, as the first stage of communism, and
   transition from formations where pre-capitalist social
   forms predominated and capitalism was not yet complete
   (the 'non-capitalist path to socialism' for the then colonies and semi-colonies). And although the historical past
   and the social interweave in different countries created

different conditions and demanded different concrete methods of transition to socialism, the world situation then obtaining made it possible to fit these conditions and methods into the two directions and it also seemed possible to map out the main contours of these two typical roads of socialist revolution and socialist construction. But the past half-century has radically changed the situation. It is now no longer possible to talk of two typical roads from capitalism to communism. And if, for example, the USA, Great Britain, Japan, Italy cannot be aligned along one path, then what are we to say of India, Brazil, Ethiopia and Algeria, where the differences are greater still? The problems facing the communist movement in the Third World as it is today, with its enormous variety – the theoretical and practical problems – differ in principle and complexity from those of the colonies and semi-colonies that faced the Comintern in its pre-Stalin years, and they are extremely individual in each of the countries. But in almost all the countries of the Third World three circumstances form the chief social context within which they will have to find and work out their separate paths to communism: The general economic and cultural backwardness and poverty of the people, often entailing the starvation (and death from starvation!) of vast human masses, yet usually accompanied by a rapid growth in population. National and nationalist antipathies, prejudices, ambitions and pretensions are natural companions of the new forms of state, when they are expected to copy traditions inherited or borrowed from capitalism or to imitate Stalinist models. And, finally, the Third World countries, compelled by their backwardness to seek aid (technical, economic, cultural and military) both from the capitalist and the so-called socialist world and yet wanting to keep their independence, try to avoid either a capitalist or a Soviet (or Chinese, etc.) perspective.

Such are the three worlds into which contemporary humanity falls. They are distinguished quite clearly, socially and territorially (although, of course, not without intermediate shadings). We see that in the last quarter of our century

the historically ripe transition from a capitalist to a communist social formation on our earth has got much more complex
than it was in the first quarter, even without the victory of
Stalinism. But to approach the question of the struggle for
communism in this three-tiered world, one further fundamental circumstance of a general character has to be taken into
consideration – fundamental and general, because it forms
the background, if not the subsoil, for the existence, the
coexistence, development and interplay of these three worlds.
I have in mind the following:

On the general plane of history our period is the era of the
emergence of universal humanity: we stand on the threshold
of the *universality* of humanity. It is more than a matter of a
world market, which was created in the nineteenth century,
or of a world economy, as it came into being between the
nineteenth and twentieth centuries when the imperialist
powers split up the world and fought over its division, or of
the general political involvements brought about by the
world wars and peaces and accords between states characteristic of the twentieth century. As the end of our century
approaches, our planet, despite its national and political
divisions, is in the final analysis defined by the economic and
political relations and connections of a global dimension
(and, in many ways, global organisation), which link up its
separate and regionally demarcated parts. And in this
economic and political context, and facilitated by it, the
scientific-technical revolution is getting under way – a phenomenon which (unlike the industrial revolution of the end of
the nineteenth and beginning of the twentieth century) is not
limited and specialised, but universal, not regional, but
global – betokening the *growing universality* of man and his
existence. The component elements, the accompanying
results and consequences of this revolution are as follows: the
reality and actuality of a single world science on and for the
entire planet; general accessibility in principle of world
standards of production technique, etc.; universality of means
of information; freedom of movement and contact of people
across state frontiers; education systems with the same principles throughout the world; mutual influence and involvement of artistic creation throughout the world; increasingly

unified criteria of welfare and civilisation across the globe; and so on. And one cannot but conclude that, after long millennia of division, seeming axiomatic and fundamental, the varied societies that make up mankind have been led, at last, by the laws of their own development to take on the task of transforming themselves from an agglomerate of societies which arose and developed separately upon the earth, into a diverse but unified and single human society – into real *Humanity*.

But is this task a real one? Is the transition by mankind from a national to a cosmopolitan plane feasible? Or are the concepts 'humanity' and 'universality' incompatible by their nature and the task of creating a single and whole world humanity a beautiful fairy-tale, a utopia? And won't the necessarily supercharged attempts to solve this task bring such insoluble contradictions, such destructive antagonisms in their train as to lead human progress into a blind alley and bring the existence of humanity to an end?

Certainly, if one starts from the present divisions of our planet among the three groups of states described and projects them forward several decades, then such pessimism may seem justified. In our *present* state of division any cosmopolitan reconstruction of human life on our planet to replace the exhausted national plane, with which the twentieth century confronts us, is bound to lead to great-power suppression of smaller nations and great-power rivalry over the fruits of such suppression. Then there is the enormous, if not decisive, significance of the Stalinist perversion of the socialist revolution and the degeneration of socialism, which has given new life to capitalism on earth. The capitalist world has seized the initiative and is creating the models for the scientific-technical revolution of the twentieth century, while the so-called socialist and 'Third' worlds have to follow along behind capitalism, to copy its models and 'assimilate' its achievements with whatever success they can muster. But *this* path and *these* models pervert and irrationalise the historical sense of the scientific-technical revolution. They carry to an extreme the depersonalisation of man and the mechanisation of his life, consciousness and culture. They deform, destroy and trample down earthly nature – and in addition to this dehumanisation and denaturalisation of the human person, they drive the technical revolution itself into an incessant arms race of monstrous proportions, which in the end must threaten the human race with annihilation. Hence all the many and many-hued eschatological moods and expectations at a time when humanity has reached the threshold of self-realisation as a *world* humanity.

But no less justified than the pessimistic prognosis is the optimistic one, which sees in the present state of humanity, full of antagonisms and tragedy, not a blind alley and a closing-down, but a *transitional phase* on the historical path of the material and spiritual progress of mankind – certainly difficult and confused, but nevertheless a deep and irreversible transition to a higher form of human existence and humanity. And it is to elucidate *this,* optimistic, prognosis and the conditions for its realisation that these articles are concerned. Their perspective is not the indefinite extension of the present division of the world into three parts, as outlined above, but the possibility that this division can be put an end to. These articles do not see the future of humanity in the preservation and perfection of the forms of sociality (in the sense both of social being and social consciousness) on which the present tripartite division is based. They suggest looking for ways and means of moving to new forms – forms belonging to socialism as the first phase of communism. For only communism, starting with its first phase of socialism, can open the way to a post-national, cosmopolitan plane of human construction, which is neither anti- nor supra-national, but which preserves, develops and creatively combines indigenous national traditions; an *international plane* which communism serves and where it can uncover undistorted potentialities for the world scientific-technical revolution. Marx and Lenin knew already that communism, even in its first stage – socialism, is not possible in a single country. Communism requires a world humanity – and a world humanity requires communism. To refuse to move to communism, that is to its first stage – socialism – can only bring human history to a close when it is time for it to become cosmopolitan. Communism, already in its first, socialist phase, opens up the *genuine history* of humanity. And in the light of this genuine history all the

complexities, confusions and (alas, only too often) inhumanities of the preceding paths of the separate nations, living and
long dead – the entire preceding journey of the human
race – appear as a *prehistory*.

* * * *

Let us see then what *resistances* have to be overcome in our
time, if we want to make a new move towards communism.
We deal with ideological resistances and they are of three
kinds.

First, there always will be and always have been those who
have grown up in the traditions and spiritual atmosphere of
capitalism, who carry within themselves the ideals and
attitudes of the bourgeoisie, who fight for bourgeois ways of
life and ideology and would never dream of the possibility or
desirability of changing the capitalist order for a communist
one. These are old, inveterate, so to speak, naturally-given
enemies. We cannot discuss these people here.[5] But we cannot
help pointing out that they are assisted by those social-
democratic circles, who oppose socialism to communism and
the struggle for communism, i.e., who see socialism as a way
of perfecting and ennobling contemporary capitalist society.

Secondly, not the least, but maybe the greatest obstacle to
seeking out new paths to communism in our time is Stalinism
and its boundless propaganda (at all levels and for all
consumers!). A half-century ago in the Soviet Union the
beginnings of a post-October movement to socialism were
crushed and uprooted, and during this half-century the
Soviet Union has travelled further and further away from
socialism, losing the basic and elementary features of socialism as the first stage of communism. Yet Stalinist (and more
cunningly, neo-Stalinist) literature portrays Soviet society as
that of fully-built socialism, which is already building communism. It is only by unmasking and pointing out this
falsification and deception that we can find a path to
communism.[6]

This, of course, does not only apply to countries calling
themselves socialist or moving towards socialism. The Communist Parties of the capitalist countries (developed and

under-developed) still fail (do not wish?) to understand, and shy away from recognising, that only by separating themselves from anti-Leninist, Soviet pseudo-socialism will they be able to restore and preserve the traditions of October and the interest and trust in communism betrayed by Stalinism. Such recognition is decisive in these countries, if any movement towards socialism is to be organised. Until they understand and accept this the Communist Parties of the capitalist world must remain cut off from the struggle for a socialist society as the imediate task of the day. And this task has been replaced by new variants of the task of the workers' movement in the nineteenth century – struggle for the improvement (or at least preservation) of the welfare and rights of the working class in the capitalist world. Even the most independent Communist Parties – the Spanish and the Italian – remain stuck in this position. Quite recently (speaking in Livorno) Carillo and Berlinguer called the countries of the Soviet camp 'socialist' (see *Unita* 13.6.75), adding the conciliatory and ineffectual sophistry that while the Stalinist path and 'variant' of socialism may be proper and natural for Russia and similar countries, we Western Europeans would take a different path and provide a different 'variant'.

And *thirdly,* we cannot ignore an as yet not very numerous, but growing anti-communist force. In fact, we need to dwell on it in some detail, because it contains people who formerly took part in the revolutionary struggle. When, as a result of Stalinist degeneration this struggle produced a society of political totalitarianism, deliberately and calculatedly isolated from the progressive processes and currents in the rest of the world, a society with endemic stratification and sharp material inequality, with low productivity of labour, low quality of production and services and general economic inefficiency, with inevitably backward conditions and standard of living, with a coerced ideological and spiritual uniformity – these people were unable to remain fighters for communism, and sooner or later lost belief in the sense and point of such a struggle, whether on the plane of practical-political programmes or of scientific theory and the general course of history. These former ideologists of a Marxist communism took over the Stalinist identification of present-day Soviet society with socialism and the beginnings of communism, and in rejecting this society forsook the struggle for communism.

Some came to the conclusion that, as a result of the Stalinist perversion of social development and the consequences of this perversion, humanity had lost the opportunity given to it in the twentieth century of overcoming capitalism and realising its millennial dream of a communist social order on earth. Such, for example, was the emotional pessimism of the late Austrian Communist, Ernst Fischer, at the end of his life (under the influence of Czechoslovakia 1968?), who inclined to the view that a restored capitalism was much more likely to lead to the extinction of humanity than to communism. Others go further, considering that the choice of communism has lost its meaning, not simply because of the absurdities and inhumanities of the Stalinist experiment, but because this experience itself, as the first of its kind historically, has demonstrated the absurdity and unreality of the idea and ideal of communism. The Pole, L. Kolakowski, for example, maintains that the essence and moving force of the struggle for communism is an attempt to combine the three highest social values: ideal equality, ideal freedom and ideal efficiency. But such an attempt, he argues, is unrealisable because it is inwardly contradictory: 'Absolute equality can be set up only within a despotic system of rule, which implies privileges, i.e., destroys equality; total freedom means anarchy, and anarchy results in the domination of the most physically strong, i.e., total freedom turns into its opposite; efficiency as a supreme value calls again for despotism, and despotism is economically inefficient above a certain level of technology.' Kolakowski concludes: communism is finished. 'I have not for many years expected anything from attempts to mend, to renovate, to clean or correct the communist idea. Alas, poor idea! ... This skull will never smile again.'[7] A third group tries to stay at an intermediate position. They do not discard the idea and aim of communism, but seek justification in the present historical situation for abandoning the struggle. The Yugoslav, Djilas, for example, declares: 'The decisive mistake of communists is to go on developing the revolution, which in present-day circumstances has nowhere further to go. All attempts to keep communism alive are doomed, because the historical conditions which brought communism into being no longer exist. All that remains is external power plus the play of concepts which have long lost their original sense.'[8]

Therefore, if humanity's journey to communism, interrupted a half-century ago, is to be resumed in the last decades of the twentieth century, there are three kinds of opponent to be reckoned with:

- all the varieties of capitalist anti-communism.
- Stalinism, which pretends that its pseudo-socialist society constitutes the first steps to communism and that these only need consolidating and perfecting for full communism to be achieved.
- the abandonment of the struggle for communism put forward by the increasing number of disenchanted communists.[9]

If this struggle is to succeed, then it must be free of textbooks and nostalgia, in other words dogmatism. The return to the Leninist sources of the struggle for communism *via* a half-century break is a matter not only of strategy, but of theory and, if you like, world-outlook. Such a return must not and cannot mean repeating all the steps and devices appropriate to the first years of the Russian October revolution and the first years of the Comintern. And the problem is not simply that (as has been shown above) the world-historical situation has fundamentally changed since then and therefore the political methods which grew naturally out of the first socialist revolution in a huge and diverse, backward and ravaged country and which were practically appropriate for its development then, are now inappropriate and simply unacceptable. The problem is that in the light of subsequent history some of the political methods used then appear mistaken – those which enabled Stalin to deform them bit by bit and, under the mask of fidelity, to turn them into their opposites: from methods of building to methods of forsaking socialism. One of the prerequisites and ideological foundations for renewing the battle for communism is a deep, critical analysis of the beginning of this process while Lenin was alive.

133

We have entitled our subject 'Communism and the Soviet Union at the End of the Twentieth Century'. We may finish our first, introductory article with the enumeration given of present opponents of communism, who enter visibly or invisibly into any discussion of the subject. The next article will deal with the problem of transition to socialism – or more exactly, to socialism as the first stage of communism – from the social order now existing in the Soviet Union (and, with a few inessential variants and divergences, in countries following the Soviet path). And we shall bear in mind that the significance and resonance of this transition goes beyond the Soviet Union. Once the movement from Stalinist pseudo-socialism to genuine socialism has begun, it will directly and indirectly affect the course of the *world* socialist revolution, providing new perspectives and content and so smoothing the way for constructing the first phase of communism on a *world* scale.[10]

To round off the present introductory remarks we should also like to say the following:

As in all historical processes, so in the movement to communism (and its first stage – socialism) setbacks, postponements, zigzags and retreats – even prolonged and profound ones – are all possible. However, history does not only preserve what has been achieved, but what – according to the laws of history – might have been, and in the final analysis is destined to be, achieved. The path to communism is historically irreversible and if, because of Stalinism, it has not yet reached its destination and perhaps will not in the twentieth century, we still have a right to think that it will do so in the twenty-first – in the lives of our children and grandchildren.

Nevertheless, this process will not happen by itself, and time does not wait. The terminal period has arrived for Marxist-Leninists to come out with a genuine communist alternative to Stalinism. And we are tardying, yielding place to non- and anti-Marxists who are putting over capitalist or retrograde alternatives. We would remind the reader that this battle was begun by Marxists and for a long time fought by them alone, in isolation, and that the best and boldest of them were physically destroyed by Stalinism. It now devolves upon a new generation of Marxist-Leninists, who are appearing even in our country against all the odds but at the behest of history, to take over the struggle against the Stalinist perversion of Marxism and socialism, to make the struggle a historically realistic and victorious one, which will lead (we repeat, on a world scale) to socialism as the first phase of communism.

There is no place for delusion – it will be a difficult and long struggle. It will require not only intellectual fearlessness and moral purity, but basic human courage and selflessness – and sacrifice. But it does not befit a revolutionary communist to step aside from this truly great task of history.

More than a half-century ago, standing on the threshold of the first wave of the world socialist revolution and preparing to meet it, Lenin called upon the revolutionary forces to swim 'against the current'.[11] Today, as a new wave approaches, we communists must once more swim *against the current*. But as before this will be against the current *on the surface* of events and relations of forces. At the heart of things, then as now, it is a movement *along a deep current of human history* and therefore in the long run unconquerable and justified.

NOTES

1   The quotation is from Lenin *Our Revolution (On the notes of N. Sukhanov)*, 16 January 1923, Complete works, vol. 45, P. 279 [Russian].

2   These are: the scientific-technical revolution of the twentieth century, which poses anew, and seeks new solutions for, the problem of the material-productive basis of existence and the development of contemporary human society; the planning and regulating of production and its distribution socially and internationally; the increase in material welfare of the masses on the basis of the 'consumer society'; the important economic and political gains and cultural growth of the working class in capitalist countries, for which there is no previous comparison and is largely unexpected, as well as the participation by workers' organisations in the taking and implementation of decisions at a government level, which is influential and strongly felt in certain spheres; international economic, political and cultural organisations and associations as well as the freedom of inter-state communication and movement of people and the freedom of international information in the capitalist world.

3 Cf. A. Zimin's article 'The Nature of Soviet Society' in the second number of *XX Century* (see *Samizdat Register I*).

4 This is evident from just the following peculiarities of Maoist 'socialism' (which in China is dated from 1957) and its 'dictatorship of the proletariat': In economic policy the formula: 'agriculture is the basis for the development of the national economy, industry its leading force'. The administrative structure is divided up into proportions of 20 per cent power at the centre, 80 per cent in the localities. The 'people's communes', which unite tens and hundreds of thousands of peasant and worker families (sometimes entire districts and, in principle, towns), combine production and administration ('unity of power and economy') and exist and work according to the principle of 'self-reliance'. The ideology of egalitarianism and the leading role of the principle of economic equality, achieved by reducing to a minimum the worker's material incentive and the role of money in the remuneration of work. The wide and active participation of the masses in the struggle against the bureaucratisation of power (method of periodic 'cultural revolutions') ...

5 But there is one question, of an individual but not insignificant order, that cannot leave a Soviet (and not only Soviet) fighter for communism untouched. There are two remarkable sons of post-revolutionary Russia, very different in political and world outlook, both born and raised in the USSR, who have served their country and still seek to serve it with their enormous talents, each according to his understanding of patriotism – Solzhenitsyn and Sakharov. Do these belong with the capitalist opponents of communism? Yes and no. *Yes,* because the one is a rabid enemy of communism and longs for capitalist restoration of the most reactionary kind, while the other is studiedly indifferent to the problem 'capitalism or communism?' and dreams of their 'convergence'. *No,* because their irreconcilable exposure of the immorality and inhumanity of Stalinist society and their heroic struggle for the rights of man in this society have, despite their intentions, helped those fighting for communism.

6 Speaking here of Stalinism, we also have in mind (in one or another form) its quasi-Stalinist variant – Maoism.

7 L. Kolakowski 'My Correct Views on Everything', *Socialist Register, 1974* (London, Merlin Press, p. 20).

8 Quoted by K. Shtrem from a conversation with Djilas in *Kontinent* 1, 1974.

9 If one may use a political term which arose in the pre-revolutionary social-democratic party, obviously for a different reason, then one might describe these former communists as 'liquidators of the struggle for communism'.

10 The author hopes to deal with the movement to communism in the present capitalist and 'Third' worlds (depending on accessible material, etc.) in the third and fourth articles.

11 Lenin used these words for the title of a collection of articles by himself and Zinoviev written during 1914-16 to clarify 'the ideas of the

international socialist revolution' as it approached 'its first victory on 7 November (25 October) 1917' (Preface to the Collection: G. Zinoviev and N. Lenin *Against the Current,* March 1918, Complete Works [Russian], vol. 36, p. 124). Communist survivors of the period remember well this thick five-hundred-page book, which during Lenin's life became one of the programmatic works and handbooks of Leninism. Of course, the Stalinists and neo-Stalinists struck it out of their falsified history of the communist movement.

From a Philosophical Diary

A. BECHMETIEV

Concrete humanism and abstract classism

The noise raised from time to time in the press about 'abstract humanism' may at first sight appear the product of misunderstanding, a mistake of theory, merely the improper use of a word. Indeed, abstract humanism is usually the name given for concrete humanism – feelings of kindness, compassion, conscience, etc., without any clear underpinning of class interests and directed towards a living, individual person.

> Forgive me, I'm sorry for old women,
> But that's my only failing ...

> [M. Svetlov]

The author of *Kakhovka* and *Grenada* may well ask to be forgiven: his humanism lies outside classes and is therefore abstract. For example, he comes across a blind, enfeebled, old lady at a street crossing, supporting herself with difficulty on a stick, and he helps her across without considering whether she was a komsomol in the twenties or a maid of honour at the imperial court. The poet is on a dangerous path, because pity for an old lady is a very concrete feeling.

Abstract humanism is concrete. It addresses itself with

138

compassion and support to a real, living person – to you, to me, to him.

By contrast, so-called 'class humanism' is abstract. It treats a person only as the representative of a particular party, group, class and dismisses his individuality, personality, peculiarity. In the light of class arithmetic even senseless cruelty is understood in some higher sense – can be reckoned into the department of humanism.

For example it is well known that in 1918 Stalin arranged to shoot and drown a group of war specialists under arrest – former White officers, on a barge at Tzaritsyn. (From both a military and a political point of view there was no necessity for this; the enemy – if he was an enemy – was disarmed and powerless.) Such 'humanism' must without doubt be considered 'class' humanism, but where is the concreteness? We are faced with an entirely abstract class humanism. In *The Quiet Don* Sholokhov tells of the fate of Grigory Melekhov. Everyone who reads this novel sympathises with Grigory ... But how many Grigorys were on that barge, sunk at Tzaritsyn? *The Quiet Don* is the song of songs of 'abstract' humanism, whatever its demented author may now say.

The coryphaeus of all the sciences further developed his conception of class humanism in the 'dekulakisation' campaigns of the countryside and in the liquidation of the 'fifth column' in the country and the army, as people like Kochetov have obligingly explained. Any concreteness went out of the window: abstract classism struck people down right and left, making no distinction between peasant, army commander, engineer or writer.

In present-day conditions the struggle against abstract humanism, if one sweeps aside verbal ornamentation, seems to have very little to do with the social antagonism of classes. Here the demands of classism are mostly artificial, only window-dressing – veritably 'abstract classism'. The bards of literary 'classness' are interested only in one thing: to reject the unconditionality of such categories as goodness, justness, conscience. Their general acceptance would prevent one from sleeping quietly and enjoying one's bread and caviar. Hence the hatred for 'abstract' humanism, the desire to convince us that everything is conditional: good and evil, justice and dishonour. The relativity of morals comes to the rescue, equalising honesty and baseness, courage and cowardice. 'For me not one flea is evil – they're all black and they all jump,' says Gorky's old man, Luka. If you evaluate everything according to the advantage of a given stratum, class, state, then there is no moral judgement, no personal moral responsibility. It is easy and convenient to accommodate this 'abstract' classness to personal advantage. Eat, drink, get rich on the quiet, just don't forget to glorify a little louder those on whom access to the feeding-trough depends.

That roughly is the character of present-day 'classism', the practical essence of the battle against 'abstract' humanism.

10 March 1966

Dreaming as a social problem

After the fall of Krushchev solemn proclamations were made about a realistic approach to economics: there was to be an end to seductive slogans, phrases, 'idealistic' appeals, the economy was to be built in accordance with objective and actual stimuli: material incentives, the state of the market, etc. As has happened many times before, we went back to our ABC and started from first syllables: an analysis of phenomena in economic policy should precede conclusions, recommendations and seductive plans. Thy will be done, O Lord!

Can this be the end of the epoch of adminstrative romanticism? During the last years of the Krushchev adminstration illusory thinking carried a perceptible load of fantasy and 'idealism'. We are all of us prone to this, but here it had taken on hyperbolic proportions. For example, the following calculation was made: in such-and-such a collective farm in such-and-such a district a hectare of arable land yielded such-and-such a harvest. The rest is schoolboy arithmetic. If all the collective farms of the region produced the same amount on all their land, the sum total would be ... And in the country as a whole?! Oho! Or: a particular corn-cob has so many grains. If all the collective farms in the country grew

140

a similar corn-cob, we would fill up the country with fodder. Why didn't this happen? Presumably because of inability or, worse, unwillingness to work. Those who were unable required the example of the advanced workers. The unwilling had to be made to work. Krushchev's speeches, often quite sincere, veered between visionary enlightenment and police aggressiveness.

The newspapers added and multiplied, getting drunk on desired figures, seeing them on waking, deluding themselves with pictures of abundant communism, the advent of which was announced for 1980. Dream far outstripped analysis and the capacity for real and sober accounting of basic conditions and factors. This was especially striking for agricultural utopias: conditions of different latitudes and topography, the material incentive of the workers, agronomic knowledge – all was put aside. The important thing was to inspire and be inspired by a vision.

The visionary administrator recalled the daydreaming Manilov, seeing himself as general, while his peasants, upon whom he had lavished every favour, were busy selling their various wares in small stores set up on the new bridge he had erected ... and while in the corner of his drawing-room there stood a broken-down armchair, of which guests had to be warned that 'it is not yet ready'.

The good-natured dreamer has always something attractive and ennobling about him – not for him the low prose of life. 'I'm only a worker, I'm only a worker in mag-ic', as the song has it, which you hear endlessly churned out on the radio. There is no lack today of 'dreamers', who include philosophers, men of letters and journalists, who have made a packet out of romanticism and magic. It pays to play the romantic!

But our First Romantic, now nicknamed 'Subjectivist and Voluntarist' by the newspapers, so as it were punishing him for the abstractness of that other *ad hominem* label 'cult of personality', was an authentic, sincere dreamer. The only trouble was: he never set a limit to his dreaming and carried it over from daily life into affairs of state. Harmless as an individual trait, dreaming becomes the scourge of God when the whole country and people become subject to the whims of the dreamer's imagination. It spares no one. Cherished in the sweetness of solitude, the dream breaks down as soon as it hits reality, and no sooner the dreamer realises this than he grows furious. A corrida begins – a ferocious battle between the dreamer and reality. Deceived in his expectations, he hurls himself with the fury of a bull at the arena of life, wrecking and destroying everything in his path. Nothing remains of his good nature and nobility. He takes revenge for his unrealised and trampled dream. And, as if he is not himself to blame, he looks around for culprits. Then, scarcely quietened down, he recommences his castles in the air. And every time, like a drunkard, a drug addict, he has to stupefy himself with the censor of hope and fame ever more radically and recklessly, the crueller his most recent failure.

Dreaming is noble and can evoke sympathy from many as long as it expresses itself in suitably idealised forms. The farther away that the dreamer's sphere of activity is from the cares of real life, the better. And the more that real life has to depend on the visionary, the social visionary, the worse, the more dangerous. His sublime projections take their toll of real human lives.

Dreaming as a fact of psychology is connected not only with predisposition of temperament and character. It can easily be excited by lack of knowledge, material, facts. Dreaming, like floodwater, fills every hollow and depression lower than the nil mark of exact knowledge and understanding.

'One must dream,' said Lenin, repeating Pisarev's phrase. It is in the nature of human consciousness to project the future, look into tomorrow, in one way or another. As is well known, the Utopian Socialists, each according to his understanding and conception of the ideal, drew detailed pictures of the future structure of the happy island or the 'City of the Sun'. Scientific socialism renounced these illusory pictures – in favour of concrete paths and methods of struggle for the emancipation of the working class, thereby losing perhaps some of its philosophic aim. 'Scientific socialism', wrote the young Lenin, 'has never drawn any pictures of the future, properly speaking.' But the dream in its contemporary social appearance is the worst kind of utopianism. It jumps over the study of facts, and the necessity for analysing ways and methods, to a conclusion set forth in an abstract and ideal form by virtue of its remoteness. Starting from good intentions, dreaming often compensates for an absence of education and culture. Culture not only as the sum of knowledge and accumulated historical experience. But the culture of a supple, alert mind, capable of recognising the dialectics of movement, the variety of conditions, the intertwining of contradictions, the intermeshing of good and evil.

'The road to hell is paved with good intentions' – the paradox is that dreaming, such an abstract, rosy, ideal thing, is the nearest relative of dogmatism and bureaucratic rigidity. An alert mind could not exist for a moment in the same world as a bureaucratic mentality, but the 'dream' manages very well. Dream and dogma do not trouble one another, because they separate out their spheres of influence: for today and for everyday purposes strict discipline and a heavy bureaucratic style, for tomorrow – to keep up spirits – the dream. The dream even covers up bureaucracy's emasculation with its fine attire. Attached to the realm of obedience and form, Dream lends it the appearance of outward favour, spiritual substance and a stimulus to self-movement. But self-movement does not occur. For only knowledge, with eyes to see, is capable of it.

'Faith will move mountains' – no one would wish to quarrel with that. But in the final analysis it is a historically doomed stimulus of action, as are 'miracle, mystery, authority', for all their power over the people, over the 'blind mass'. Of course, they have worked in history (mostly in favour of evil) and continue to work. But even then only as a temporary bridle put upon people to make them more obedient, while they are still not 'conscious' enough to act in accordance with their personal convictions, based on knowledge. *Self-consciousness* is what will remove the remnants of faith.

Our schoolboy hero, Gorky's Danko, who shows people the way with his heart, is a fine hero, but historically doomed. How is it that only he knew the path and not others? I can guess why he was turned into a textbook hero during the Stalin period.

'One of Dobrolyubov's essays develops a metaphorical

picture: people lost in a wood and in their midst a 'super-fluous man', implanting dejection and despondency in their hearts and indulging in useless reflection, singing and moaning. And, of course, this is not an ideal example of social behaviour.

I too should like to tell a little tale about this dark wood of life. I would draw two situations. In one the hero has led the people a long way through the wood, and it has been such a torment getting through the swamps and obstructions that in the exhausting battle with obstacles they have forgotten the destination they were aiming for. The other has an optimistic ending: the hero being the first to guess where to go does not hide from the others where he saw the light, does not turn it into a revealed miracle and mystery, but tells the people honestly of all the painful details in front of them. And they start to think and help one another to find the path through the wood. And this is why they do not fall into despair, do not quarrel with one another on the way, overcome everything and are able to reach their destination. They remember the direction they took but are prepared for all the burdens of the journey – and do not despond when light fails to appear on the second or third day.

This is *self-awareness,* this is the movement of a person to himself and of society to an aim.

Dreaming does not contain the source of self-movement. It requires urging and the additives of forced discipline or belief in miracle and authority. As a means of mastering reality dreaming depends on general, abstract, approximate considerations. That is why it wages war on facts and firm knowledge, which it finds unbearably pragmatic.

It is said that in economics and economic life a realistic approach is now at last taking the place of fantasy and dream and that on its banner are inscribed the words: exactness, knowledge, concreteness. Apparently, that habit of taking a single, attractive example and turning it into a fetish, an alluring abstraction by ignoring the variety of conditions, is receding into the past. Generalisation, they say, is ceasing to puff itself up and strut about, inhabiting a world prior to experience and outside facts. And no longer, we are told, will a 'law' drawn from one felicitous example be allowed to suppress all the other one hundred thousand different examples. Indeed, if only!

But if you are going to introduce a realistic approach into the economy, you can't keep to old ways of thinking in politics, philosophy, ideology, literature. And the 'dream', 'education by example', by illusions, continues to form the basis of our approach to life.

But ideology is homogeneous and will not tolerate such a division. It is impossible to take a radical step towards realism in the management of the economy, if the old, illusory methods are retained in the education of the masses: dream, the enthusiasm of lone heroes or the abstract 'inspiration of the masses'. Otherwise, either it won't happen in the economy (a realistic course depends on the direct and conscious participation of the masses, of the people, and is unrealisable without this condition), or we shall be forced, at last, to change the old methods of education which never really caught on and pleased the teachers rather than the pupils and which today have totally collapsed, like an empty shell.

One would like to be optimistic and hope that the change in methods of 'education' and the reform of ideological dogmas is something unavoidable. The only question is: will this happen sooner than later and what will be the cost we shall have to pay in terms of mistakes, failures and losses for the conservative thinking of those who find it easier to use the rusted but familiar weapons, which have already been discarded in the economic sphere.

So far the only protest against dreaming has come from statistics, whenever it has been allowed to see the light. And, of course, from literature, which cannot help reacting on the basis of living experience. When 'Subjectivism and Voluntarism' were making their fantastic multiplications and calculations, literature pointed modestly to 'single facts' that contradicted them, as if to say: what about this? What about the Northern village? asked A. Yashin in *The Vologodsk Wedding*. What do you do with the total lack of interest in social labour among collective farmers? queried F. Abramov in his sketches *Round and About*. And the answer they got: slander, contempt for our life, until the same facts were made public in Central Committee resolutions on troubles in agriculture.

4 January 1967

Ends

The events of our history over the last half-century have fastened attention on the question of means: means are not indifferent to ends, bloody terror and cruelty do not lead to the promised land of happiness, unjust means can alter a good end along the way and so on.

Philosophers and sociologists have paid less attention to the question of *ends*. There is a tradition here, rooted in the struggle between 'scientific socialism' and 'utopianism'. The utopian projects of the 'City of the Sun', setting out detailed rules for the world of the future, the 'crystal palaces', the prophetic dreams of Chernyshevsky's heroine – all of these were naive attempts to put into accessible and tangible form the general idea of an earthly paradise and the universal happiness of men. Marxism is generally credited with having posed the question of ways and means of struggle concretely in place of the yearnings for the future and the illustory prophecies to be found in the utopian systems.

But the question of ends did not thereby disappear, that is of universal and fundamental ends, not partial and temporary ones. However paradoxical it may sound, Marxism has been concerned with the question of ends least of all, evidently assuming that in general terms these were firmly understood and familiar, indeed self-explanatory, and that given their remoteness did not require any special concretisation.

But do not a lot of people think consciously about what communism is, about the future society for which so many sacrifices are being made? Shouldn't we know more exactly what is being talked about? Otherwise, we are sailing in the same bark, pulling at the oars in a friendly spirit, when suddenly we find out that one of us thinks that he is going to Saratov, while another imagines it is Astrakhan. No one thought of working it out in advance.

146

If the classics of Marxism spent little time on the problems of ends, contemporary theoreticians show no concern about it at all. We are very familiar with the word 'communism', but we understand the meaning far less. It is enough to recall a remark of N. S. Krushchev in one of his speeches that under full communism the role of state and party would increase, and no one, of course, objected. It was simply forgotten, erased from consciousness that communism had formerly been considered, by even the most orthodox sources, a society of free people, a society where it was taken for granted there would be no classes, no state, no party.

Go along the Nevsky on a public holiday and at every corner you will find streamers with the message: 'our aim is communism'. What do people think, when they read these words? Or do they think at all? They simply accept in advance the combination of words given to them, and an aim, however conventionally formulated and unthought-out, seems to be something that it is in people to need.

In 1916, at the Third Congress for Experimental Pedagogy in Petrograd, Academician I.P. Pavlov delivered his programmatic speech 'The End-Reflex', where he said:

'The end-reflex has an enormous importance for life, it is the basic form of life-energy in each of us. Life is only beautiful and strong for someone who his whole life aims at an attainable, but never attained, end, or who goes from one end to another with equal zeal ... Conversely, life will lose its hold, once an end disappears.'

The word 'communism' contains a social end-reflex. It calls to action and serves practice well. Its very lack of definition and incomplete inventory of aim makes it all the more attractive, because it allows people to individualise their ideal and introduce into it an element of their own understanding of happiness. And yet a social aim should be outlined more clearly to guarantee against perversion on the way.

The only thing that seems unquestionable and that has fixed itself in the consciousness of the masses is material abundance and distribution 'according to needs' under communism. But, in the light of industrial development in the twentieth century, isn't such an ideal narrow, isn't it 'bourgeois'? Contemporary capitalism in Sweden, Japan or the USA promises to reach material abundance before we do. The problem of inequality will remain, but, most likely, it will be problem of differences between the rich, provided with all the benefits of life, and the super-rich bathing in luxury, i.e., some kind of conflict between 'good and better'. But the aim of life? And its meaning? Communism has promised us it, and the question of ends remains the sharper, the more it seems to be exhausted by the level of material well-being.

The question of social aim as super-aim, 'aim of aims' (J. Dietzgen) is connected not only with economics and social structure. Its kernel, its heart is the philosophy of a person. What does the 'blossoming of human personality' under communism mean? How is it attained? What elements in history contribute to it? What in this respect does the 'bourgeois freedom of personality' mean? What becomes of morality and art in the perspective of the future? Is it possible to speak of moral self-perfection as the goal of a communist personality? Etc.

Perhaps it is not possible at present to answer every such question. But to facilitate an answer the question should be posed in a clear, unambiguous objective form, and so stand in expectation of a worthy response.

20 June 1969

Ethics and super-aim

Ethics has always occupied a modest and subordinate place in the hierarchy of Marxist concepts. The fault lies perhaps in a confusion of concepts. There is applied morality, everyday ethics, and one floor below there is etiquette as a form of polite manners. But that is not all that is contained in the word. The individual behaviour of a person is always determined by the structure of his feelings and outlook, his conception of the meaning of life, of immediate and distant goals. And it is here that ethics as part of philosophy finds its proper sphere – in its consciousness of the end and meaning of human life, the life of a single person and of his behaviour and ideals.

I have already remarked that Marxism considers the question of *ends* as too abstract and conceives them only in general terms, such as: a classless society, a society of material abundance where distribution is carried out 'according to needs' and a person is given the opportunity for the limitless and free development of all his spiritual potentialities.

Disdaining liberal idealism, despising actionless mouthings about 'goodness', 'conscience', 'brotherhood', Marxism has concentrated its attention on real ways of liberating working people from exploitation, that is on how to get to the radiant goal. Marx studied the economic structure of class society, its social history in order to show what might be humanity's real way into classless society.

In so doing, little attention was paid to one thing: The 'philosophy of practice' required sanction from the philosophy of end. This end is not simply an idealised future, graspable in general words by reason. An end is the conscious behaviour of people corresponding to the end, it is the principles of their relations to one another *in the process of attaining* the end, more briefly it is social morality, ethics.

The end should not be alienated from the process of its attainment, otherwise one gets what Kant warned against in his paradox on freedom:

> I confess that I cannot agree with one opinion which is held sometimes by very intelligent people. It is that a certain nation (at the present moment striving for lawful freedom) is not yet ripe for freedom, that the serfs belonging to the landowners are not yet ripe for freedom and that the people in general are not ready for religious freedom. But the point is that on such an assumption freedom will never arrive, for it is impossible to be ripe for freedom unless one is already free: it is necessary to be free beforehand in order to be able to apply one's energies on behalf of freedom. The first attempts are characterised, of course, by a certain crudity and are linked with the more or less onerous condition, with the danger, compared with the earlier authority and tutelage of some over others. But

to be ripe for reason is only possible by one's own efforts and these efforts are only possible on the basis of personal freedom.

[*Religion Within the Limits of Reason,* last part.]

Marxism, in pursuit of the economic side of things, has treated morality in exactly this fashion, as something unripe and therefore inessential. It has recognised in morality only a class-limited content, although it has made some inconsequential reservations about 'the simple laws of morality and justice, by which private persons should be guided in their mutual relations' and ideally nations too. (Cf. K. Marx and F. Engels, Works, vol. 16, p. 11.)

Clarification of the principles on which a future society is based, not only socio-economic, but moral, is evidently no idle task. Essentially, only this can disclose the *end* which justifies struggle and revolutionary action.

One cannot say that Marxism has ignored this side of things entirely. The writings of Marx and Engels of the first half of the forties are full of suggestions as to how the future order of things might look and on what principles they would be constructed. But the more their theories get concretised, the more abstract this end appears, and the interest in social ethics disappears altogether.

25-27 June 1969

Revisionism

If Marx and Engels had the proud right to review all the data and conclusions of the social sciences existing before them, then by the same token they provided the basis for a critical review of their work, when the time came. Marxism, after all, is not a religion and its leading lights are not gods. And review does not mean refute, it means checking so as to be able to keep all that is valuable and alive and get rid of what is antiquated, dead and mistaken. But checking – terrible to say – is revision. And so woe betide anyone who dares to

150

engage in this, for he will be a 'revisionist', not just in terms of a dirty label, but in his very essence.

The achievement of Hegel's philosophy, according to Engels, was that 'it *once and for all* broke with all notions about the final character of the results of human thought and action' (*Ludwig Feuerbach and the End of Classical German Philosophy*). Once and for all! The clearest example of revisionism was given by Marx and Engels in relation to all the philosophic and cultural traditions existing prior to them.

The philosophic role in classical Marxism

Marx's and Engels's ideas on the ends of the communist movement, on the future society, on the character of human relations inside it are touched on mainly in their very earliest works: *The German Ideology* and the *Economic-Philosphical Manuscrips* of 1844. *The German Ideology,* alongside references to the economic premises governing relations between people under communism, speaks of 'the necessity of the free development of all in solidarity with one another' as the highest moral principle. Marx was interested then in what would become of people's 'consciousness of mutual relations' among individuals, if there disappeared from it self-sacrifice, 'the principle of love' and egoism.

Very soon, however, the founders of Marxism lost interest in these problems. An important role here was played by the cirumstances of the concrete polemical struggle with the 'true socialists', such as Karl Grün and Moses Hess, and also with Proudhon. Marx proceeded further and further with his materialist understanding of history, elucidating the relationship between economics and class interests, the significance of the proletariat's struggle for real changes in the socioeconomic structure of society. From this point of view all talk of morality, of mutual relations between people, of socialist principles of justice, of freedom of personality, etc., began to be treated as useless if not harmful chatter, diverting the working class from the real paths of struggle. 'Miserable, moral brew', 'tear-stained socialism' – is how Marx and Engels referred to attempts to create a socialist ethics. In the years 1845-7 the polemic with the 'true socialists' was hotted up by the fact that Moses Hess and his friends slipped into openly reactionary political positions and were prepared to compromise with the Prussian government. And so evidently they deserved the venomous gibes of the young Marx.

These polemical fights of their early years left Marx and his closest friend with a distrust for the concept of morality. Class interest and class struggle appeared to them as the only indubitable objectivity, analogous in many ways to the struggle for existence in the world of living nature: any 'universally human' moral element merely served to obscure, with conscious or unconscious hypocrisy, this essence of relations between people that Marx had discovered. All the subsequent activity of Marx and Engels – the founding of an economic theory (*Capital*) and the materialist understanding of history, revolutionary practice, the creation and consolidation of the International – caused them to quarrel with whatever moral doctrines arose in the socialist movement.

But the question itself, as if deliberately put aside by Marxism in the forties and forbidden serious study, remained open. Engels acknowledged this in part in his letter to Carl Schmidt of 21 September 1890.

A polemical spirit and the desire to consolidate Marx's socio-economic theory moved Engels more than once to an excessively sharp, inflexible, undialectical formulation of the question of the role of consciousness, of the 'superstructure', inclusive of morality, which was always allotted the most secondary and dependent place. This is particularly striking in *Anti-Dühring* and *Ludwig Feuerbach*. One memoirist relates how Marx would always burst out laughing whenever anyone spoke to him of morality.

Engels ridiculed Dühring, who thought that the moral world, 'like the world of general knowledge has its impassable principles and simple elements', that moral principles in a certain sense 'stood above history'. Naturally, it would be absurd to maintain that anyone held in his hands the formula for 'eternal morality', 'eternal justice', especially 'in completely ready-made form' – here Engels is right. But he is obviously not right when, in the heat of polemic, he also rejects the possibility (which he accepts for the category of truth, where relative truths accumulate and move towards absolute truth) for each class morality, with all its historical limitations, to contain elements or 'particles' of 'eternal' and absolute morality. Engels argues in an extraordinarily illogical and undialectical way, when he maintains in *Anti-Dühring* that morality is always and fatally class-bound and that there are not and cannot be even elements of a future morality in previous human history.

'Morality standing above class antagonisms', we read here, 'and all memories of them, really human morality, will become possible only at such a stage of development of society, when the antagonism of classes will not merely be overcome, but also forgotten in daily practice' (*Anti-Dühring,* Moscow, 1966, p. 92).

But how can that be? If class morality is always equal to class interest, then how and out of what elements can the morality of classless society be formed? Or will we have to wait for a declaration that the material-technical basis of communism is ready and then we can allow ourselves the luxury of building new relations and new ethics?

But that does not happen in history. Particularly in that part of history which is connected with culture, that is with the slow, organic assimilation of a new level of human relations – just and free.

In this way there has developed in Marxism, at the very centre of its theory, a sizeable 'hole', roughly plastered over with the formula of 'simple norms of morality and justice'. What was rejected in the theory had to be retained, at least in part, for practical everyday needs. Are we not indeed building an amoral society?

The consequences of the incompleteness of the 'philosophy of practice', as Marxism has sometimes called itself, were very serious. People at the head of a political movement, class and party were able to free themselves from all general moral considerations. In Nechaev's *Catechism of a Revolutionary* we read: 'Moral for him (the revolutionary) is everything which helps the triumph of the revolution. Immoral and criminal is everything which prevents it.' The decision of *what* exactly was necessary for the revolution Nechaev, like every leader, reserved for himself, laughed at 'eternal' moral rules, was certain that he had behaved morally when he killed the student Ivanov in the park grotto and was ready 'for the sake of the revolution' to kill another hundred thousand Ivanovs without flinching.

'We do not believe in eternal morality, and expose the deception of all fairy-tales about morality', 'Class struggle continues, and our task is to subordinate all interests to this struggle. And we subordinate our communist morality to this task,' – said Lenin, addressing the youth in 1920. Indeed, morality was subordinated to the tasks of class struggle, and when Stalin, having formulated these tasks to the party for a quarter of a century, unleashed mass terror, there was no moral hold either for him or his myrmidons. Marxism had foreseen everything, cleansing itself of subjectivity, following out the objective laws of economics, classes, social struggle. It did not foresee that by casting off all aspirations for an 'eternal' and 'universally human' moral ideal it had opened the way to pitiless and amoral caprice.

Moral is that which advantages my class, my party. It is not such a large jump to saying: what advantages me.

14 July 1969

Obviously, when Marx got angry with bourgeois philanthropy and the 'high-flown phraseology' of the 'true socialists' or Proudhon, he could not predict the conclusions that his followers would draw from his (polemical) attacks on morality. And in practice Marx and Engels rarely denied the importance of moral judgements. Often, without noticing it, they spoke (in the *Communist Manifesto*, for example) not only of the advantage or disadvantage of a class, but of the nobility and baseness and similar 'abstract' moral categories. Evidently, to think outside the categories of traditional (however approximate) moral judgements is simply not possible for a normal person.

Strictly speaking, the polemic of Marx and Engels with Proudhon and his followers is based on a protest against turning moral dogmas into causal impulses of human development. It is clear to Marxism that history is moved much more by the socio-economic side, by material interests and the struggle of classes. And in this sense any law of 'eternal justice' must appear so much idyllic rose water.

But matters are different for the philosophy of ends. The fact that certain moral rules, however approximately formulated and continually distorted by class prejudice, are preserved in the course of history has enormous significance for the working-out of human ideals. The slogan of justice, freedom, goodness – for all its apparent abstractness and vagueness – retains its appeal for the majority of people. Dialectics consists perhaps in the fact that, in an antagonistic society, moral rules and norms are all the time and at every moment distorted, deformed and doomed in some way to express greedy class interest, and yet they retain their significance as the formulation of ideals and ends in history.

For example, the words 'liberty', 'equality', 'fraternity', fixed by the French revolution, were a thousandfold traduced, prostituted and emptied of meaning in subsequent bourgeois history, and yet they retained their enormous significance as the expression of a social and moral ideal. Many aspects of a universal human ideal were first formulated in the Enlightenment period. While Rousseau in France wrote of equality as the original happy condition of man, Kant in Germany defined his moral imperative. Its basis was that an individual person could in no circumstances ever be a means, only an end.

Marxism grew out of Hegel and his theory of the subordination of the individual to historical necessity, the subsuming of the individual under the process of the grand movement of the absolute idea. This could lend itself to an openly anti-human use. But in terms of the end which Marxism set itself – the emancipation of humanity and its future flowering – it had to accept, intuitively or consciously, Kant's conviction that man is the measure of all things and an end in himself, and not a means for achieving even the most dazzling of ends.

15 July 1969

More on the idea of justice

Engels ridiculed the slogan of justice and equality, put

forward by Dühring on behalf of his 'sociality'. He pointed out that the idea of equality was historical, that it was merely the *negation of inequality,* that therefore it contained no positive 'eternal' content. He says the same, a little less convincingly, about the idea of justice. Justice is as it were merely a shadow, a negative idea, the restoration of a normal correlation of forces upset by injustice.

Is this true?

Equality was known to people as a *social* condition at the time of primitive communist society. Subsequent stages in history (slave-owning, feudal, bourgeois societies) may be defined and appraised as exploitative in comparison with this primitive equality.

How do you measure justice? There is rather another relationship here: that of man with the animal kingdom. An animal does not know the feeling of justice. This is a purely human and social feeling-awareness. It creates the life-conditions of man as a *social* being.

At its source the principle of justice is egoistic: I allow you to live only because I want to live myself; I respect your interests so that you do not encroach upon mine, etc. The principle of sharing booty, the principle of collective defence – of members of the tribe or the gens, was, as it were, utilitarian. But in the course of human development this principle could acquire a relative autonomy, assume the aureole of a 'noble idea'. And this is the first and most important element of morality – the victory of the human in man.

1 August 1969

If thought has reached a certain frontier, it is impossible to drive it back to make it think as it did formerly, even if the intimidated thinker so desires.

Questions, guesses, puzzles – such are the genres of my 'philosophical diary'.

3 August 1969

From a Philosophical Diary

The 'superstructure'

Those philosophical values which, according to Marxism, belong to the sphere of the 'superstructure', which is wholly determined by the basis, in fact have a much more complex relationship with the latter. Undoubtedly, they are in part linked to the economy, to productive relations and needs, to class interests – but only in part and the least significant part in terms of the future. What is called the superstructure has its own relative autonomy and priority in the form of traditions of spiritual culture.

The word 'superstructure' is formal and inexact, pointing to the supposedly secondary character of what is primary from the point of view of the development of the human race and at least as important as the economy. It is not the superstructure, but the structure, the building itself, the underground foundation which the basis serves.

Engels writes that 'consciously or unconsciously, people draw their moral attitudes in the final analysis from practice, from the practical relations on which their class position is based, i.e., from the economic relations within which production and exchange take place'.

Let us agree that that is the rule, although mediated by 'the final analysis'. But why is it that there are always thinkers, artists, philosophers who rise above these concepts, who break out of their class norms? How, for example, did Marx and Engels themselves manage? Engels was not just a small manufacturer ... Why were they not bound to their material interests and how did they express a point of view and morality, which was not bourgeois, but, as it were, 'proletarian'? And isn't it such people, who are able to diverge from the laws of their class superstructure, who create the valuables of human thought and culture?

12 August 1969

More on dogma

'There is not and cannot be any non-class morality, science or art.'

157

'Philosophy is as partisan today as it was two thousand years ago.'

'It is impossible to live in society and be free of it.'

'Every diminution of socialist ideology, every departure from it means a strengthening of bourgeois ideology.'

'There is not and cannot be any position *au-dessus de la mêlée.*'

The directive tone of these sentences, a thousand times repeated and rammed down the throat, the incantations, political maxims, strict taboos are aimed at nipping in the bud any desire to examine the state of things consciously. Much of what for Marx and Lenin was a temporary slogan, a tactical move, a polemical exaggeration, even simply a spontaneous thought attracts the mediocre ideologist, who likes a crude definiteness in everything and makes it the basis for doctrine.

Nevertheless, I shall try some examination. Can you live in society and remain free of it? Obviously, to be absolutely free is not possible; dependence will inevitably show itself in one form or another. But to rise above one's society, social background and environment, one's material interests is not only possible, it constitutes the basis of all spiritual progress. Otherwise, if you imagine that everyone depends on all and that all consists of 'everyones', then you get some kind of Push-Pull with a false imitation of movement. Dead necessity, as it were from the cradle, enslaves people and incapacitates them for original thinking and behaviour, robs them of hope for change.

It is true that in the mass people are not free of society and the influence of their class and background. But whatever is worthwhile in philosophy, morality, politics, art does not depend blindly on surrounding circumstances and is able to look into the future. Men of science, art, philosophy spend all their time trying to break through the limits of a narrow class outlook imposed on them by their society and background. And they are important to the extent that they succeed; they themselves can move human history forward and not simply float along passively in its current. Such were Tolstoy and Shakespeare, Aristotle and Kant, Marx and Lenin.

3 September 1969

Progress

Recent research has upset the comforting notion of the gradual movement of humanity, of progress, of optimistic evolution inculcated by the nineteenth century. Civilisations and developed cultures have been pointed out, which have perished without trace and without influence for the subsequent evolution of humanity; there have been and there are societies with humanist inclinations and the most ferocious satrapies and tyrannies – and none of this develops in a steady, step-by-step way, according to the ways of evolution, but often catastrophically and each time differently. It seems sometimes that there is no progress and that development occurs not according to the 'Marxist spiral', but in a circle.

But what if there is an undiscovered law here of a more subtle connection, a more complex evolution, which still retains an optimistic prognosis of history and does not deny a law of progress?

Of course, the theories of progress and evolutionism of the nineteenth century, Spencer and Mikhailovsky, today seem like pauper's broth. It now appears that everything occurs more tragically, variedly, terribly and profoundly than was apparent to even the most perceptive thinkers.

But I want to think that today's scepticism towards progress will not last. It is a transitional state on the way to something new, to a more complex and comprehensive understanding of the movement of humanity. In ten to fifteen years perhaps a new, dominant philosophy will arise, a new explanation of life, on whose threshold we stand today. It will probably combine and correct all that is fruitful in scientific socialism, the natural sciences and religious (Christian) consciousness.

*   *   *   *

Rousseau posed the question: does morality progress in human history? It would appear there is no progress. The successes of civilisation do not bring any spiritual flowering. The advanced socialist systems reveal a new despotism.

The memory of our generation is scarred by the First World War, the Civil War, Auschwitz, Magadan and Hiroshima. Humanity lives among monstrous disproportions: improvements in life, raising of the material level, unprecedented progress in science and technology and constant wars, hunger in the backward areas of the world and the comparatively slow progress of moral concepts.

But perhaps there is no progress at all in the sphere of spiritual culture. Perhaps humanity is slipping backwards.

But let us recall the epochs of savagery, barbarism and slavery, let us recall the medieval Inquisition, the burnings at the stake and the slave-galleys, let us recall the Crusades, the refined executions, the quarterings, the guillotine, the burning of witches, the cholera and salt-mine revolts, etc.

Let us remember that not so long ago in our own history, only thirty to forty generations back, we tore a prince limb from limb, tying him to the top of a birch-tree; we drank wine out of the skulls of the enemy; that there were Polovtsians and Pechenegs, violations and rivers of blood, Ivan the Terrible and his *oprichnina*, Peter the Great writing his decrees, as Puskhin put it, 'with the *knout*'. Let us remember the Arakcheev settlements, the Central Asian expeditions sanctified by Vereshchagin's 'apotheosis of war' – a mountain of skulls – let us remember the crushing of Poland and Hungary, and all our previous history will appear a terrible scroll of villainies and crimes.

Where does moral progress show itself here?

I do not wish to idealise the present. The last half-century has its toll of tragedy. But nor do I think one should embroider the past and in the light of the terrible August of 1968 bury socialism and with it any idea of human progress.

A man who has once been deceived by a woman stops believing in love and is inclined to think it does not exist anywhere in the world.

The attitude to socialism of some of our protesters is that of rejected and angry lovers. They cannot even bear to hear the word. And in their injured subjectivity they throw at its head all the sins and disasters of humanity and of our age.

Social progress proceeds slowly, with disappointments, subsidences and returns to the past.

As for the progress of moral consciousness, if it takes place, and I think that it does, it moves like all deep processes in living nature: so slowly that we scarcely notice it.

Accustomed to dealing with clocks that show the hours of the day, we see clearly the movement of the second hand. But imagine that we have before us a huge dial that shows time in terms of centuries. However much we might stare at the end of the giant steel arrow poised somewhere between the figures XX and XXI, we should not be able to notice the slightest movement. Does that mean that the clock has stopped or is going backwards?

The technical revolution of the twentieth century, the unprecedented acceleration of the tempo of development, the shrinking dimensions of the earth and its gradual unification into one large, though as yet quarrelsome, family by means of global information and transport – isn't this the prologue to an epoch of new spiritual development?

7 September 1969

Why do I write about this?

Why have I gone in for philosophising? Why do I write about all of this? I am not a philosopher and am liable to be reproached for dilettantism. I am not a philosopher, but I think, and I cannot not think.

My advantage, perhaps an illusory one, is that for me this is not only a question of pure thought taken from other general theories, but a question imposed upon me by life and therefore my own.

Many theories of Marxist orthodoxy I accepted as axiomatic out of intellectual inertia, and only gradually did I notice how little they concorded with my concrete experience, observations and moral awareness.

I believed and preached that morality is class-determined, that philosophy, history and literature are partisan and, which is quite understandable, found plenty to confirm these judgements. And today I am prepared to agree that they contain a part of the truth, but only a part, not the whole truth. Only one of the 'applications', but possibly not the chief one.

There is Lenin's well-known example of dialectics in his polemic with Bukharin: a glass is a 'receptacle for drinking', but it is also a glass cyclinder, and, if you throw it at somebody's head, it is an instrument of 'polemic' and so on. Lenin is correct, the glass has many properties, but they are not equally significant. The main point of a glass remains: it is a vessel for drinking. All the other properties are either partial or ones it was not meant to have.

Morality is class-based, art is class-based, philosophy is class-based. This is one of their qualities, but not the chief one, it is not the purpose of morality or art. But who would deny that they can be used against their purpose and use literature, say, as a 'missile' to throw at somebody's head? Although a stone, bullet or cannon ball would be more suitable.

Morality, reason and art must be measured according to general human yardsticks – that is what is most important about them. Obviously, in every age they express the spirit of their time and therefore the parties, classes, etc. But you cannot measure them solely by the immediate historical measuring rod. Their basic measure is the progress of the entire human race, the measure of the free person of the future, living in a classless society. And in this sense reason, morality and art are more communist in their elements than any other manifestations of man in society (state, law, politics, etc.).

I found the old dogma of total classness restrictive. I tensed my shoulders, the rope snapped and fell.

21 September 1969

Commodity Number One

(Part Two)

A. KRASIKOV

Translated by Brian Pearce

No tax is paid joyfully. But the vodka tax, the levying of which accompanies the state's selling of alcoholic drinks, is paid with the greatest willingness, indeed with craving and self-oblivion, one might say. How could one possible resist increasing such a tax?

From early times the drink-shop was a state institution. A wine monopoly held by the Russian state (vodka was formerly known as 'grain wine') existed, along with farming-out of the drink trade, all through the seventeenth century and the first half of the eighteenth. Then, for a century and a half, there was only the farming-out system, then an excise, and at the end of the nineteenth century the wine monopoly was reintroduced. In Soviet Russia this monopoly forms one constituent of an over-all state monopoly of all kinds of production, to which there are very few exceptions. Private production of vodka is severely penalised.

The ways in which the state has obtained revenue from vodka have changed in the course of time, but the essential character of the vodka trade has not changed. It is interesting to see what instructions were given to tavern-keepers three hundred years ago. A minimum level of earnings was laid down for each tavern, anticipating the economic plans of our own time. And the orders were to obtain money from the tavern trade 'with an increase on previous years': there you are, planned growth from year to year! If they did this, the tavern-keepers were promised that they might, in return, 'expect to receive the Tzar's favour': what is this but a bonus for over-fulfilment of the plan? The Tzar's directives laid it down that 'heavy drinkers are not to be driven away'. Drink, Orthodox Christians, drink as much as you like!

The plans were fulfilled so successfully that the Tzar and the Boyars themselves became alarmed at the incredible increase in drunkenness. In 1652, in the reign of Alexei Mikhailovich, 'Regulations for Taverns' were introduced which included several progressive measures. The number of taverns was reduced. A 'heavy drinker' was to be allowed only one cup of vodka. During fasts and on Sundays, and on Wednesdays and Fridays as well, the taverns were to close, and on the remaining days they were to remain open only until mass-time.[1]

Nevertheless, the 'Regulations' maintained in force the same requirement as before that tavern-keepers' receipts must increase from one year to the next. Oh, Russia!

Campaigns against drunkenness have never been pursued too persistently in Russia, and that was so on this occasion. Already in 1659, only seven years later, it was again laid down that heavy drinkers were not to be driven away from the taverns.

To drink and drink until he lost consciousness completely, that was what the entire system of the vodka trade taught the Russian man for hundreds of years. The craving for 'a hair of the dog that bit you' on the morning after a drinking-bout is a distinctively Russian phenomenon. Our way of 'taking a drop to get rid of my hangover' is unknown to most other peoples who are far from shunning alcohol. The Russian word for it *(opokhmelyat'sya)* cannot be translated into other languages except by a phrase. Evidently, peoples who do not drink so heavily and so wildly as we do have no need of such a word.

The tradition of drinking oneself under the table is also the popular tradition most profitable to the state.

I shall not discuss the extent of the profits made in this way in the distant past. I shall merely try to establish, approximately at least, the dimensions of the gains and losses from alcohol in the USSR, in so far as these are reflected in official statistics.

Let us analyse the table headed 'Commodity structure of retail turnover in state and cooperative trade' in the collection of statistics entitled *Narodnoye Khozyaistvo SSSR v 1972 g.* (p. 584). It shows the increase in expenditure on the purchase of various goods. Everything that people eat is enumerated most conscientiously, even salt being given a separate column, although it accounts for less than one-seven-hundredth of all purchases of foodstuffs, the total amount of which in 1972 came to 96.5 milliard roubles. Of what people drink, however, only tea is named, though this article occupies no great place in the expenditure – considerably less than one per cent (0.7 per cent). All other beverages, from kvass to vodka, are merged in an unspecific and all-embracing column under the neutral heading 'Other foodstuffs'. But this column depicts such a lot of money (30.9 milliard roubles, or 32 per cent of all expenditure on foodstuffs) that one can only wonder what sort of statistics we have here, lumping nearly one-third of the data into a category called 'others', without even explaining, between brackets, what these 'others' are. This is just as though, when totting up the urban population of our country, after listing such towns as Abakan, Aktyubinsk, Alma-Ata, etc., right on until Yalta and Yaroslavl, but omitting all towns with a population of more than a million, that is, Moscow, Leningrad, Kiev, Tashkent, Kharkov, Baku, Minsk, Gorky, Novosibirsk, Kuibyshev and Sverdlovsk, one were, without naming them, to lump the population of those towns together under the heading: 'other towns'. And yet the inhabitants of the largest towns of the USSR, lumped together in this imaginary comparison as 'others', make up not 32 per cent, like those 'other foodstuffs', but only 15 per cent of the country's total urban population.

Isn't this a strange sort of statistics? Mustn't it alert the reader to the possibility that the compiler is trying to dissemble for some purpose? The careful reader of the table of commodities inevitably asks himself what that purpose can be. The answer is self-evident: so as to conceal the amount people spend on alchoholic drinks. This is indeed a startling amount, as we shall now see.

The corresponding tables of the statistical year-book mentioned, during the first few years that it was published (it began appearing in 1956: before that time nearly all statistics were treated as secret), always included a column headed 'Other foodstuffs', which could not, for reasons of space, be listed in detail, but down to 1963 mention was made, in brackets, of some of the goods, of secondary importance (of *secondary* importance!), which were included in it: 'coffee, spices, mushrooms, vitamins, soya-bean products, etc.' – 'etc.' meaning goods of even less financial weight than those named. The amount of money shown in this column remained insignificant from one year to the next, as was to be expected of a grouping of secondary items: about 3 per cent of the total sum spent on foodstuffs.

Drinks other than tea and coffee were in those years shown in a special column of the table, although they were all merged together as 'alcoholic and non-alcoholic beverages'. It had not by any means been decided to reveal *all*: that was the style of those years of 'the thaw'. But let us be grateful even for what was revealed.

Starting in 1964, the column 'Alcoholic and non-alcoholic beverages' is no longer there. It has disappeared from the table! However, the column 'Other foodstuffs' has increased more than tenfold in one year, and thenceforth it goes on showing improbably large sums. The previous enumeration in brackets (coffee, spices, mushrooms, etc.') has, of course, also vanished. Nothing is specified – all we are told is: 'other foodstuffs'.

Collating several year-books (for example, those for 1962, 1963 and 1964) we observe that the renovated column has grown by the same amount that previously was shown in the drinks column. The statistical manipulation here is not a matter of falsifying the figures – it is not always expedient to do that – but of merging two columns into one and thereby hiding from the people the rapidly increasing expenditure on drink.

As a result of the merging of two previously distinct columns ('Other foodstuffs' and 'Beverages') we are deprived of the possibility of discovering how much Soviet consumers are actually spending today on those secondary commodities which previously were included in the list of 'Other foodstuffs' – coffee, spices, mushrooms, etc. It would be idle, though, to suppose that it amounts to much more than before. What has happened to this item, all of a sudden? To make sure, let us try a comparison with tea – that one per cent of all expenditure on foodstuffs which we calculated earlier as accounted for by tea increased in the twelve years 1960-72 two-and-a-bit-times, from 329 million roubles to 685 million, but nevertheless lagged behind the over-all increase in expenditure on foodstuffs: whereas in 1960 expenditure on tea made up 0.77 per cent of this total, in 1972 it made up only 0.71 per cent. And this was not coffee but tea, – the national drink of the overwhelming majority of the peoples of the USSR.

Nevertheless, let us assume that all the secondary commodities, from coffee to mushrooms, have maintained, unlike tea, their previous position in the total expenditure on foodstuffs, namely, 3 per cent. For 1972 this would mean 2.9 milliard roubles. Deducting this sum from the present nameless, faceless column 'Other foodstuffs', which amounts, as already said, to 30.9 milliard roubles, we obtain the figure of 28 milliard, corresponding to expenditure on all beverages (other than tea and coffee) without distinction, whether alcoholic or non-alcoholic. Let us now try to sort out these beverages.

Without bothering the reader with detailed calculations, I will take the quantity of soft drinks bought every year as amounting to between 8 and 10 milliard litres, in other words, an average of 80 bottles, or 200 glasses, of kvass and other soft drinks per person. This is greatly overestimated: whoever buys such a lot of soft drinks? In the countryside and the smaller towns they are hardly sold at all, whereas alcohol is sold everywhere. Also, people consume these drinks mainly in the summer. If we take 18 kopecks as the average price of a litre of non-alcoholic beverage (which is also an overestimate: mineral water costs 20 kopecks a litre, but kvass and aerated water cost only half, or even one-third, as much) we get the figure of 1.8 milliard roubles. Making this a round figure, and so overestimating yet a third time, we get 2 milliard roubles.[2] That would seem quite enough: we have taken expenditure on soft drinks to come to three times as much as expenditure on tea, which people drink in winter and summer alike.

And so we must deduct from the present column of 'other foodstuffs', in addition to the money spent on items properly included in it, such as coffee, also two milliard roubles spent on soft drinks. What remains is 26 milliard roubles, spent by the people on the purchase of alcoholic drinks in state and cooperative shops. Home-distilled vodka (*samogon*), home-brewed beer and other do-it-yourself drinks, together with domestically-produced wine, which is made in great quantity in Georgia and Moldavia, I have included in none of my calculations, owing to the lack of indices for them in official statistics.

Though there are no indices, it is worth quoting the authoritative opinion of an outstanding Soviet economist, the late Academician Strumilin. In the article by him and Professor Sonin, 'Alcoholism and the Fight Against It', published not long ago in the periodical *Ekonomika i organizatsiya promyshlennogo proizoodska (Economics and Organisation of Industrial Production)*, No. 4, 1974, we read: 'The present over-all consumption of *samogon* probably amounts to a figure not less than 50 per cent of the amount of vodka consumed.'

Even so, making it my rule to use only official figures, and not assumptions, I prefer to work with the precise figures of Soviet statistics – and of foreign statistics in those cases only when they have been quoted in the Soviet press.

With only a little difference from the figure calculated by analysing the table 'Indices of retail prices' (p. 602 of the same year-book), we find that the population spent on alcohol not 26 milliard but one milliard more – 27 milliard roubles. This confirms that my calculations were very cautious.

The figure of 26 or 27 milliard roubles signifies over a quarter (27-28 per cent) of total expenditure on foodstuffs in state and cooperative shops. And if we compare it with *all* the money spent in state and cooperative shops, this expenditure on alcohol came, in 1972, to 15 per cent of the total.

For 1970 the sum spent on alcohol, calculated in the same way, amounted to 23 milliard roubles. No small increase in two years: and this is confirmed by figures for the annual growth in the sale of alcohol products which will be mentioned later.

On no other commodity does the Soviet people spend 26 or

27 milliards every year. Apart from this, sums exceeding 10 milliard roubles are spent only on clothing and underwear, taken together (16 milliard in 1972), and on meat and sausages, also taken together (14 milliard). Expenditure on all other items is immeasurably less. For example, on footwear, 7 milliard: on textile fabrics, a little over 5 milliard: on printed publications (books, textbooks, newspapers, periodicals), less than 2 milliard (1.951 million) – almost fourteen times less than the figure for alcohol. This is the stern language of figures.

*   *   *   *

During the fifty-six years since the Revolution it would have been possible – what was needed, above all, was a more sincere desire to do this! – gradually to wean our people at least from the old national habit of drinking themselves unconscious, if only this had not run counter to the direct financial interests of the state. 'The state's interests are higher than any other consideration,' proclaimed *Pravda* in the title of its leading article of 28 August 1974. The financial interests of the state hold the producers of vodka in a grip no less powerful than that which vodka itself has upon its consumers. The state has never enjoyed such a fabulous income from the alcohol business as it enjoys today.

In Tzarist times, before the First World War, the population of Russia spent 900 million roubles a year on vodka. Of this sum 200 million roubles represented the cost of production, and 700 million, i.e., more than 77 per cent, was taken by the Treasury.

The exact figures of net revenue from the alcohol turnover today are known only to a very small group of those in charge of this trade. The cost of production of alcoholic drinks has been made a jealously guarded state secret, no lower in classification than any military secret.

Nevertheless, every drinker (like, indeed, every non-drinker) knows that the cost of production of vodka is relatively less than that of any other commodity. The state's revenue is extracted, for the sake of greater obscurity, bit by bit under several different financial headings: producer's profit, trade profit, wholesale price, retail price, and, finally, the turnover tax, that fattest of all the items of state revenue. In my article *Commodity Number One* I tried to penetrate the palisade constituted by all these headings and work out the cost of production of vodka, but this time I shall confine myself to a simpler, even merely approximate, calculation.

In the publication *Narodnoye Khozyaistvo SSSR v 1972 g.*, which I have quoted, there is a table called 'Index of state retail prices' (p.602). In this table the prices of goods in 1940 are taken as 100. The price of alcohol products in 1972 is shown as standing, in relation to that figure, at 265. Be it noted that the statistics are for alcohol products as a whole, and not for vodka alone, the price of which has risen, as compared with pre-war, more than the average price of alcohol products generally.

Let us suppose that in 1940 the state supplied alcohol out of pure love for its subjects, without taking any profit over and above the costs of production, transport and trade. Let us further suppose that, in the thirty years since then, the productivity of labour in the vodka and wine-making industry has not risen, nor has the cost of production fallen. Let us suppose, finally, that no new kinds of cheaper raw material have been brought into use in vodka production. Given this supposed, although, of course, improbable, set of circumstances, the cost of production (assumed to be equal to the selling price, taken as 100 in the table) would have come to about 38 per cent of the present selling price (which is given in the table as 265) – 100:265 = 38:100. The profit, therefore, would be 62 per cent.

But it is absurd to suppose that in 1940 alcohol was sold at cost price. After all, the trade in vodka was carried on in order to obtain additional resources for industrialising the country (more about this later, with a quotation from Stalin), and from the very beginning a substantial profit was extracted from it. Perhaps not so much from wine as from vodka, but on the average it would not be an overestimate to reckon that 30 per cent of the selling price of alcoholic drinks in 1940 represented net income for the state. Consequently, cost of production (plus other expenditure) accounted at that time for 70 conventional units. But today these goods are sold for

265 such units. The cost of production, therefore, is 70:265, or 26 per cent, and the proportion going as revenue to the state is 74 per cent.

Total purchases of vodka at the present time amount, as I have calculated, to at least 26 milliard roubles. Of this sum, 74 per cent, or 19.2 milliard, is net profit to the state. Later I shall test this figure, deduced from suppositions, against other calculations.

The state's revenue as a whole amounted in 1972 to 175 milliard roubles. One-tenth of this was derived from alcohol.

Nineteen milliard roubles is a very large sum of money. Such a sum is not to be sneezed at. Let me cite, for comparison, a few figures from the expenditure side of the state budget for 1972: to health and physical culture, for example, the sum allocated was 10 milliard, to social insurance 8.3 milliard, to general schools of all kinds 7.6 milliard, to science 7.3 milliard (cf. the year-book quoted, p. 727).

The temptation constituted by the profits from alcohol is irresistible. How can it be suggested that such a huge item of revenue be abolished? What would you replace it with? But if it can't be struck out of the budget, one can at least try to strike it out of sources of information. The most important thing about the alcohol trade, its profitability, is being enveloped in ever-greater secrecy. The secret of drink is being protected from those who are its defenceless victims.

For purposes of comparison it will be very useful to give a (far from complete) list of the serious economic works about the drink problem in the old Russia which were published in the ten years before the Revolution: P. Tsytovich, *Piteinaya monopoliya pomeshchikov Polshi v svoikh imeniyakh* (The Drink Monopoly of the Polish Landlords on their Estates), St Petersburg, 1907; S. A. Pravdin, *Vliyanie urozhayev na potreblen-iye alkogolya v Rossii* (The Influence of the Harvests on Alcohol Consumption in Russia), Moscow, 1911; *Trudy I Vserossiiskogo s'yezda po bor'be s p'yanstvom* (Proceedings of the First All-Russia Congress for Struggle against Drunkenness), three volumes, St Petersburg, 1910; V. K. Dmitriyev, *Kriticheskiye issledovanii o potreblenii alkogolya v Rossii* (Critical Investigations into the Consumption of Alcohol in Russia); D. N. Voronov, *Alkogolizm v gorode i derevnye v svyazi s bytom naseleniya* (Alcoholism in Town and Country, in Connection with the Way of Life of the Population), Penza, 1913; by the same author, *Zhizn derevni v dni trezvosti* (Village Life during Days of Abstinence), Petrograd, 1916; M.I. Fridman, *Vinnaya monopoliya* (The Wine Monopoly), a fundamental work in two volumes.

The list of books of this kind could be lengthened many times over, while still remaining within the period 1906-16. Yet for the last forty years – forty years, not ten – it is impossible to name a single economic study devoted to the present state of affairs as regards drink in the USSR.

The tragic problem of drunkeness in the USSR is not to be exhausted in a few pages. For this subject a dozen volumes of rigorous scientific analysis – sociological, historical, economic – would be required, at least, and not merely works at the popular-medicine level to which all anti-alcohol propaganda has been reduced in our country.

*   *   *   *

Drinking has become a national calamity in the USSR but not because so many litres of alcohol per head of population are consumed here every year. In terms of *that* index we probably lag behind France, where all, including adolescents and women, drink a weak wine with their meals, treating it as a drink for the table, just as we take Narzan water, say, with our lunch. There they drink while they eat, but here we eat a snack while we drink.

And not always do our people eat a snack with their drink, either. This is what I was told by a geologist who worked for many years in the Salekhard area, where, under Stalin, it was planned to lay an immense Northern Railway, running from the north Ural area right up to Norilsk, but where in fact they only managed to leave in the tundra many tens of thousands of corpses of prisoners (or, maybe, hundreds of thousands: who counts them?) before they abandoned this hopeless 'dead rail'.

The local inhabitants, Nentsi and Mansi, drink not vodka but raw spirit, for it is unprofitable to send vodka to the far north. My informant saw a woman come out of a shop carrying a bottle of spirit, swallow a good half of it, and then take a mouthful of snow. He saw a baby at the breast being given some of this spirit, while its mother explained: 'He's crying because he wants a drink.' And the child did indeed fall asleep.

It was the Russian merchant who first introduced the minority peoples of the north to strong drink. But he only began the process ...

An article entitled 'Economics and Alcoholism' in *Nauka i Zhizn* (Science and Life), no. 7 of 1974, quoted this from a report by Dr (of Economic Sciences) M. Sonin. In a typical contract of service with a domestic servant in France it is laid down that the servant shall be allowed between 16 and 30 litres of wine every month by her employers. 'And yet French housemaids are not drunkards,' the learned economist tells us, in spite of the fact that these women drink as much as a litre of wine a day. That's the point – *what* is drunk and *how* it is drunk.

Let us call to witness also the Soviet journalist O. Orestov, who spent six years in England. In his article in *Novy Mir,* nos. 7 and 8 of 1974 he writes: 'During those six years I do not recall a single case when I encountered a really drunk person in the street ... To give the English their due: though they drink regularly, they don't try to get drunk or strive to "finish the bottle", but know their limitations. Even on holidays, drinking is not carried on to the point of inebriation.'

Since in the West, including the country that drinks most, namely France, they drink in a different way, not at all as we do, it is foolish to make a comparison in quantitative terms – so much alcohol consumed per head of population, there and here. Such a comparison is no better than demagogy.

The comparison we need to make is with ourselves – with ourselves as we were in the past, and not with anybody else. If we compare present-day drinking with the pre-revolutionary situation we really do discover something serious.

As an average for Russia as a whole, according to the article 'Wine' in the *Large Soviet Encyclopaedia,* first edition (Vol. 11, 1930), the greatest consumption of vodka was recorded a hundred years ago, in 1870: 0.93 *vedra* or 11.4 litres per year per head of population (a *vedro* [literally, 'bucket' – Trans.] is 12.3 litres). Translated into pure alcohol, this means 4.6 litres.

Consumption of vodka was highest in the western provinces, where it was cheapest, and lowest in the central provinces. In the following two decades the government introduced taxes on vodka which were uniform over the whole country and this had the effect of reducing consumption in the western provinces and increasing it in the central ones. Over-all consumption of vodka began to decline, coming down to 0.57 *vedra* per head in 1893.

However, making alcohol dearer cannot serve as a regulating measure for long. Eventually it loses its effect. This duly happened, and in the 1890s the level of drinking began to rise once more. By 1913 consumption per head had reached 0.63 *vedra* (7.75 litres), or, in terms of pure alcohol, 3.1 litres.[3]

Over a period of twenty years (1893-1913) the increase was thus 10 per cent – a figure not to be compared with the rate of increase in our own times, as I shall show later.

If historians were to study the victorious advance of vodka, that would probably be more useful and beneficial for the people than studying Suvorov's victories in Italy. It is no vain saying that the hardest conquest to make is the conquest of oneself.

*   *   *   *

The foregoing pages were all based on generally available statistics. In addition to these, however, there is also information for internal consumption ('for in-service use', as this form of classification is called); for instance, reports and surveys which circulate only within the Ministry. From a report of this kind, compiled in Glavspirt (the Chief Administration of the Alcohol Industry) in 1968, I shall now try to draw some conclusions, in order to compare these with the ones I managed to mine from the depths of the ordinary Soviet statistics.

The 'service' information mentioned relates to the production of vodka in Russia and the USSR in the period 1913-67, and forms a concise history of vodka's triumphal march.

When we think about the direct influence which the development of a branch of the economy like this can have on the spiritual life of the people, their character, their morals, and even their general way of living, we inevitably arrive at this thought: the increase in vodka production affects the soul of the Soviet people more directly and powerfully than the development of any of the most important branches of heavy industry, even though the economic quantities involved are not at all comparable. In engineering, for example, in 1968, 8.7 million persons were employed, and in vodka production a few more than 42,000, that is, only one-two-hundredth as many.

It is all the more interesting to study the table set out below, showing production per head of vodka and other alcohol products in millions of decalitres (a decalitre is ten litres, called in international statistical usage a 'dal'). Notes are appended to some of the figures in this table, as not every reader, probably, will remember the events in the general history of our country which find reflection in the development of the vodka trade.

Years	Million dals	Years	Million dals	Years	Million dals
1913	118.9	1939	109.5	1955	116.9[7]
1928	55.5	1940	92.5[6]	1956	122.5[8]
1929	55.2	1945	44.3	1957	140.2[9]
1930	61.8	1946	50.8	1958	145.4
1931	78.8	1947	41.4	1959	137.3
1932	72.0[4]	1948	30.1	1960	138.1
1933	70.0	1949	48.3	1961	145.7
1934	70.2	1950	62.8	1962	162.0
1935	70.7	1951	76.8	1963	168.9
1936	77.6	1952	81.1	1964	176.5
1937	89.7[5]	1953	95.4	1965	188.8
1938	109.2	1954	108.5	1966	198.7
				1967	213.6

As we know what the population of the USSR was in all these years, it is easy to calculate how much vodka this meant per head of population in each year. In 1913 it was 7.5 litres per person (the *Large Soviet Encyclopaedia* gives a higher figure, 7.75 litres, a difference of 250 grammes), and in 1967 it was 9.1 litres. To this must be added wine and beer, which are drunk much more than in Tzarist times. There is also *samogon* (home-distilled vodka) to be taken into account. Before 1915 people did not make it, but after the Tzarist Government, at the beginning of the First World War, put a ban on vodka, they began to do so, and in 1918-20 the Ukraine was practically swimming in the stuff.

In the period 1950-67 a significant reduction – to one-sixteenth of the earlier amount – took place in the output of the kind of vodka called, simply '40 degrees'. On the other hand there was an over-fiftyfold increase in the output of new varieties: '*Moskovskaya Osobaya*' (Moscow Special), '*Stolichnaya*' (Capital), and then '*Ekstra*' (Extra). It is difficult to say whether the purpose was to please the consumer's taste, but one can affirm with complete assurance both that '*Moskovskaya Osobaya*', '*Stolichnaya*' and other such brands are cheaper to produce, and that the turnover tax weighs more heavily upon them. The turnover tax contributes to making the difference between the wholesale and the retail price of a commodity. This difference is very great, espcially in the case of vodka. The turnover tax goes in its entirety to the Treasury. All prices, wholesale and retail alike, are fixed beforehand by the state, quite independently of the producers or the trade organisations, and this, of course, applies to the turnover tax as well. The enterprise is allowed to manoeuvre within the limits set by the wholesale price: it can reduce its cost of production (in this case, the cost of producing alcohol and vodka), and if it manages to bring this cost down below the level of the wholesale price, the enterprise makes a profit – otherwise, it is 'unprofitable', and makes a loss. However odd this may seem from the standpoint of common sense, many vodka factories worked for long years at a loss, and were given state subsidies. Thus, the profit from producing the ordinary, old-time 40-degree vodka was nil, and so was the loss. Only in a few factories did they make a profit of 20 kopecks per decalitre. The profit on the new brands ('*Stolichnaya*', etc.) comes to 43 kopecks per decalitre, for the USSR as a whole.

The cost of production of vodka is (for ordinary 40-degree vodka), between 3 roubles and 3 roubles 93 kopecks per decalitre, or, as an average for the country as a whole, 3 roubles 63 kopecks. Among the factors determining the cost of production of alcohol (and, therefore, of vodka) a specially important one is, as with any other commodity, the price of the raw material (potatoes, grain, molasses, waste-products from wine-making, etc.), and this differs widely between different parts of the USSR.

I am not sufficient of an expert in matters of drink to be able to explain why the cost of production of other, more fashionable vodkas *(Stolichnaya', 'Osobaya,* etc.) comes, taking the country as a whole, to no more than 3 roubles 9 kopecks per decalitre, that is, 31 kopecks a litre. This figure is, however, absolutely official, even if little known.

What is most interesting, though, is the situation with the turnover tax. On ordinary vodka it ranges from 19 roubles 68 kopecks to 42 roubles 48 kopecks a decalitre. But the selling price, before the price increase, was 47 roubles 99 kopecks a decalitre, that is, 4 roubles 80 kopecks a litre.

From the new brands, which have now almost completely ousted the former '40-degree vodka', the turnover tax extracts a great deal more – as an average for the whole country, 49 roubles 56 kopecks, out of a selling price of 55 roubles 94 kopecks per decalitre (before the price increase.) This means that for every litre sold, at 5 roubles 60 kopecks, 4 roubles 95 kopecks went straight into the state's coffers. That was the situation in 1967.

I shall come back to the question of the turnover tax when we consider the year 1972, but, for the moment, let us have a look at the level of consumption of vodka as between the different republics. Here, the report does not cover *all* kinds of vodka: it excludes brandies, liqueurs and also some secondary varieties. Altogether, though, out of the 213.6 million decalitres mentioned above, it covers 202.3 million, and so is a quite representative figure.

This is what we find when we relate the figures given for the separate republics to the size of their populations in 1967 (these figures are given for only eleven of the republics). Consumption per head of population in the USSR as a whole was 8.6 litres. By republics, in descending order, it was as follows: Kirghizia, 11.4 litres; RSFSR, 10.3; Estonia, 10; Lithuania, 8; Kazakhstan, 7.8; Byelorussia, 6; Ukraine, 5.9; Uzbekistan, 3.4; Tadzhikistan, 2.9; Moldavia, 2.1; Georgia, 1.8.

Nearly all these figures are capable of explanation. In the republics where wine is produced (Moldavia, Georgia) they don't drink much vodka. In Byelorussia and, especially, in the Ukraine, where most of our sugar factories are situated and the waste-products of sugar production are easily come by, home-distilling of vodka from this very cheap and convenient raw material is widespread. In Central Asia they have not yet learnt to drink 'in the Russian way'. In Kazakhstan and Kirghizia it is not, of course, in the main the Kazakhs and Kirghizes who drink – though I cannot explain what specific conditions in Kirghizia cause such a large quantity of vodka to be drunk per head of population in that republic.

Reviewing all these figures and comparing past and present we see what tremendous victories have been won by vodka in the fifty-two historic years depicted in the little table given above.

Let us now endeavour to calculate, however approximately, what the situation was in 1972. In the last ten years shown in the table (1957-67) the rate of increase of vodka production was 3.8 per cent per year in the first half-decade and 5.7 per cent per year in the second. The rate of increase was on the upgrade. If we extrapolate this tendency for the five years after 1967 we find that in 1972 between 25 and 28 per cent more vodka was being produced than in the earlier year.

For caution's sake, let us take the lower of these figures. This gives 267 million decalitres. Our hypothetical figure is clearly an underestimate, since in these same five years the amount spent on alcoholic drinks, calculated by the method already known to the reader, increased not by 25 but by 45-46 per cent, as we have seen in the previous pages. It is hard to suppose that so great an increase in expenditure can have occurred as a result of increased prices alone. In all probability, a lot more than 267 million decalitres of vodka were produced in 1972. Even that figure, however, means 10.8 litres of vodka per person.

Again, this figure does not take account of wine, of which 293 million decalitres were manufactured in state enterprises in 1972, i.e., nearly 12 litres per person. (Domestic wine-making is not recorded.) Translated into terms of alcohol, the two drinks, taken together, work out at 5.8 litres per person. (Let us not regard beer as an alcoholic drink, for this purpose – even though our people can drink themselves insensible with it.) Altogether, the vile Tzarist monopoly, with its maximum 1870 consumption of 4.6 litres of alcohol per person has been left far behind.[10] Not to mention the year 1913 with its mere 3.1 litres!

We cannot but deduce, from the increase in the quantity drunk, the increase in the revenue this brought to the state. The cost of production, as stated above, is not at all large – something of the order of 3 roubles, or a little more, for a decalitre. The profit which the producers are allowed to make is also not large, as we have seen.

When the price of alcoholic drinks was raised we must presume that there was no change in the cost of producing them. Nor was there any change in the overhead expenses of trade, and if the profit increased it did so only to an insignificant extent. It was 43 kopecks a decalitre – let's say 50. An excessive increase in the profits made in any line of production (dependent not only on efforts made in the sphere of production but also on the wholesale price previously laid down, from on high, for the article concerned) inevitably leads to complacency on the part of the heads of the industry concerned and deprives them of the stimulus to improve production and raise the productivity of labour in the enterprises entrusted to their charge. For this reason the wholesale price of products is so fixed as to bring economic pressure to bear on the producers constantly to concern themselves with improving their indices (of productivity, economy, technology, etc.).

When a retail (selling) price is increased – and, once again, this must not be confused with the wholesale price! – only one item in the state's revenue can undergo perceptible change, namely, the turnover tax. If, at the old retail price, the turnover tax on a litre of *'Stolichnaya'* amounted to 4 roubles 95 kopecks, how much must it come to at the new, higher

179

price? Unquestionably, all, or nearly all of the extra amount goes in payment of this tax.

Using the figures of the report we have been examining, it is possible to calculate that the amount of the turnover tax on vodka alone, disregarding wine, was in 1967, long before the increase in the prices of alcohol products, more than 10.1 milliard roubles. In that year, as we see from the handbook, the total amount contributed by the turnover tax to the state budget was 40.1 milliard. Vodka alone, therefore, without help from wine, supplied more than a quarter of this item of revenue. This commodity is indeed convenient beyond compare: it calls for very little trouble, and yet gives brilliant results.[11]

It is not so easy to calculate the amount that the turnover tax has produced in recent years, as a result of the growth in the demand for alcohol and the increase in its price. Let us try to do this, even if only approximately. Suppose that the consumption of vodka increased during five years by no more than 25 per cent: that would, by itself, mean an extra 2.5 milliard roubles paid in turnover tax in 1972, in addition to the 10.1 milliard of 1967. But the price increase, even if it led at first to a certain fall in purchases of vodka, nevertheless all went in turnover tax, as mentioned already. The increase came, for vodka alone, to an average of 20 roubles per decalitre, or 2 roubles per litre. Let us assume that this increase had such a marked effect on the demand for vodka as to bring it back to the 1967 level, or lower still, to the level of 1962. Even in that case the additional sum paid in turnover tax would have been 3.75 milliard roubles.

Altogether, then, it would appear that the revenue from the turnover tax charged on vodka amounted in 1972 to 16.3 milliard roubles. We have not yet worked out the turnover tax obtained from the sale of wine. This is, of course, much less than the tax on the new brands of vodka, but, all the same, a lot of wine is sold. Let us try to calculate this figure as well.

I will show the ratio between the retail price of different brands of vodka and the turnover tax charged on them in 1967. Here are precise figures, based on the data provided by Glavspirt. On 40-degree vodka, the tax was 55 per cent of the price; on *Osobaya, Stolichnaya* and other expensive brands it was 88 per cent; on sweet liqueurs it was 75 per cent; and on brandy it was 47 per cent. The cost of producing wine is high compared with that for vodka, and there the ratios are evidently close to or even lower than in the case of brandy, which is itself made from grapes. Let us assume that not 47 but only 30 per cent of the average retail price of wine goes in turnover tax. If we take the average retail price of a litre of wine as 2 roubles 50 kopecks (i.e., cheaper than vodka by as much as it is weaker, since otherwise it would not be to the consumer's advantage to buy it), we find that the tax on wine amounts at the present time to no more than 75 kopecks per litre, or 7 roubles 50 kopecks a decalitre – only one-tenth as much as on vodka. Could it be even less?

Given this (obviously underestimated) assumption, the total amount of the turnover tax on wine comes to 2.2 milliard roubles, and the total amount of the turnover tax received by the state from the sale of vodka and wine to 18.5 milliards. This is close to the figure I deduced in the preceding section of my article: 19 milliard roubles. It is a little less because in all my calculations I kept to the lowest of my hypothetical figures.

*   *   *   *

So then, we are now acquainted with the Treasury aspect of the drink question. But alcohol combines the purely fiscal function of pumping money from the pockets of the citizenry into the state's strongboxes with another, ideological function: that of bringing a little consolation to the people and drowning their thoughts in the bottle. Alcohol, provided it is taken in substantial doses, creates that good feeling about which our papers have begun to write so much. It makes the drinker a real man, in his own eyes, removes his sense of inferiority and exalts his ego. In a situation where man's personality counts for nothing, alcohol gives him an illusion of his own importance.

It is precisely the ideological aspect of drunkenness that is most dangerous for the country's future. It finds reflection in the productivity of labour, in work (or, rather, anti-work)

181

habits, and in the growth of delinquency. But it is not for us, Soviet people, to meditate on these matters. Of all the effects that alcohol has, the only one that it is proper for us to think about is its effect on the liver. This is probably the reason why we need to have 'sobering-up stations', but do not need to establish anything similar to the American National Institute on Alcohol Abuse and Alcoholism. (The only Union Republic where there are no 'sobering-up stations' is the Armenian SSR: there you see no drunks in the street, because they drink in a different way from us.)

The Director of the American National Institute on Alcohol Abuse and Alcoholism, M. Chafetz, recently wrote (see the newspaper *Sovyetskaya Rossiya*, 16 July 1974) that in the USA there are now 10 million alcoholics, and that abuse of alcoholic liquor, leading to loss of working time, increased expenditure on public health and expensive accidents, costs the country 25 milliard dollars a year. *Pravda*, 29 July 1974, also printed this news, with the further information that three years ago the figure for losses due to abuse of alcohol, now 25 milliard, stood at 15 milliard dollars.[12]

The figure of 15 milliard dollars, which is already, as we see, out of date, also figures in the article, 'Economics and Politics', quoted above from No. 7 of the periodical *Nauka i Zhizn*. The author of this article hastens at once to make this reservation: 'America's losses provide, of course, no pattern for us, and direct, crude analogies would be pointless.' Do not imagine, dear readers, says he, that *we* suffer such losses.

And I do not think so, either. I believe in the strength of the socialist system and the beneficent influence exerted upon men, not excluding drunkards, by our Soviet way of life. Furthermore, I recall the old, true-to-life saying: 'What's good for the Russian is deadly to the German.' Those who first said this evidently had in mind a glass of vodka, swallowed in one gulp, after which the drinker sniffs a crust of bread and then swallows a second glass, likewise in one gulp. (Cf. Sholokhov's story, *One Man's Destiny*.)

So neither the 15 milliard dollars nor the 25 milliard dollars lend themselves to purposes of comparison. We must approach these figures in our own, Soviet way, concluding that, apart from 'sobering-up stations' we need no other national institution for combating alcoholism. And there is no need for us to talk about the matter in speeches and reports.

Stalin spoke frankly about vodka for the first and last time in his interview with foreign workers' delegations on 5 November 1927 (*Works,* Vol. 10 [English edition, p. 237 – Trans.]): 'When we introduced the vodka monopoly we were confronted with the alternatives: *either* to go into bondage to the capitalists by ceding to them a number of our most important mills and factories and receiving in return the funds necessary to enable us to carry on, *or* to introduce the vodka monopoly in order to obtain the necessary working capital for developing our industry with our own resources and thus avoid going into foreign bondage.'[13] Later in this interview Stalin said [p. 238 – Trans.]: 'We introduced it [the vodka monopoly] as a temporary measure', and declared that at the time when he was speaking, in 1927, vodka produced a revenue of 500 million roubles, but that 'at present our policy is gradually to reduce the production of vodka. I think that in the future we shall be able to abolish the vodka monopoly altogether,' he concluded.

The logic of reality proved stronger than Stalin's optimistic forecasts. As in many other matters, life showed their unsoundness. There is no question today of putting an end to the vodka trade, which Stalin spoke of as something temporary, though half a century has now passed since it was revived in 1923. The 'temporary measure' has become a permanent calamity.

Already in those days, in 1927, warning voices were heard, saying that the path of raising revenue from vodka would never lead upward but always down, and any profits made from drink would inevitably turn into the greatest misfortunes both for the people and for that very 'industry' for the sake of which they were collected. Stalin did not want to listen to those sober voices – and the results confront us today.

The figure of revenue from vodka quoted by Stalin, 500 million roubles, represented one-tenth of the total state revenue of that time, which was 5 milliard roubles. The demagogic way the question was posed – either enter into bondage to capitalists or sell alcoholic poison to our own people – tells us merely that Stalin could not see any other paths but these two. Like every pragmatist, he sought only an immediate effect, without being able or even wanting to think about the further consequences. And yet the experience of the Tzarist Government's ban on vodka during the First World War was already well known. In 1914-15 cessation of the sale of vodka had increased the productivity of workers' labour by 7 per cent – according to some calculations, by even more than that.

To accumulate revenue for the state by means of a tax on alcohol means resorting to the very worst sort of the worst type of tax, the indirect tax, which always weighs more heavily on the less well-off than on the prosperous. Even if we assume that the lower-paid drink only the same amount as the higher-paid, it remains true that the share taken by alcohol in the family budget of the former is larger than in that of the latter category. Those who suffer worst from drunkenness are not the drinkers themselves but their wives and children, as has long been known. For this reason any increase in *direct* taxation, which nowadays always takes the form of taxation in proportion to income, is a more just, a more expedient and a more far-seeing measure than 'obtaining working capital', as Stalin put it, from the drink trade.

Actually, Stalin only spoke brazenly of what others do without talking about it.

In recent decades nobody has raised this question in its full magnitude in any speech (I have already mentioned the absence of books). In Tzarist Russia they did not fear to hold an All-Russia Congress for Struggle against Drunkenness and to publish its proceedings, which I have mentioned in the list of books I gave earlier. A congress like that, of course, cannot be a sort of gala affair, with speeches full of eulogies. Since those unforgettable times when, in 1934, the Seventeenth Party Congress was held, and there and then was christened 'the congress of victors' (which in no way hindered Stalin from shooting the majority of the delegates soon afterward) – since those days a definite style for occasions of that sort has become established, a style to which a congress for combating drunkenness would hardly lend itself.

All the same, a Decision of the Central Committee of the

CPSU on the struggle against drunkenness was promulgated: that happened in June 1972. Set forth in a hundred lines in *Pravda*, it was entitled: 'On Measures for Strengthening the Fight against Drunkenness and Alcoholism'. The decisions of the supreme organs in our country are not subject to criticism, and God preserve me from violating this Soviet tradition. Most of the space in this decision is taken up by measures 'for extensive development of mass work', 'intensification of propaganda against alcohol', free showings of anti-alcohol films, and 'improvement in the organisation of cultured leisure activity' (one paragraph is devoted to this, all the rest being allotted to the strengthening of mass work and propaganda).

Since then, photographs of the swollen liver of an alcoholic have begun to embellish public places. Only in those places where drinkers usually drink – in the doorways of the shops that sell alcohol – do we, for some reason, never see these pictures. Why drive away the heavy drinkers?

As for administrative and economic measures for combating drunkenness, these are set out in another decision with the same title, adopted by the Council of Ministers of the USSR in that same week, on 16 June 1972. 'The State Planning Commission of the USSR, the Ministry of the Food Industry and the Councils of Ministers of the Union Republics are instructed to see to it that, in the annual plans, measures are taken to ensure a reduction in the production and consumption of alcoholic drinks and a considerable increase in the output of wine and beer.' So runs one of the main points in the decision (from which, incidentally, we see that wine and beer are not officially regarded as alcoholic drinks: though the output of alcoholic drinks is to be reduced, that of wine is to be considerably increased). Furthermore, the Councils of Ministers of the Union Republics are instructed to look into the question of limiting the hours and days when vodka can be sold, as I have mentioned already.

Nothing was said in either of these decisions about the increase in the prices of alcoholic drinks. This is known to be a promising and well-tried method of combating drunkenness. Its only weakness is that it is effective just as long as, and no longer than, the time the people need to get used to the new price. And our people are an obliging lot – they get used to many things.

I shall speak later of how the people have actually reacted to this concern for their sobriety, when I come to analyse the annual figures for the consumption of alcohol. Before tackling that question, let us consider the concomitants and consequences of drunkenness.

*   *   *   *

Among the consequences of drunkenness, mentioned also by the American Chafetz, are motor car accidents which destroy thousands of lives. In a long article devoted to the dangers connected with road traffic in our country (*Pravda*, 8 October 1974) the head of the State Automobile Inspectorate of the USSR Ministry of the Interior, V. Luk'yanov, says: 'When we analyse breaches of the traffic regulations it is not difficult to determine one of the chief causes of these offences, namely, alcohol. About a quarter of all road-transport incidents are due to pink elephants ... When talking of alcohol in this connection many people usually have in mind only the drivers of cars. However, the proportion of incidents caused by violations of the traffic regulations by pedestrians, mostly drunk, increased from 7.6 per cent in 1971 to 8.2 per cent in 1972.'

That's clear enough: one-quarter of all accidents are due to alcohol, and one-third of these the fault of drunken pedestrians. But what is not clear is the actual number of accidents. The article quoted only percentages, except for one, solitary absolute figure. To quote: 'In Irkutsk Region, for example, the number of accidents increased by one-third in eight months. The number of persons killed was 318, and another 1,375 were injured.'

Irkutsk Region is certainly not the region of the USSR richest in motor cars. But since the official figures speak only of this region, let us endeavour to compare them with the figures for the victims of motor transport in the West, about which our papers write indefatigably.

Irkutsk Region had on 1 January 1973 a population of 2,381,000. This means that in one month one person in 60,000 was killed in a motor accident. In Italy, with 55 million inhabitants, in August of this year 825 people were killed in motor accidents *(Pravda,* 2 September) – which means one in 66,000, a better monthly figure than in Irkutsk Region. In Paris, according to *Literaturnaya Gazeta* (see the entire page devoted to this question in the issue of 9 October 1974), 300 people are killed every year in car crashes, that is, one person in every 120,000, every month – which is just half as bad as the situation in Irkutsk Region, even if we consider only Paris without its suburbs. If we include the suburbs (from the passage in *LG* it is not clear whether 'Greater Paris' is meant, or not), then the figure is one out of every 320,000, or one-fifth as bad as in Irkutsk Region. *Pravda,* which takes great interest in the number of victims of car accidents in the West and is constantly telling its readers about them, gave the latest information on this subject in two successive issues, 7 and 8 December 1974, dealing with crashes in Denmark and in Belgium. If we relate the number killed to the total population, we obtain for Denmark the figure of one in every 54,000, and, for Belgium, the figure of one in every 63,000.

Finally, let us compare ourselves with the USA, that classic land of the motor car and of the disaster, where every day, according to *Pravda* of 15 August 1974, 150 people are crushed to death under wheels. In relation to the population of 210 million that means, on a monthly basis, one in every 46,500. If we consider the enormous difference in the development of motoring in the West and in Irkutsk Region, these comparative figures are quite simply terrifying. Why, in only eight months, has the number of accidents in Irkutsk Region increased by one-third? Clearly, the roads cannot have deteriorated to that extent in so short a period. A different explanation seems sounder – the number of built-up areas has increased, and with it the circulation of motor cars. By how much it has increased I do not know, but it certainly has not reached the level of Italy, and it is, of course, far below the level of Paris or of the USA. According to the authoritative statement by the author of the article, about a quarter of the incidents were caused by pink elephants. We know that supervision by the militia is considerably better in big cities than on the roads of spacious and remote regions, so that the average figure of 'one quarter' needs to be differentiated: in Moscow much less than a quarter, in a faraway region much more than a quarter. And the amount of road traffic in such a region has only to increase somewhat for the graph of those killed on the roads suddenly to make a sharp upward turn.

And so we see that our well-being, constantly vaunted in our newspapers, does not stand up to statistical analysis, when even just one corner is lifted of the curtain that hides the truth about the realities of life in our country.

* * * *

Let us now turn to the other concomitants of drunkenness. These are concomitants, not consequences: where low productivity of labour and delinquency are concerned, vodka is not the first cause, the basis, the soil from which these phenomena grow. That soil is something different, which we are not allowed to name, and I shall not touch upon it. Alcohol serves as a sort of fertiliser. It is spread over and dug into the soil from which these phenomena grow. We sow the seed, and we produce this fertiliser on a generous scale and sell it at a big profit in hundreds of millions of bottles, accompanying our trade with unctuous newspaper articles about the harmfulness of alcohol. The item has been ticked and the measure carried out. Here in *Literaturnaya Gazeta* is a whole page (10 July 1974) headed 'Stronger Than A Dry Law', in which there is everything except one thing, namely, an analysis of the drink question.

This page of *LG* opens with a dramatic letter from somebody living in Minsk. 'My proposal is derived from personal experience of a more than ten years' struggle against my son's alcoholism and my observation of other boys from our yard – I know five lads like him. How many are there in our whole town? How many in the whole country?'

Indeed, how many must there be if there are six 'lads' (he must mean youths) in a single yard? In truth, we have no need of an institute for combating alcoholism.

And the father of the alcoholic lad writes, and *Litgazeta* quite seriously prints his letter:'We should isolate alcoholics in settlements where a "dry law" should be applied strictly, with no exceptions. These inhabited localities should, of course, be subject to proper supervision. I am firmly convinced that if an alcoholic is unable to obtain drink, then within a month or two he will become able to work and live normally. But it is enough for him to drink ten grammes and he's dragged down into the abyss, and everything is ruined.' Later he adds: 'Loving kinsfolk would willingly agree to go and live there with them.'

'Proper supervision' of such inhabited localities means that they must not be too extensive, territorially speaking, since otherwise they could not be supervised, but at the same time the inhabitants must be close-packed, since otherwise too much building would be called for. In short, what is meant is an area under guard, equipped with barbed wire, watch-towers, sentries and guard-rooms, in the absence of which there can be no 'proper supervision'. Also, of course, searches in the guard-room: it would be all too easy to bring in a bottle in one's pocket. The loving kinsfolk would also be searched. After all, out of pity for their own dear child they might bring in those very ten grammes which would cause the thing to start all over again ...

So, then, what it comes to is a concentration camp! And people are to be sent there for life, or at any rate without any period of detention defined in advance: the alcoholic is to remain there until he is completely cured. And the cure in question, seeing that a mere ten grammes could wreck it, is highly uncertain.

This camp is not only to be a place of indefinite detention but also one subject to particularly strict supervision, since the ordinary sort, as we know, permits vodka to be brought in without any difficulty. This, then, is the project introduced via the pages of *Literatunaya Gazeta* – and *LG*, that guardian of humanism, does not even notice what sort of psychology underlies this proposal, which, incidentally, has long since been put into practice in the form of the exiling of 'parasites' to remote areas of our great Motherland. All that is required is to widen the circle of persons liable to exile and to put the remote areas in question (hamlets, villages, districts) under 'proper supervision'.

The psychology of combating every social evil (and personal

evils, too: don't wives take complaints to various authorities about their unfaithful husbands?) by means of administrative pressure, and tightening up what in our country is called order, has long been firmly established among us. 'People have become insolent, there's no order any more – under Stalin there was order!' – this is a sentiment we hear expressed quite often. Persons who regard themselves as models of order, in the sense of fulfilment of orders from above, want to lock everybody else up under proper supervision. In this way all problems will be solved, an insuperable barrier will be erected against drunkenness, and with the decline in drunkenness there will also come a decline in delinquency – against which, however, the fundamental struggle is waged in zones which are subject to very good supervision.

What a close connection exists between drunkenness and delinquency is known to all. A few niggardly figures about this are given in the article in *Nauka i Zhizn* already mentioned. Thus, according to statements by the President of the Supreme Court of the RSFSR, L. M. Smirnov, 55.8 per cent of all robberies, and 69.3 per cent of all acts of brigandage. Neither of these social ailments can be discussed without taking the other into consideration.

The fight against crime is carried on more vigorously than the fight against drunkenness: crime is not profitable, but, on the contrary, causes heavy losses. A huge apparatus is maintained for the purpose of eradicating crime, the cost of which is, of course, kept absolutely secret. The extent of crime is an even closer-guarded secret than that of drunkenness: where alcohol is concerned we can manage to find at least a few scanty figures, but for crime we have only, at best, percentages, those cosiest of all numerical data.

In his day, A. Vyshinsky, as Procurator-General of the USSR, gave to those who came after him a worthy example of how to juggle with percentages. In 1936, at the Eighth Extraordinary Congress of Soviets, he drew such a happy picture that it seemed as though another five years would see the prisons empty, so that the warders would have to be retrained for some less demanding trade. 'If we take the number of persons convicted in the first half of 1933 as 100,' said Vyshinsky, 'then in the first half of 1936 the number of persons convicted in the RSFR will be only 51.8 per cent, and in the Byelorussian SSR only 24.5 per cent. There has also been a reduction in the number of persons convicted in the Ukrainian SSR and in the Transcaucasian and Central Asian republics ... If we take the number of offences recorded in the first half of 1934 as 100, for the Union as a whole, then in the first half of 1936 the corresponding figure comes to 59.8 per cent. In the same period the number of unarmed robberies fell to 66.4 per cent, that of armed robberies to 69.8 per cent, and that of thefts to 35.2 per cent. These figures testify to tremendous progress made, to one of the greatest victories of socialism' (*Izvestiya,* 29 November 1936).

So, then, the number of persons convicted in Byelorussia declined to one quarter of what it had been, in a period of three years. With such tempos as this, crime, declining by three-quarters every three years, ought by the time of Vyshinsky's blessed decease [1954 – Trans.] to have shrunk to no more than 0.05 per cent of what it was in 1934. And yet, *forty* years after his speech, it is so much more than 0.05 per cent that no precise figures are published about it anywhere. Percentages are sometimes quoted – very much less optimistic ones, though, than those which Vyshkinsky dispensed so boldly. But percentages without a single absolute figure are not information but a substitute for information, useful only for show, and therefore widely employed for that purpose alone.

In the whole of 1973 and the first half of 1974 the periodical *Sotsialisticheskaya Zakonnost* (Socialist Legality) published only one article containing some figures, expressed in bald percentages, to confirm this proposition that crime is steadily declining in our country. Just as it began to decline in 1934, in Vyshinsky's time, so it has gone on declining and declining ever since, and yet somehow has not got down to zero level. In issue No. 7 of 1973 of the periodical mentioned there is an article by a member of the collegium of the Office of the Public Prosecutor of the USSR, P. Kudryavtsev, entitled: 'Experience in the Fight against Crime in Estonia'. Let us transcribe the passages referring to the decline in delinquency.

In the Estonian SSR in recent times, together with a general reduction in crime, fewer and fewer serious offences have been committed. For example, in 1972 as compared with 1970 the number of cases of premeditated murder fell by 38 per cent, cases of grievous bodily harm by 24 per cent, rape cases by 17 per cent (and, in comparison with 1967, by 40 per cent). Such widespread offences as malicious hooliganism occurred much less frequently – 50 per cent less than in 1967 – while petty hooliganism declined by over 30 per cent.

After the phrase acknowledging that malicious hooliganism is a widespread offence comes the good news of the next achievement: 'Whereas in 1967 theft of citizens' personal property, embezzlement and hooliganism accounted for more than 62 per cent of all offences, in 1972 their share of the total had been reduced considerably, to 43.4 per cent.' Further, 'in 1967 cases of hooliganism made up 24.7 per cent of all offences, but in 1972 only 11.5 per cent'.

An inspiring picture! But here is a question to which I can think of no optimistic answer: since, in a particular year, thefts, embezzlement and hooliganism made up 62 per cent of all offences, and then fell to 43.4 per cent, this must mean that all the other offences, which previously made up 100 minus 62, that is, 38 per cent, have now risen to 100 minus 43.4, that is, 56.6 per cent. The same applies to hooliganism, for which a specific figure has been given: since it occupies a smaller space among the total number of offences (11.5 per cent instead of 24.7 per cent), this must mean that the other offences have come to occupy a larger space – instead of 75.3 per cent (100 minus 24.7), they now occupy 88.5 per cent (100 minus 11.5).

It turns out badly when a writer treats his readers as cretins incapable of doing a simple subtraction sum. This is the inconvenience of the method of depicting a situation in terms of bald percentages alone – any attempt to hide some shameful part of the truth by means of those little percentage symbols inevitably uncovers some other, equally shameful part.

It is easy now to understand the method by which crime is always being reduced in our country. On crime in the West, however, most detailed information is given in the periodical mentioned, as in our press generally. Here we find the number of drug-addicts and the number of murders, thefts and burglaries – and not in percentages, either, but in unambiguous direct figures, taken from official sources. It emerges from all the figures given that crime is increasing in the West. Official organs in the capitalist countries do not fear to publish figures testifying to the increase in crime. And yet *we* refrain from showing our achievements in d'.ect figures. What strange modesty!

Izvestiya of 4 July 1974 contained the following note: 'More than a million crimes were committed in 1973 in England and Wales. According to figures published in the annual report of Britain's police, the number of crimes in which force was used went up by 18 per cent as compared with 1972. Expenditure on the upkeep of the police in England and Wales came to £425 million in 1972-3.'

Since crime is declining in our country there is no point in letting us know how much is spent on the upkeep of our militia. That's a state secret. About Britain, however, we learn from the quotation just given, in addition to the figures for crime, another very interesting fact: apparently the British police report to their people every year ('figures published in the Annual Report of Britain's Police'), and thereby also to the whole world, since the paper in which the report appears is read everywhere.

Thus, in trying to emphasise British criminality, *Izvestiya* unintentionally told its readers about British democracy.

We find a similar communication, this time about Japan, in *Pravda* of 29 June 1974: 'During the past year, 1,190,549 offences were committed in Japan. These figures are given in the White Book of Japan's national police administration.' The Japanese police too, then, report to their people and to the whole world – and not in a newspaper article, but in a special White Book, and in precise absolute figures.

In our country the people can also find something out from the periodical *Sotsialisticheskaya Zakonnost*. In the article already quoted it is said: 'Statistical analysis shows that a considerable number not only of petty breaches of the law but also of dangerous crimes are committed by adolescents.' That's what it says, though without precision as to what this 'considerable number' may be, for the Soviet reader is not allowed to analyse the statistics for himself: the facts are still lumped together like 'other foodstuffs'.

Young people, as is well known even without newspaper articles, make up the bulk of what are called hooligans. But it is not easy to find the source of this malignant social ulcer, hooliganism. Is it rooted in the fact that youngsters follow the example of their elders, and cannot but follow them, in becoming addicted to alcohol? Or is it due to their getting out of hand and becoming 'insolent', as the admirers of Stalin's order claim? But, if that is the case, *why* have they got out of hand? That is hard to discover without deep-going social investigation, of which the people stand in great need, but which is not wanted by those who sell alcohol and yet conceal the amount consumed, and who fight against crime and yet shy away from reporting to the people on the progress of their struggle, in direct and honest figures.

Without a social analysis of a social disease the latter cannot be cured. Though by its widespread character comparable to cancer, this disease differs from that one in the low degree of applicability of surgical treatment. And in any case, to operate on the patient on the assumption that what he is suffering from is not cancer but, at worst, a polyp, is inadmissible here.

* * * *

Drunkenness, crime, hooliganism belong to the category of social diseases on which everyone tries to form an opinion, and has the right to do so, even without having comprehensive figures at his disposal. Where questions of high policy are concerned, or discussions about the rights of man, one may shrug one's shoulders and say: 'It doesn't concern me', or: 'It's over my head.' But one can't shrug off hooligans, or those six alcoholic lads living round a single yard. Everyone wants and needs to know: is this trouble getting worse, or is it decreasing?

In so far as crime and drunkenness are undoubtedly complex phenomena and it is impossible to imagine crime declining while drunkenness increases, we have the right to judge of these two phenomena by examining, with a certain measure of confidence, that one of them on which at least a few figures have leaked out. Let us consider the question which seems to me to be of the greatest importance: which way is the situation developing, what is its dynamic? Let us try to work with the statistics at our disposal more seriously and, above all, more honestly, than did that supreme guardian of honesty and conscience, Procurator-General Andrei Yanuarevich Vyshinsky.

As regards alcohol, the question formulated above can be answered only in this form: is consumption of this commodity increasing or not? We are not in a position to judge how increased consumption is related to what is drunk – whether or not consumption varies with variations in the character and content of drinks. It may be thought, however, that the centuries-old traditional way of consuming alcohol is not subordinated to the modernisation of what is drunk, but, on the contrary, subordinates that factor to itself. If someone has the inveterate habit of drinking himself unconscious, it is of no great significance whether he drinks diluted alcohol, or vodka, or beer mixed with vodka, or fortified wine. We shall therefore consider all alcohol products together, in the way they are given in the statistical volume *Narodnoye Khozyaistvo SSSR v 1972 g.* which has been frequently quoted from already. From the big table on page 555 I have taken only the eight largest items.

Increase in the sale of the principal articles of general consumption in state and cooperative shops (in comparable prices): in percentages of 1940

	1940	1960	1965	1970	1971	1972	1973[14]
All goods	100	326	425	646	690	737	775
Foodstuffs	100	264	360	511	540	570	598
Meat products	100	531	661	958	11-fold	12-fold? 11.6-fold?	11.9-fold
Alcohol products	100	200	283	439	472	501	534
Non-foodstuffs	100	436	567	894	966	10.5-fold	11-fold

	1940	1960	1965	1970	1971	1972	1973[14]
Clothing and underwear	100	394	530	878	936	977	987
Leather footwear	100	536	507	785	811	844	895
Radio sets and radiograms	100	27-fold	32-fold	37.6-fold	37.5-fold	38-fold	38-fold

In this table many other goods are named besides alcohol, and the sale of nearly all of them has grown faster than that of alcohol products. An idyllic picture is given. Although consumption of alcohol has risen (to a figure something over fivefold that of 1940), this is, so to speak, only a result of the general increase in prosperity. It can be said that our people buy nearly eight times as much as before the war, but that, though they do buy more vodka, they buy only five-and-a-bit more of *that* than they bought pre-war. Whereas, look, they buy thirty-eight times as many radio sets as in 1940 (the table, be it remembered, is given in comparable prices, so that upward or downward changes in price do not affect the indices shown).

But is it correct to calculate the dynamic of development from a starting-point so far behind us as thirty-three years? Is this a conscientious procedure? Does it show the present tendency? And can we take as 100 the pre-war year 1940, when the overwhelming majority of goods (meat, clothes, textiles, footwear, furniture, etc.) were then in short supply, and some had hardly begun to be produced (knitwear, radio goods, motor cycles), whereas vodka was not in short supply in those days, and was in no sense a new product?

From any point of view we know it to be wrong to take 1940 as the starting-point for a statistical comparison. This table does not show the current tendency but gives a distorted (and, of course, deliberately, not accidentally, distorted) view of that tendency. The picture becomes much truer to life if we take as starting-point a year that is nearer to our own time. In the table this could be 1960. We shall not need to add any new data to the table, but merely recalculate it, taking the figures for 1960 as 100. Here, then, is the table adjusted to show percentages of 1960:

	1960	*1965*	*1970*	*1971*	*1972*	*1973*
All goods	100	133	198	212	226	238
Foodstuffs	100	136	193	204	216	226
Meat	100	124	180	207	226?	224
products					210?	
Alcohol						
products	100	142	220	236	250	267
Non-foodstuffs	100	130	206	223	242	253
Clothing and						
underwear	100	134	223	237	248	251
Leather						
footwear	100	142	220	228	237	251
Radio sets and						
radiograms	100	118	140	140	141	141

This is the true picture of the current dynamic of purchases by the population: not a fivefold growth for one commodity (alcohol) and a 38-fold growth for another (radios), but a more-or-less uniform increase in all purchases, though with 'consumer durables' lagging behind, as happens in real life and not as in life re-shuffled by means of cunning statistical sleight-of-hand. It is especially important that, by beginning our calculation in 1960, we obtain a picture of the *recent* past, not of the long-distant past, and on this basis can understand what is happening today and get an idea of what will happen tomorrow. What leaps at once to the eye is that alcohol is in the lead. In 1973 its increase over 1960 was 167 per cent – more than clothing, purchases of which, it needs to be observed, increased especially fast because purchases of textile fabrics increased only very slightly. (I do not quote the figures, so as not to overburden the argument: cf. the handbook for 1972, p. 555.)

In the light of these irrefutable figures, taken from official statistics, the assumptions I made in previous pages regarding the increase in the sale of vodka in 1972 (an increase of 25 per cent in five years) look extremely cautious. The amount of growth I allowed for was obviously an underestimate and, consequently, I also underestimated in my assumption regarding the amount of turnover tax derived from alcohol

(18.5-19 milliard roubles). Thus, from the statistical hand-book, studied with the attention which any scientific work deserves, we have managed to extract the information which it was designed to keep hidden in the depths of its tables ...

But let us return to our commodities.

In fairness I must add that certain commoditie which are enumerated in the handbook, but which I have omitted, have in the last few years outstripped alcohol in the rate at which demand for them has increased. These are mainly goods the large-scale production of which, or the sale of which through state shops, has developed only in the most recent period: jewellery, knitwear, stockings, furniture, earthenware and glass crockery, eggs and cheese. Of these, only knitwear constitutes a substantial magnitude (7.8 milliard roubles' worth was sold in 1972); the rest cannot be regarded as being among the most important commodities. But neither knitwear, nor furniture, nor any other commodity challenges the leading position of alcohol. This remains what it was, namely, Commodity Number One.

To be more precise, we could say that alcohol is men's Commodity Number One, and knitwear is the commodity with which, so to speak, the women try to emulate the men's achievement. But what a huge difference in quantity there is between them! On the men's side, 26-27 milliard roubles, and on the women's only 7.8 milliard. (Some of the alcohol, of course, is drunk by women; but so also is some of the knitwear worn by men.) And what about the future prospect? Even allowing for the factors of fashion and comfort, knitwear is a commodity which gives a longer period of use than alcohol, which is bought and drunk simultaneously. The 'knitwear explosion' will soon come to an end, and the long queues to buy imported woollen jackets will, let us hope, get shorter (to be replaced by queues for something else). Knitwear will become a more or less common-or-garden commodity, and the market for it will reach saturation point. But will the market for wine and vodka reach saturation point?

As for clothing, furniture, meat, cheese, etc., the same people spent considerably more on these goods than in 1960. The general growth in material well-being in all the developed countries of the world has been enormous, and could not but affect our country along with the rest. It is one of the consequences of the scientific and technical revolution which has enveloped the whole world. It had become simply impossible for the Soviet people to lag too far behind the British, the Finns, the Swedes, the Hungarians and so many other peoples. We had to pull ourselves up to their level, and we have begun to do this. The consequence is that a Soviet citizen who previously had two pairs of shoes has now acquired four: instead of two suits he has bought three; he has got himself a TV set; he is starting to eat pineapples and oranges, and so on.

The increase in the purchases made by Soviet people proceeds along the following channels: increase in the quantity of goods available which previously were in short supply, appearance of new or modernised goods (knitwear, silk underwear, tape recorders, motor cars), modernisation and improvement of foodstuffs (white bread, imported fruits, meat).[15]

In all these cases – and they cover the overwhelming majority of purchases – the purchasers involved are the same people as ten and twenty years previously. It is just that each person buys either more than he used to, or something better, or something new. The number of consumers increases only by as much as the population increases – that is, over the thirteen-year period that concerns us, by 17 per cent. This increase was, of course, reflected in the increase in consumption, but was only a small element in the latter.

The increase of 167 per cent in the consumption of alcohol was also due only slightly to the increase in the population. Other factors were at work here. What were they?

They can hardly have been the same ones that led to an increase in sales of suits, knitwear or meat. Unlike the position with those goods, our market has been more than adequately saturated with alcoholic drinks since early times. It would also be silly to suppose that the same persons who, thirteen years ago, drank, say, four bottles a month, have now begun to drink ten. Some of them have certainly increased the amount they drink (whence comes the increase in alcoholism) but what we are concerned with is the total amount of vodka and wine purchased, and not the purchases made by alcoholics.

The headlong increase in the consumption of alcohol throughout the country cannot have been affected by 'old' purchasers. It is not that the thirst of all the drinkers has increased so inordinately – more than two-and-a-half times in these few years – but simply that additional millions and millions of people have been drawn into drinking. It may be that every heavy drinker is taking a little more than he did before, but in the main the increase is due to new drinking cadres.

In the article already quoted, by Academician Strumilin and Professor Sonin, 'Alcoholism and the Struggle against it', in *Ekonomika i organizatsiya promyshlennogo proizvodstva*, 1974, no. 4 we read this: 'Investigation of a clinical group of alcoholics showed that 28 per cent of the men became acquainted with alcohol before the age of 15, 65 per cent before the age of 18 and 80 per cent before the age of 20.'

Even if the group studied was not very large, the figures quoted are highly significant. There can be no doubt that they reflect a dynamic which is common to the country as a whole: young people are increasingly being drawn into the consumption of alcohol. Inevitably we recall those six alcoholic lads in one yard, about whom a reader wrote to *Literaturnaya Gazeta*.

This is the new factor which decisively alters the nature of the alcohol problem.

And such are the peculiarities of our socialist way of life that the drawing of young people into indulgence in drink is facilitated precisely by a government measure which, as is clear from the decision of 16 June 1972, was intended to reduce drunkenness, namely, increasing the output of wine. The intention was admirable; but hell is paved with good intentions.

The 'level of assimilability' of wine is considerably higher and more easily surpassed than that of vodka: wine is not unpleasant, does not smell of fuel oil, does not burn the throat, and does not immediately go to the head. Vodka's shortcomings in the matter of taste have rendered it unattractive to young people and women. But now everything has been arranged in the best possible way. The State Planning Commission and the Ministry of the Food Industry have been instructed to bring about 'a considerable increase in the output of wine and beer' not so that we may admire the labels on the bottles, but in order that we may drink what will be in them. A considerable increase, note, had been achieved even before 1972. Whereas in 1960 less than 78 million decalitres were produced, by 1965 production was nearly twice as high (134 million) and by 1970 it had doubled again (268 million), but by 1972, though production was substantial (293 million), the rate of increase was not what it had been – it had noticeably slackened. Thus, the guiding instruction promulgated in the decision 'on measures for combating drunkenness', proved, as is always the case, very timely and wise: increase the output of wine! Actually, we have seen a nearly fourfold increase in twelve years, not to mention the fact that imports of wine from the fraternal People's Democracies have also increased substantially.

Wine adds colour and savour to the stream of those facile pleasures on which it is so easy to let oneself float and float along. This stream of pleasure easily carries away young drinkers. The cheering properties of wine are just what pleasure-seeking young people require.

Introducing youngsters to wine is also a leading factor in promoting the consumption of Commodity Number One. There is a terrible dynamic here, fraught with many dangers. The names of the closest concomitants of drunkenness are all too well known.

The frightful Russian tradition: 'If you drink, drink to get drunk', which is presented as a sign of our national prowess and generosity of character, really testifies to a different sort of 'generosity', namely, the wide extent to which the national calamity of drunkenness has developed.

Any calamity becomes doubly dangerous when people refuse to admit its existence, or when they start deliberately to conceal its extent. The problem of drink, in addition to its medical and economic aspects (about which I say nothing, for these reasons: the medical aspect is adequately explained in the papers and posters to be seen in polyclinics, while the economic aspect cannot be discussed owing to the complete absence of official data), has become also a moral problem.

This moral problem includes, besides the usual accompaniments of drunkenness (hooliganism, crime, parasitism, squandering the money needed for housekeeping, break-up of marriages,[16] wounding of children's souls, and so on), also *lying*. This is employed on a grand scale, concealing the truth about vodka and wine and reinforcing intoxication by alcohol with the intoxication of the people by means of incessant blarney about our moral superiority over all other nations.

There thus arises before us a moral problem which is not simple but, so to speak, double: the ulcer of drunkenness, with all the social ills that accompany it, and the concealment of this ulcer by a coating of official optimism, manipulation of statistics, propagandist complacency, official self-satisfaction, and a general attitude of tolerance towards the hell of alcoholism (and not only of alcoholism?).

It is difficult to raise up a dam against the time-honoured mighty river of vodka and wine which flows, broadly and freely, across the boundless spaces of our motherland, but it is even more difficult, perhaps, to stop the river of empty verbiage which is poured out instead of truth, so as to prevent the people from appreciating the full depth of our national losses through alcohol. To start with, what is needed is to cut a chink, even if only a small one, in the thick curtain of lies which hides the problem of drunkenness, and this I have tried to do to the best of my ability.

Of profound importance is the fact that the problem of drunkenness brings us right up against another problem, which is far from being a cause of suffering and pain to everyone, namely, the problem of the suppressing of information.

It turns out that these two problems are connected – and how closely connected!

The suppressing of information about alcohol, information which it is so vitally necessary for the people to have, since they cannot get out of their plight without it. It is possible to express a serious opinion as to the measures that need to be taken to combat it only if one knows the facts. The suppressing of this information is dependent upon a 'temporary' measure which was introduced in the early years of the October Revolution, namely, the censorship. Just as the sale of vodka was introduced on a temporary basis, so was the censorship. And while the vodka law has lasted fifty years, the 'temporary' censorship has lasted fifty-five. But that is another story. Or perhaps they are both parts of the same story?

Afterword

This article had already been completed when the latest issue of the handbook *Narodnoye Khozyaistvo v SSSR,* that for the year 1973, was put on sale. It confirms the computations I made before it became available. The table printed on p. 638, showing 'Increase in the sale of the most important consumer goods in state and cooperative shops (in comparable prices)' is very revealing. In this table the starting-point is taken as the year 1965, unlike the practice in previous issues (in my article calculations were made on the basis of the figures for 1960). It is not worth reproducing the entire table, which fully agrees with my own, given on p. 197 of this article. The conclusions that can be drawn from it are that in 1973, as compared with 1972, the sale of alcohol products increased by 6.2 per cent, whereas that of meat increased by 3.4 per cent, of clothing and underwear by 2.1 per cent, of knitwear by 5 per cent, of radio sets by 2.5 per cent, of footwear by 6.5 per cent, and so on. The sale of TV sets fell by 10 per cent and that of bicycles also fell, but there was a remarkable increase in the sale of light cars (40 per cent more than in the preceding year). However, the motor car is not by any means an article of wide general consumption in our country, and does not define the profile of the typical Soviet consumer. As the table is given only in percentages, it remains unknown how many of the 917,000 light cars produced in 1973 were sold to buyers within the USSR, and how many were sold abroad. However, this is not the most important of the figures kept from us by the statistical handbook: figures for the revenue from the sale of alcohol are a great deal more significant.

The table mentioned is given, as we see from its heading, in comparable prices, so that price changes do not affect its indices, and we must face the fact that the 6.2 per cent increase in the sale of alcohol is indeed the true index of the consumption of this commodity.

So, then, alcohol continues to be Commodity Number One. It continues to hold that position despite the fact that in 1973, according to the latest figures (see *Narodnoye Khozyaistvo SSSR v 1973 g.* p.323), the output of wine declined sharply: in 1972 it was, as already mentioned, 293 million decalitres, but in 1973, strangely enough, it was down to 207 millions. Whether because the grapes did not ripen or for other reasons, the directive regarding 'increased output of wine' remained hanging in the air. Our economy is far from always law-abiding, and this is especially true of its agricultural branches.

* * * *

Some friends have asked me: But what can you suggest should be done, concretely?

To begin with, these two measures are needed, at least:

(1) Make available to everyone the figures showing the revenue received by the state from the sale of alcohol. This would be doing no more than Stalin did on the eve of the tenth anniversary of the October Revolution. He told foreign workers' delegations on 5 November 1927 (and this was printed in the Soviet press) the extent to which it had been possible to 'obtain working capital' from the sale of vodka. Why not tell us the current figure?

(2) Permit the publication of books and studies devoted to the problem of drunkenness in its full dimensions. This would be doing no more than the Tzarist government allowed to be done by men whose hearts grieved for a people whose rulers had been pouring drink into them for centuries.

Can it be that what the Tzarist government allowed to be published about vodka cannot be allowed today by the most democratic government in the world?

NOTES

1   Limitation of the days and hours when vodka can be sold is regarded today as a measure that can reduce drunkenness. By the decision of the Council of Ministers of the USSR, dated 16 June 1972, 'On measures for intensifying the struggle against drunkenness and alcoholism', the Councils of Ministers of the Union Republics were instructed (according to *Pravda*) 'to examine the question of restricting or suppressing the trade in vodka and other alcoholic drinks with a strength of 30 degrees or over, on rest-days and holidays, and to take the appropriate decisions in accordance with local conditions'. In the seventeenth century, limitation of the days and hours when vodka could be sold played an important part. Bottles were not yet being made in Russia, so that it was not possible to take vodka home, and only a rich Boyar could keep it in barrels in his house. The common people could not drink anywhere but at the bar of a tavern. Restricting a 'heavy drinker' to only one cup, or serving vodka only until mass time, was a really effective measure. The first Russian glass factories, which appeared in the seventeenth century, manufactured utensils for the Tzar's table: glass was considered a luxury. In present-day conditions, however, when alcohol is sold in glass containers convenient for keeping the stuff, prohibiting the sale of drink on certain days or during certain hours affects only those people who even on holidays do their drinking not at home but in the yard-entrance.

2   I gave similar but more detailed calculations, for the year 1970, in my article *Commodity Number One,* which was read by only a small group of friends. There I took expenditure on soft drinks as being one milliard roubles, but now, so as to avoid any underestimation, let us (clearly *over*estimating) say *two* milliard.
    As regards mineral water, an article by the USSR Minister for the Food Industry, V. Lein, in *Pravda* of 8 July 1974, gives a descriptive account of the production of Borzhomi water. Every day, says the Minister, over a million bottles of it are made available to consumers. They could manage a larger quantity, he says, but 'what holds us back is the loading, which is done by hand. The bottles have to be stacked one by one in the trucks, because there are no cardboard containers: the enterprise is very poorly supplied with cardboard. Many examples of this sort of situation could be given.' The Minister does not tell us what proportion of the bottles, stacked in the trucks like firewood, get broken in transit, or who eventually pays for this amazing system, in which what matters is the plan: we fulfilled our norm and loaded the stuff on the trucks, even if it is now all smashed to smithereens!
    About the vodka industry, which also comes within his province, the Minister said nothing at all in his long article. He would probably not have kept mum about it if it had been contracting. Silence is sometimes more eloquent than words.

3   Before the Revolution, wine made from grapes, and also beer, occupied a very small place in the consumption of alcohol by the people. Wine-growing developed in Russia only in the early years of the twentieth century, but even then the amount of wine made for marketing was only 16 million decalitres, or about one litre of wine per year per head of population.

4   It is not difficult to understand the reduction in tempo beginning in 1932 – due to collectivisation and the sharp decline in the harvests. Official statistics have good reason to conceal the harvest figures for those years – e.g., in the 'jubilee' issue of the statistical handbook *Narodnoye Khozyaistvo SSSR* for the year 1972, on p. 218 we find the harvest-figures for 1909-13 and for all the years of Soviet power between 1922 and 1972 *except* the years 1928-36.

5   The sharp increase in 1937, and especially in 1938, is also explicable: 1937 was a year of good harvest. Where did the grain go? Into vodka!

6   In order to understand the decline in 1940 we need to remember the non-aggression pact made with Hitlerite Germany in August 1939. A lot of grain was sent to Germany: the special trains that carried it were still running on the last day before the war [i.e. the German attack on the USSR – Trans.].

7   We are approaching the harvest-figure of Tzarist times!

8   We have surpassed it!

9   The sharp upward leap corresponds to the excellent grain and potato harvest of 1956.

10   To the figures drawn from our statistics we ought to add a probable figure for the consumption of *samogon,* based on the opinion of Academician Strumilin, which I quoted earlier, namely, that *samogon* accounts for a quantity of alcohol not less than 50 per cent of that which goes into vodka. This means about another two litres of vodka consumed in the form of *samogon.* Altogether, a minimum of 7.5 litres of pure alcohol per person per year.

11   It calls for very little trouble even on the part of those who grow the potatoes used to produce alcohol. Potato-picking has been carried out for a long time now, as we all know very well, by townsfolk: by students, workers, office-workers, and scientists. One-sixth of all the state's purchase of potatoes in 1967 (1,908 thousand tons) went to make alcohol. When he places a bottle of vodka on his table, the scientist, like the worker and the office worker, can with justification declare that it contains a drop of his labour, too.

For some time now, though, raw sugar (not the waste-products of sugar production) has been being processed for alcohol. Before 1965 very little of this was used, but in that year 87,000 tons of raw sugar were turned into alcohol. A year later this amount had grown to 425,000, and in the following year it was 387,000. What happened in those years? It is not hard to understand: Cuba began to sell us her sugar. Thank you, Comrade Fidel! He helped us out!

12   *Pravda* was so concerned about alcoholism in the USA that it reprinted five months later, word for word, a good half of the note on the subject

it had published on 5 February 1974. For lack of space I do not reproduce these curious duplicate passages, and refer the reader of *Pravda* to his back-numbers of February and July: let him find the pages and compare them.

13 I quote literally: *izbezhat' inostrannuyu kabalu* [a clumsy expression here rendered as 'avoid going into foreign bondage' – Trans.]. No one was ever allowed to correct Stalin.

14 The figures for 1973 are, of course, not taken from the 1972 volume. Their source is the recently issued short statistical handbook entitled *SSR v tsivrakh v 1973 godu* (The USSR in Figures in 1973) which appears every year a few months before the publication of the main work, by the same publishing house, *'Statistika'*, and under the same editorship. All the stranger, therefore, is the following disparity: for the item 'Meat products' *Narodnoye Khozyaistvo* shows a 12-fold increase in 1972, whereas *SSSR v tsifrakh v 1973 g.* though reproducing all the other figures for the previous years, makes an exception of the sale of meat-products, and shows for 1972 not a 12-fold but an 11.6-fold increase (I have given both figures, followed by question-marks). If this means that there was a mistake in the main publication (probably the computer miscalculated!) then this should be commented on in the next issue of the smaller book: 'We have corrected an inaccuracy.' This is an indispensable rule of conscientious scientific work – which, as has clearly been seen, is something alien to the editors of the collection of statistics concerned. Incidentally, this inaccuracy, translated into money terms, was a matter of 465 million roubles, since the sale of 'meat products', evidently meaning meat and sausages, brought in more than 14 milliard roubles in 1972.

15 I think it proper to single out the consumption of meat in order to compare this with the consumption of alcohol. One must not be over-impressed by the figure of 124 per cent for the growth in the sale of 'meat products' (which means not only meat but also sausages) in state shops as compared with 1960, or by the 12-fold increase since 1940. Meat is sold on the market not only by state shops but also by collective farmers, and if the sale of it has increased 12-fold in state shops since 1940, that does not mean at all that the whole population of the USSR has begun to consume twelve times as much meat as before the war. That would be an absurdity, such as could cloud the thinking only of a child. With vodka, however, it really is the case that the amount sold through the shops and the amount consumed fully coincide, for only the state sells this commodity, through its own trade network. (No attention is paid here to *samogon*, which from the start I have excluded from my calculations.)

The average increase in the consumption of meat per head of population is given in other tables in the same statistical handbooks (*Narodnoye Khozyaistvo SSSR v 1972 g.*, p. 557, and *SSSR v tsifrakh v 1973 g.*, p. 190). For some reason they do not show the year 1940, though 1913 is there (28 kilogrammes per head). In 1950 the figure was 26 kg, that is, it was still not up to the pre-Revolution level: in 1960 it was

40, in 1970 – 48, in 1972 – 51 (an increase of 6 per cent in two years), and in 1973 – 52 (an increase of 2 per cent in this year.) There was no 12-fold increase, of course, and no mention of anything of the sort. What these figures show is the consumption of *meat*. (Our statistics, unlike, for example, the British ones, include in one and the same column, under the general heading of 'meat', also lard, poultry and by-products, as is mentioned in brackets.)

In the tables, however, where we read of a '12-fold' growth, only part of this meat is represented – that part which passes across the counters of state and cooperative shops. By however much this part has increased, it still tells us nothing about the increase in consumption. The actual dynamic of the people's consumption of meat is shown only in those tables which show their average annual indices as figures 'per head of population'. For the 13 years we are considering, the increase came to 30 per cent: from 40 kg per head it rose to 52 kg. So let us put that on record: between 1960 and 1973 the increase in the consumption of meat was 30 per cent, while the increase in the consumption of alcohol was 167 per cent.

16 According to a selective inquiry mentioned in the article in *Nauka i Zhizn* already quoted, 40 per cent of all divorces result from drunkenness, and a tendency is observed for the proportion of divorces due to this cause to increase.

Editor's Note

A. Krasikov is one of the pen names of Mikhail Baitalski (he also used pen names: Baikalski, Domalski and sometimes wrote anonymously for *samizdat*). The Editor is very sorry to inform readers that Krasikov-Baitalski died on 18 August 1978 at the age of seventy five. He was born in the Ukraine in 1903. At the age of sixteen he took part in the Civil War as a private in the Red Army. After the Civil War he started to write and worked as journalist in the Ukraine in Donbass region. In 1927 he was arrested as a 'Trotskyist', but released in 1928. In 1929-34 he worked as journalist in Kharkov and then in Leningrad, but in 1934 during the first purge in Leningrad he was dismissed and started to work as a metal craftsman at the plant in Leningrad. In 1936 he was again arrested and spent five years in Vorkuta (Polar region) where the railroad was under construction. During the war he was released and served in the Soviet Army until the end – was among soldiers who reached Berlin. After war he again worked as metal craftsman in provincial towns. In 1950 he was again arrested and sentenced to fifteen years – the accusations were again the same – 'Trotskyist'. He was released and fully rehabilitated in 1956.

From 1958 he lived in Moscow. Baitalski-Krasikov started to write for *samizdat* in 1959-60. From 1965 he contributed some essays to *POLITICAL DIARY* – a *samizdat* journal which was edited by myself and he gave me some of his memoirs which were anonymous, but which I quoted often in my book *Let History Judge*. Krasikov-Baitalski was a very gifted essayist and poet; one book of his poetry was published in 1962 in a Russian publishing house in Israel under the pseudonym D. Seter (*My Spring will Come*). His essay 'Russian Jews Yesterday and Today' had been well known in *samizdat* and was partly published in *Political Diary*. He also wrote a *samizdat* book *Notes for Grandchildren*. It is difficult now to compile a list of Krasikov-Baitalski's works because he often used different pseudonyms. He was a kind man, talented author, serious thinker and good historian. I hope that a collection of his essays and works will be published in due time. His relatives have expressed the desire that his real name be now known to enable us to collect his works in future.

Comparative Mechanisation of Agriculture in the USSR and Other Countries

(Summary of an Unpublished Article
by the Economist M. B. Davydov)

Almost forty-five years ago Stalin declared: 'We are becoming a country of metal, a country of automobilisation, a country of tractorisation. And when we place the USSR in a motor car and the peasant upon a tractor – let the honourable capitalists, pluming themselves on their "civilisation", try and catch up with us. We shall see then which countries can be called backward and which advanced.' (3 November 1929, *Problems of Leninism*, Moscow, 1962, p. 305.)

As we know, it is only now that the Soviet Union is really getting into a motor car. And in quantity of heavy and light vehicles, as well as quality and extent of automobile routes, the USSR still lags very much behind Western Europe and the USA. But we shall not discuss cars here. Below we shall examine only part of the promise; namely, how the peasant has been put upon his tractor and how the 'honourable capitalists' have caught up with us. The light vehicle is after all an impermissible luxury for many countries. Tractorisation on the other hand is one of the foundations of present-day agriculture; the development of agriculture is unthinkable today without the tractor.

At the time when Stalin pronounced the words quoted above, the capitalist countries of Europe, like the Soviet Union, essentially had no tractors – they numbered in the ten thousands. Even ten years later, i.e., in 1939, England had

210

only 55,000 tractors, France 36,000, Germany (within the Federal Republic borders) 20-25,000, Italy about 30,000. Only the USA had really taken the path of tractorisation – with over 800,000 tractors in 1929 (see the handbook, *Agriculture in Capitalist Countries,* Moscow, 1959).

But for the USSR tractors were especially necessary. The collectivisation of agriculture would have become senseless, if the young *kolkhozes* could not obtain hundreds of thousands of tractors in a short period. One has to remember that in 1929-30 the setting-up of the collective farms was accompanied by a catastrophic drop in head of working livestock. If in 1916, despite the war, there were 38 million horses in the Russian countryside, in 1932 the *kolkhozes* had only 12 million horses.

Tractorisation in the USSR certainly went ahead energetically in the thirties. If in 1928 the country had only 27,000 tractors, by 1932 it already had 148,000, i.e., more than all the major countries in Western Europe taken together. By 1937 the USSR had 456,000 tractors. But thereafter the tempo of tractorisation dropped sharply, which was connected in the first place with the development of war industry. During the war the tractor fleet for agriculture decreased sharply, and even by 1950 there were only 595,000 tractors available for agriculture. Only after ten years, in 1960, did the number of tractors employed in agriculture exceed one million, and after another ten years, in 1970, did it reach two million physical units. (Data on the number of tractors taken from the statistical year-books of the Central Statistical Board.)

This increase in no way corresponded with the needs of our agriculture. In the first twenty-five post-war years the growth rate of our tractor fleet considerably lagged behind that of every developed capitalist country. As a result, tractorisation and other indices of agricultural mechanisation showed our country to be way behind the 'honourable capitalists'. If we leave out of the comparison small, low-powered tractors and calculate according to the number of tractors per 1000 hectares of arable land and long-term planting, we can put together the following illuminating table for the situation in 1970.

Country	Tractors in agriculture (thousands)	Arable land and long-term plant-ing (thousand hectares)	Tractors per 1000 hectares of arable land and long-term planting
1. Switzerland	73.0	386.0	189.0
2. Netherlands	156.4	867.0	180.0
3. German Federal Rep.	1371.0	8076.0	170.0
4. Austria	249.0	1581.0	157.00
5. New Zealand	95.5	774.0	123.0
6. Norway	90.0	814.0	110.0
7. Belgium	85.5	850.0	101.0
8. Ireland	84.0	1147.0	68.2
9. Denmark	174.6	2676.0	65.5
10. France	1240.0	19101.0	64.5
11. Great Britain	444.4	7261.0	61.1
12. Finland	155.5	2722.0	57.0
13. Sweden	170.0	3053.0	56.0
14. Japan	278.0	5510.0	50.5
15. Italy	614.7	14930.0	41.2
16. German Demo-cratic Rep.	149.0	4806.0	31.0
17. Czechoslovakia	136.0	5334.0	26.1
18. USA	4562.0	192318.0	23.7
19. Rep. of South Africa	220.0	12058.0	18.2
20. Greece	60.0	3631.0	16.5
21. Canada	631.6	43767.0	14.4
22. Poland	213.6	15326.0	14.0
23. Spain	259.8	20626.0	12.5
24. Hungary	68.9	5594.0	12.3
25. Bulgaria	53.6	4527.0	11.9
26. Romania	107.3	10512.0	10.2
27. *USSR*	1977.0	232809.0	8.6
28. Yugoslavia	66.9	8205.0	8.1
29. Australia	335.0	44610.0	7.5
30. Argentina	180.0	26028.0	5.8
31. Mexico	92.0	23817.0	4.9
32. Turkey	104.4	27378.0	3.8
33. Brazil	99.4	29760.0	3.3
34. India	63.0	17849.0	0.38

The present table is put together on the basis of Soviet and foreign statistical handbooks. For some countries (the USA) the data is given for 1969, for Greece for 1968. The tractor fleet for the whole world in 1970 was 15,330 tractors, so that the countries not shown in the table, as is easily calculated, had at their disposal a little more than 5 per cent of all tractors.

The USSR occupies only the twenty-seventh place in the table. One might, however, assume that Soviet tractors were put to better use than in capitalist countries. But this is doubtful, because in matters of care and maintenance of agricultural machinery the USSR is well behind the majority of countries in the West. The power of the tractor fleet is another matter. The Soviet Union produces more powerful tractors than the majority of Western countries. It is desirable, therefore, to supplement the table given above with an account of the power of the tractors in terms of horse-power per 100 hectares of arable land. This table will be smaller than the preceding one, because many countries do not have sufficiently exact statistical data on the power of different tractors. After quite complex calculations, details and method of which we shall omit here, we obtained the following table (from data for 1970):

Country	General power of the tractors	Horse-power per 100 hectares of arable land and orchards
1. German Federal Republic	34.8 million horse-power	430.0
2. Belgium	3.6 "	423.0
3. Great Britain	16.0 "	220.0
4. France	41.3 "	216.0
5. Japan	10.4 "	189.0
6. Italy	25.5 "	171.0
7. German Democratic Republic	6.0 "	125.0

Country	General power of the tractors		Horse-power per 100 hectares of arable land and orchards
8. USA	209.3	million horse-power	109.0
9. Czechoslovakia	5.5	"	103.0
10. Canada	28.5	"	65.0
11. Hungary	3.5	"	63.0
12. Bulgaria	2.2	"	49.0
13. *USSR*	111.6	"	48.0
14. Romania	4.7	"	45.0
15. Poland	6.8	"	44.4

In these two tables we quote data for 1970. But little has changed during the five subsequent years. Although the provision of tractors for agriculture was quite considerable – in 1970 it had exceeded 300,000 and in 1975 had reached almost 350,000, the annual growth of the country's tractor fleet for the ninth Five Year Plan came to an average of only 60,000 a year. A huge number of tractors are written off for scrap every year before their time, and the new supplies scarcely replace this loss.

It is, of course, possible to say that the countries of Western Europe enjoy an excessive supply of tractors. But this is not quite the case. It is true that the countries of Western Europe and Japan, not having ploughland to waste, practise a more intensive agriculture than the USA and Canada. But even comparison with the USA does not help us. Soviet economists usually say that in the USA where small farms predominate, tractors and other machines get worse use. This is untrue. It is difficult to imagine a civilised country where agricultural technology is more misused than in the USSR. In addition, according to American figures, roughly 75 per cent of agricultural production in the USA is accounted for by large and medium-sized farms with a productivity of more than 15,000 dollars a year, the majority of such farms comparable in size with the brigades and sections of our *kolkhozes* and *sovkhozes.* Furthermore, the huge dimensions of our *kolkhozes* and *sovkhozes* do not offer much room for technology. The point is that over a large section of our country (excluding only virgin land and the Southern regions) agricultural production is very fragmented. Small and irregular plots of arable land overlap with pasture, hayfields, woodland and shrub, etc. In some regions of the non-black earth zone there are up to 30 contours for 100 hectares of arable land. But the area of one contour of arable land comes to a little more than three hectares. And where there are 10 contours for a 100 hectares, as for example in the Novosibirsk district, this presents a major obstacle to the rational use of technology. This situation can only be remedied by melioration to which the USSR is only now advancing.

The manufacture of more powerful tractors in the USSR has not improved the situation very much. For example, DT-75, T-74 and T-78 tractors are roughly 30-40 per cent more powerful than the earlier DT-54 and DT-55 tractors. However, the daily output using the more powerful tractors is only 11 per cent higher in the *kolkhozes* and 7 per cent in the *sovkhozes.*

Economic studies often quote figures to show that one tractor in the USSR works longer during a year and tills more land than in the USA or other capitalist countries. This is correct. But it is certainly no achievement. On the contrary, it is a serious deficiency, hampering our country from accomplishing its basic agricultural tasks well and rapidly. It is the lack of tractors and other agricultural machinery which causes our corn harvest to drag out for 25-30 days with an attendant loss of grain of up to 20-30 per cent. We quote the following figures.

It can be calculated from Central Statistical Board data that each tractor works 216 shifts a year in the *kolkhozes* and 173 in the *sovkhozes.* With a seven-hour shift this produces an average of 1,360 hours work for the entire country. From foreign sources we learn that one tractor in the German Federal Republic works 430 hours per year and in the USA 420 hours. We cannot therefore boast about our 'rational' use of tractors. In the USA and West Germany, simply by having a sufficient quantity of tractors, farmers carry out sowing and harvesting more quickly as well as all other agricultural tasks. And in the USA and West Germany a tractor performs twice the number of agricultural tasks *in one working hour* as in the USSR. It is worth pointing out that over the ten years 1960-70 the continuity of work performed by one tractor in the USSR diminished by 7.5 per cent. This insignificant drop has annoyed the academics of the All-Union Lenin Academy of Agricultural Sciences. However, one can only welcome it, because it means that a tractor's work is approaching shorter hours.

The question arises – when will the USSR surpass the USA in terms of tractor power per 100 hectares of arable land? If we go by the growth rate of the tractor fleet in our country over the last fifteen years, then it will require seventeen to twenty-five years.

What has been said above about tractors may also be said about other mechanical means of agricultural production. In much agricultural machinery the USSR lags even further behind the capitalist countries, particularly in the mechanisation of stockraising. We scarcely use any motorised loading-vehicles. In country districts of the USSR made-up roads are twenty times fewer than in the USA, where the overwhelming majority of fields and farms connect directly with made-up roads or at a distance of no more than half a mile.

To conclude our article on the problems of the mechanisation of agriculture we shall look at some problems of that part of agriculture which is totally unmechanised and depends almost wholly on manual labour. We have in mind the personal plots of the *kolkhozniki,* subsidiary holdings belonging to workers and employees and *kolkhoz* land which workers and employees may use. The number of personal plots and holdings of this kind comes to roughly 23-4 million. Their size is limited by law and cannot exceed 0.3 hectares for *kolkhozniki* and 0.25 hectares for agricultural specialists, workers and employees. (We are not taking into account the millions of tiny garden plots used by workers and peasants in suburban zones, which vary from 400 to 1000 square metres in size.) The proportion of land at the personal disposal of the *kolkhozniki,* of workers and employees in the *sovkhozes* and agricultural specialists is very small: 1.5 per cent of all agricultural land and 3 per cent of arable land. However, these plots occupy quite a significant place in gross agricultural production. For example, in the 1973 bumper-crop year gross agricultural production using the comparable price-scale of 1965 came to 97.8 milliard roubles. Of this the *kolkhozes* accounted for 39 milliards and the *sovkhozes* 29.8 milliards. Personal ancillary production accounted for *29 million roubles*. We see, therefore, that production on personal plots is as much as in the *sovkhozes* (on an average annual scale it is even greater) and not much less than in the *kolkhozes*. These figures appear particularly striking if we recall that in 1973 the *sovkhozes* had more than 110 hectares of arable land, while personal, ancillary households did not have as much as seven million. In other words *kolkhozniki* and *sovkhoz* workers extract *13 times more* agricultural produce, in terms of roubles, from a single hectare of personal land than from one hectare of *kolkhoz* land and *16 times more* than from one hectare of *sovkhoz* land! If the huge areas of our *kolkhoz* and *sovkhoz* lands were used even half as intensively as the private plots, then the USSR today would be producing an agricultural yield of 600-700 milliard roubles annually. How does one explain such intensive use of the private plots? First by the material incentives for *kolkhozniki*, workers and employees. As is well known, these plots produce little in terms of commodities. Almost the whole of production in these personal plots goes towards feeding the *kolkhoz* families and the *sovkhoz* workers; the little left over is sold at the markets. These plots are in practice the only source of supply for agricultural workers of meat, milk, poultry, eggs, potatoes, vegetables and all other products except bread. In the present day, work in the *kolhoz* or *sovkhoz* is remunerated almost everywhere monetarily rather than in kind. This is why the *kolkhozniki* and *sovkhoz* workers give the *maximum of labour and effort* to their small plots. It is well known that in the post-war years several attempts were made to cut down the private-plot cultivation of *kolkhozniki*, workers and employees. It was presumably supposed that if the *kolkhozniki* and *sovkhoz* workers spent less time on their own land they would work better in the fields of the *kolkhozes* and *sovkhozes*. These attempts unfailingly produced a deterioration in nutrition and a drop in the general material situation of agricultural workers, causing dissatisfaction among wide masses of the rural population and in the final analysis a worsening of the situation in the countryside. For this reason each attempt to encroach on private agricultural activity had to be stopped. In the last ten years (1965-75) the general value of private agricultural production has not decreased, but risen by roughly 15-20 per cent. This is not surprising, since the *kolkhoznik* even now receives *less money and facilities from his kolkhoz* than from his own plot. So, for example, in 1965 produce from private *kolkhoz* plots came to 16.3 milliard roubles according to prices of that year. In the same year the *kolkhozniki* received a remuneration for their work, in cash and facilities, of 11.5 milliard roubles. In 1970 these figures were proportionately the same: 19.6 as against 15 milliard roubles, and for the bumper-crop year 1973: 20.4 milliard as against 16.6 milliard roubles. We have reckoned all these data on the basis of the official Year-book of the Central Statistical Board, see for example, the Central Statistical Board Year-book for 1973, pp. 53, 57, 456, 469. True, this same Year-book does publish on page 633 *Kolkhoznik family budgets,* which show that in the budget of an *average kolkhoz* family income from work in the *kolkhoz* comes to 42 per cent and income from the private plot to 29.7 per cent while the remaining 28.3 per cent is gained from work done outside the *kolkhoz* or pensions, subsidies and payments out of public funds, which include education and medicine. But these data are based on *selective research* carried out on 62,000 family budgets. It is clear that the method of selection of the *kolkhoz* families is incorrect and does not allow a true picture of the role of the personal plots in the family budgets of the *kolkhozniki.*

At the present time one should come to terms with the situation that has developed historically and with the deep-seated psychological complexes of the rural population. It would be better, therefore, to plan for an increase rather than decrease in the size of personal plots during the next ten to fifteen years. We think that it would be possible to let *kolkhozniki* and *sovkhoz* workers and agricultural specialists have up to one hectare per household. But this gradual increase in the size of the personal plot must necessarily be combined with the production of a whole range of means of *minor mechanisation,* which should considerably lighten the labour of rural dwellers on their personal plots. The enormous expenditure of labour in the private plots derives above all from the fact that no agricultural machinery can be used here apart from spades, scythes, choppers, etc. It would not be a bad idea in the given instance to borrow from the experience of Japan, where peasants with small allotments own hundreds of thousands and millions of tiny tractors and all sorts of other equipment and contrivances. In other words, what is needed here, too, is a rational form of mechanisation, which together with chemicalisation and a radical improvement of organisation over the whole of agricultural production (inclusive of all the problems of management, planning and material incentive, and the introduction of proper sowing turnover and selection) could make the USSR into one of the most advanced agricultural countries on our planet.

Losses Suffered by the Population of the USSR 1918-1958

M. MAKSUDOV

Translated by Naurika Lenner

The Tsar's orders are that one should pray for those who fell in disgrace and that the mass for the dead should be said in their name. As for those who are not specifically mentioned in this memorial, or who are mentioned only by surname or by number, 10, 20, 50,[1] it is proper to pray for them and to say: 'You, God, you know their names.'

['Memorial for those who fell in Disgrace under Ivan the Terrible' ('Sidonik opal'nykh Ivana Groznogo'), in *The Collection of the Archives Commission of the Nizhnii Novgorod Government/Sbornik Nizhegorodskoi gubernskoi arkhivnoi komissi*, XV, 1913.]

Men are the main riches of our country.

[*Population of the USSR (Naselenie SSSR)* Moscow, 1974.]

How many fell in this abyss?
How many? The question retains all its relevance; and is raised with pain and anger in the pages of the *Archipelago*. But even so ours is a generation that can live undisturbed, except when we remember the names of individual innocent victims.

We will not, however, become a people, a nation, until we have come to terms with this and with history and moved from a position of disinterest to respect for human beings and ourselves.

The aim of our study is to assess the minimum number of losses suffered by the Soviet population[2]. By losses we mean those people who disappeared prematurely, before their natural death. They include the victims of war as well as of camps, hunger epidemics, insufficient medical care, etc ... The term 'losses' in this sense does not simply mean a decrease in population, or the number of victims of repression: it corresponds to the increase in mortality, worked out as the difference between the decrease in population and a theoretical 'natural mortality'. The level of 'natural mortality' is obtained arithmetically. It is an easy calculation if the figures for population and mortality rate per age group are known.[3] For instance, the 17 December 1926 census listed 933,000 men aged 30, and the mortality rates for men aged between 28 and 32 were 0.62, 0.63, 0.64, 0.66, and 0.68 per cent[4]. This means, given a mortality level corresponding to these figures, that there must have been, at the end of 1927, 933 – (933 x 0.64 per cent) = 927,000 31-year-old-men. The number of men aged 32 in 1928 would apparently be 927 – (927 x 0.66 per cent) = 921,000. In 1929, the number of 33-year-old-men would be 921 – (921 x 0.68 per cent) = 915,000. It is just as simple to count the men aged 29 in 1925: 933 + (933 x 0.63 per cent) = 940,000, and the men aged 28 in 1924: 940 + (940 x 0.62 per cent) = 947,000, etc ...

In this way we follow the evolution of the number of men and women of each generation and thus, the evolution of the population of the whole country.[5] The resulting table reflects the natural population trends (without taking birth-rate into account) and in cases where the actual population figure provided by the census is obviously lower than that assessed, we can then speak of human losses.

The method used for this study is not new, and has frequently been employed for population surveys.[6] Yu. A. Korchak-Chepurlovskii has shown how important such fore- are in historical research:

Bearing in mind the complex level of the method and technique which have been used, the estimates of M. V. Ptukhi, of S. A. Novosel'skii and V. V. Paevskii, are still held to be of great interest for the demographic historian attempting to analyse the demographic consequences of events which have interfered with the normal population development in our country.[7]

Calculations were made for three periods: 1926-38, 1926-1918 (by the retrospective method), and 1939-58;[8] the pivot-years were fixed by census dates. We have retained the population figures obtained in the 1926 census, taking into account the correction made by Novosel'skij and Paevskij.[9] They are the authors who established the mortality rate tables which were used in our assessment. The rates from these tables have been used without modification for the 1927-38 period, but for the other periods studied, they have been either up- or down-graded: multiplied by 1.5 for the 1897-1922 period, by 1.2 for the 1923-6 period, by 0.9 for the 1939-49 period. The multipliers used were calculated on the basis of the data available for the mortality rate of those years (see table I, and table III). In conjunction with our proposed aim—i.e., the search for a minimum—we adopted figures higher than the population mortality rates published by the CSU (Central'noe Statisticeskoe upravlenie/Central Bureau of Statistics) (table II). It is useful here to draw attention to the constantly decreasing mortality in this country[10] (table II), which must inevitably lead to an overestimation of the population losses, in relation to the data available. Such a phenomenon can be observed just as easily during the relatively peaceful periods of our history.

For the 1897-1913 period, the population decrease obtained by calculation was 1.4 million more than the actual decrease; 0.45 million more for the 1923-31 period, and 2.9 million more for the 1950-8 period (table V; table IX-XI).

Given that this tendency was characteristic of peacetime, the enormous discrepancy between the actual population figure and the estimates for 1914-17, 1918-22, 1932-8, 1939-45 (of 1.7, 14.3, 7.9 and 27.4 millions respectively) can without a doubt be considered to stem from human losses. The alternation of periods of peace and periods of catastrophe is also important here, since on principle we have used the same mortality rates for all the estimates. It is significant too that the younger generations, little affected by the (political) 'measures', follow the same pattern in the years of catastrophe as they do in the years of peace (see table X and table XI).

Description of the Material Used

We believe that the CSU must provide objective material, free from any preconceived idea, since any attempt to conceal figures for whatever reason constitutes a criminal act.

[J. Stalin. Fourteenth Congress.]

Tradition demands that the author, at this point, should evoke the work of his predecessors with some contempt; and it is unlikely that a more appropriate occasion has presented itself to anyone. Amongst demographic publications of these last few years, which can be numbered in thousands, only the works of B. C. Urlanis are devoted to the question studied here. But what can be expected of him when he finally admits that his results had been predetermined by a series of party dictates? It is appropriate, of course, to take note of the remarkable progression of B. C. Urlanis's theories. He was writing in 1960: 'If we try to compare the losses suffered during the civil wars and the respective population figures for this kind of conflict in recent times, we must first consider the Spanish Civil War, between 1936 and 1939 (1.8 per cent); next the civil war in the United States (1.6 per cent), the war in the Vendée (1 per cent), and lastly the civil war in USSR (0.5 per cent). Nine years later, he already remarks: 'Therefore, in the space of three years, from 1918 to 1920, because of the number of deaths being greater than that of births, the population figure has fallen by approximately 4 per cent, and bearing in mind the losses due to emigration,

the population loss for these years has been in the order of
per cent.'[13]

Incidentally, it seems that the Civil War is no longer a
taboo subject. Thus, the authors of the reference book *The
Population in USSR*[14]—which was compiled by a collective of
particularly representative writers under the direction of A.
Ya. Boyarskii—point out in their introduction:

> The First World War (1914-18) inflicted heavy losses on
> the country's population. The number of men killed in
> action alone reached nearly two million. The Civil War
> and the struggle against foreign intervention involved
> heavy losses of human lives. People perished not just on the
> battlefields but also of hunger and disease. The birth-rate
> dropped abruptly. In the space of nine years (1914-23), the
> country's population (within the pre-1939 borders) fell
> altogether by more than 23.2 million inhabitants.

Twenty-three million: a staggering figure! Usually the CSU
indicated 7 million: 143.5 million inhabitants in 1917, and
136.8 million in 1920. Why this discrepancy? Because of an
unexpected confession, a discovery, a misprint? It is actually
more complex: in fact, there was a deduction made, from a
straightforwardly erroneous figure. In the index, the book
gives 159.2 million as the population figure for 1913, but it
does not specify that the figure covers only the present
borders. The author of the article subtracted from this figure
the number for the population in 1923, 136.1 million (i.e., for
the pre-1939 borders) and thus obtained his 23.2 million.
What is surprising here is neither the error (who never makes
a mistake?), nor the demographer's confusion about his
country's borders (this could happen given the many
changes) but that nobody was moved from a political point of
view: neither the censors, nor the publishers, nor the author
himself. Through simple arithmetic we obtained the figure
23—so be it, it is a fact, it is true that the losses were heavy.
But let the author attempt to assess the losses caused by the
great patriotic war in the same way! He does not try, and
anyhow his editor will not let him: 'We have said 20.' Not 21,
not 20.5, not even 20.2 up until now, can appear in Soviet

literature. However, there too, it seems that a shift is beginning to take place. In a 1975[15] reference book, the birth-rate figures for the years 1946-9 were published, with some delay, admittedly; it is nevertheless an important step in a more precise direction.

We note the population figures for such or such years in the CSU's[16] present publications. However it would seem more accurate to use the census results, but it is not an easy task, given the constant extension of our country's borders. This fact itself is unusual for the twentieth century, although at the same time it is in keeping with a certain historical tradition.[17] It may seem appropriate here to consider the matter in the light of some words of our great historian: 'The State was swelling—the people were dwindling' (Klyuchevskii).

The estimate by the CSU of the 1918 population figure is near that of Volkov[18], taken from the 1916 and 1917 census results. These censuses are obviously less accurate than the 1926 one. They were carried out in summer; in some *gubernii,* foreign prisoners of war were included in the census, in others they were not; men conscripted by the army were counted by questionnaire. Refugees and evacuees from western regions were an added source of confusion. It is therefore quite possible that the 1918 population figure was low (one to two million) compared with 1926. The fact that provisional results for the 1926 census were lower than the final results and show a difference of almost one million, confirms the likelihood of an underestimation in the 1918 figure. We must also consider that this low figure would lead to an exaggerated estimate of human losses in the years 1918-20; it is doubtful that the CSU statisticians have any vested interests in this. In the estimate we assume, with E. Z. Volkov, that the consequence of migration was a deficit of around 3.5 million people. However, it is not impossible that some or all of the movements could have been included in the CSU evaluation. Thus, the possible underestimation of the 1918 population in relation to the 1926 figure, and the confusion due to migration can lead to an underestimation of population losses; in the order of one to four million for the period 1918-26. The official assessment of the 1931 population figure is, it appears, less accurate than the 1926 census. It was carried out during the summer, under conditions of 'class extermination', when a large part of the rural population was scattered throughout the country and presumably very few lent themselves to rigorous surveys. We can show that the official estimate for the population figure has been lowered even during more peaceful times (1960-9). One just has to compare the directories *Economy of the USSR (Narodnoe khozyaistvo SSSR)* of 1968 and 1969 to realise that the estimates have been increased by between 100,000 and 600,000 inhabitants after the 1970 census.

Censuses count the population more accurately than official estimates but they too can include errors. The CSU does not provide direct information on this question, but it is known[19] that the control measures adopted in 1959 have had the effect of adding 1,074,000 to the first count (0.51 per cent of the total figure). Since in 1926, unlike in 1939, such controls were not the practice, it is possible that 0.5 per cent of the population were not registered (0.7 million inhabitants) – not more, apparently, since population mobility was lower than in 1959. The 1939 census was probably carried out with great concern for accuracy. Indeed, the statisticians had received from the Party's Central Committee and from the Council of Ministers the order 'to proceed to the census without an omission, without any errors'. And the fate of the 'saboteurs' who had deliberately lowered the population figure in the 1937[20] census was still too fresh in everyone's memory. On one point the 'young cadres' who had replaced the 'enemies of the people' have undoubtedly excelled: there was only a 0.006 per cent discrepancy (less than 100,000 inhabitants) between the estimated figure and the actual population; it means, notably, a lower degree of accuracy in the census's proceedings. One may ask if it would not be desirable to introduce new methods for calculation; on this matter, in 1959 the gap reached 0.4 per cent. But the 'cadres' have not understood that they have themselves provided sticks to be beaten with, and up to this day, they brag about their 'contribution to science, to methodolgy and to organisation'.[21] The 1939 census has not yet been published. First, the fragmented material published after 1959 includes the inhabitants of the western territories, and secondly, it does not even provide any information on gender or age groups. But nevertheless, it can be said that the 1939 population figure is more accurate than the 1926 census (from 0.7 to 1.5 million inhabitants); it is still possible though that it might be exaggerated by a few million. If this were the case, though, the estimate for human losses would have been correspondingly less.

The details of the 1939 population, used for projections of the 1939-58 period, are borrowed from the 1959 census, published in 1962[22]. The publication date itself gives hope that the material was not deliberately falsified. It is obvious that, as this edition was under way, the CSU officials considered it necessary to compare the 1939 with the 1959 results. This is apparently where we find the limit with the 3 million reduction in the population figure for the disputed territories. The national composition of the population for 1939 (see table VI) confirms this hypothesis. We know that over 3 million Poles lived in the disputed territories (the 1939 figure was only a million more than for 1926) and that after the war over 2 million Poles left the USSR (their number is reduced, in the 1959 census, but only by 350,000). The table does not reflect the movement of 400,000 Germans either (annexation, then departure). It would seem that the CSU's silence on post-war emigration suggests that it has already been taken into account. However, if these hypotheses are incorrect and if the estimate for the 1939 population figure does not exclude future emigrants, then the assessment of the number of human losses during the 1939-59 period is increased by the number of those who left the country during those years (2 to 3 million).

The inaccurate breakdown of age groups in the censuses also leads to mistakes. This is particularly important for the 1939 data which was divided, scaled from the fifties age group. To take the errors into account, the standard operation is to make allowances by the contents[23] or mathematical[24] method. The estimates reached in using the various correction methods have shown that the gap between them is not great (100,000 to 200,000).

More dangerous are the errors committed in the mortality

rate tables, since they are compounded during the calculation procedure. These mistakes can lead to an overestimation as well as to an underestimation of human losses. Thus, the incomplete population count in the 1926 census, mentioned above, would raise the rate. A similar effect is induced, according to Babynin[25], by the scope of the tables being limited to the European part of the country. The Eastern Republics (not included in 1926 tables) were characterised by both a higher birth-rate and higher infant mortality rate and also, it seems, by a greater vitality amongst middle-aged and elderly people.[26] In 1940 as in 1950 and in 1959, mortality in most of these Republics was lower than RSFSR.[27] Given the method used, high infant mortality is hardly shown in the results.

An inaccurate subtraction of deaths while the tables were being compiled leads to an underestimation of the rates. Some authors[28] mention one fact only: in a rural area, covering some 500,000 inhabitants, funerals omitted from the census reached, according to rural correspondents *(sel'skie korrespondenty)* approximately 2.5 per cent of all deaths. It is true that most of these were new-born babies, a fact which is not crucial for our purposes. This is why we will consider, (as we also keep in mind that the recording of deaths in towns is more accurate) that the margin of error tending to a lowering of the figure is about 2 per cent.

A certain degree of inaccuracy also comes from the fact that population figures are rounded off (to the thousand) as are the mortality rate (up the quarter of point).[29] When we statistically assess this accuracy, we notice that for the longest period (eleven years) there is an error of 80,000.

Let us now summarise. The possibility of error toward underestimating human losses results from inaccuracies concerning the movement of particular groups (2 to 6 million), and from too high a threshold of 'natural death' (4.3 millions just for peacetime). On the other hand the following factors would lead to an exaggeration of the number of human losses: inaccuracy in age-group breakdown, the defectiveness of the tables, calculation errors, inaccurate subtractions of emigrants in the years 1939-49. These mistakes represent, for 1918-22 and 1931-8 respectively, about 300,000 people; for

1939-49 between 0.7 and 2 million people. It is thus possible that we might overrate the human losses (by between 2 to 3 million) or that we might underrate them (by between 5 to 11 million).

Losses Suffered by the Population Between 1918 and 1926
The Civil War

Torrents of blood, we are told. But let us clarify this aspect of the question. No torrent of blood that flowed in the Civil War can be compared to the seas of blood that Russian imperialism spilt (on the Front) after June 19.

[V.I. Lenin: *The Russian Revolution and the Civil War*
September 17]

Russia. Always so remote, so much of a distant Northern myth. How did they live? In peace, with high ceilings, pure air, rivers unpolluted by factory sewage ... What did they eat? Fresh meat, no frozen foods, they had no knowledge of tins, and, generally speaking, we do not need to go into details: one just has to read their literature.

How did they live? Without planes, without cars, without electricity, without asphalt, without radios, without refrigerators, without medicine and above all, to come back to our topic, without various methods of birth control. And children, did they have them! Four, five, six per family. But these children died: one in four did not live to be one year old, one in two only reached the age of five. It is not so now: only one child in twenty dies before the age of five these days. It is true that there are not so many children now as there were before: less than two per family for the country as a whole,[30] and one in Moscow. This phenomenon – the decrease in birth-rate in a 3 to 1 proportion, and infant mortality in a 10 to 1 proportion – might be not only demographically but also psychologically, the most remarkable event of our century. It is true that this could be predicted even before 1917. Like many other things, it could be seen approaching, irreversibly coming forward; but it reached Russia with some delay. Inevitably this trend began in Europe where it developed, as always, ten, fifteen, fifty years ahead.

But let us go back to the population trend in Russia. The Russo-Japanese war 'cost' 46,000 men.[31] The 1910 cholera epidemic killed 300,000 people;[32] the pogroms, if we believe Zinger,[33] claimed 100,000 victims (it is possible that this figure might include the Civil War pogroms); in thirty years (1880-1910) emigration involved about 2 million people.[34] The 1914-17 war cost 1,660,000 human lives (see table III). It is worth noting that this war was not accompanied by the losses due to famine, epidemics, genocide, which were going to be so characteristic of the period that followed. On the contrary 'on average in the whole of the *gubernii* for which data was readily available, the number of deaths in the rural population even decreased during the war years ... The data provided showed that infant diseases as well as other infectious diseases were on the decline, amongst civilians, during the first few years of the war. The effects of tuberculosis, venereal disease and alcoholism amongst the civilian population also diminished.'[35]

At the outbreak of war, Russia had a population of 165.7 million (139.3 million within the pre-September-1939 borders). Over 15 million men were engaged in warfare and, of those, over 5 million were wounded, hundreds of thousands maimed. More than 3 million men found themselves in captivity and some 5 million refugees from western regions, as well as foreign prisoners of war, were scattered throughout the country. As many millions were used to fuel the furnace of civil war (table III). Table II gives an overview of the demographic events which followed. Prisoners return, soldiers are sent back to their home, the birth-rate goes up again, without, however, reaching pre-war levels. People under the jurisdiction of western countries, foreign prisoners of war, and millions of nationals (2 million Nansen passports were issued by the League of Nations[37]) leave the country. The mortality rate escalates. Spanish influenza, typhus (see table IV), and then famine, take their toll of millions of people. In 1923, the population fell by almost 8 million. Death resulting from all these diseases was on the increase. 500,000 died from tuberculosis alone (3.96 per cent) in 1920.[38] Even so it is clear that the medical statistics for that year are incomplete. Armies re-formed (in 1920, there were 3.5 million men in the Red Army, and around one million in the White Army, and various small bands.)[39] The losses resulting from the war, according to Urlanis's estimates, amount to 800,000 men.[40] We know that repressive action also played a part; Conquest (without any proof) suggests a figure of 1.5 million.

Table V provides an overall picture of human losses during that period. It shows that between 1913 and 1917, the number reached 1,700,000, a figure which fits perfectly with the data available (see table III); between 1918 and 1920, 10,180,000 and between 1920 and 1922, 3,630,000. Consequently, during the Civil War the country lost altogether 13.8 million inhabitants. In various other sources, we can find lower and higher figures. Boyarskii and, after him, Urlanis, mention a fall in population of 10 million people.[41] Strumilin, the academician, suggests a figure of 26 millions (!) between 1914 and 1922, of which 5 million were victims of the 1921 famine.[42] This figure appears to be grossly inflated, given that its author failed to take into account the decline in birth-rate over the period covered, using for his estimate the pre-war rate!

The losses amongst men were not significantly greater than those amongst women, which indirectly shows the considerable extent of famine and diseases. The difference, after evaluating the figures, amounted to 4.1 million. If we allow for the fact that even before the war, the male population was slightly less than the female (by about 700,000 in the pre-September-1939 borders), and that 1.4 million were killed in the war (without including deaths caused by disease), more than two million men died as a result of the Civil War. It is common to find a higher estimate of the discrepancy between male and female losses. Thus, in the CSU Bulletin No. 55, in 1931, it is given as 10 million; Strumilin indicates 6.7 million.[43] In all likelihood, such inflated figures stem from the fact that the 1920 census did not include Bukhara, Khiva and the Far East Republic, all of which are regions where a male population clearly predominates.

From the number of human losses calculated in this way, we must subtract the number of those who emigrated which, like Volkov, we take to be in the order of 3.5 million. There therefore remain (see table II), 10.3 million which strictly speaking can be considered as human losses. As was noted above, this estimate can be overrated by 0.4 million, through arithmetic errors, or underrated by one to four million through inaccurate calculation of the population figures and the number of emigrants.

Human Losses in the Years 1926-1938
Collectivisation. Repressive Measures

Each particular system of historical production effectively possesses its own demographic laws, which have historical consequences.

[K. Marx, *Capital*]

After the 1926 census, the material relating to birth-rate, mortality, population counts, was published every year until 1936. After that, there was a most revealing silence which, as Orwell rather pertinently observed, only underlines the importance of historical events in certain countries. For six years, i.e., 1932-8, the CSU and CUNHU publications repeated one and only one figure: 165.7 million inhabitants on 1 January 1933. The results of the 1939 census – 170.4 million inhabitants – once and forever replaced the familiar preceding figure. So minimal was their difference that the two figures were never placed alongside one another. During these last few years, material covering the years 1937-8 has appeared, delineating precisely a new period of a rather murky nature: 1931-6. These years are like the thinnest cows of the pharaoh, who devoured the previous, relatively prosperous years of the NEP. Though the aims were the same, the pharaoh's methods were more sophisticated, more efficient and even, one could say, more humane. Moreover, it is possible that responsibility should rest neither with Stalin nor with the pharaoh, but simply with the person who was then in charge of the Agriculture Department of the Central Committee. Then Stalin would neither have allowed the mass slaughter of cattle, nor would have deported the

232

dissatisfied, nor would have tried to starve the insubordinate. But history does not repeat itself and, as everyone knows, 'Soviet communism is a new civilisation.'[44] This is why

> in the kholkozes where the fields have deliberately not been ploughed or sown, there was no help available when they found themselves without food – in order not to encourage this sort of resistance – except in the most serious cases, where entire villages were saved from famine because they were dragged just in time from their native soil ...

It is because

> the Soviet government did not have workhouses and there was no time to build them. The only solution was to force the starving to leave their villages, where their presence had a demoralising influence, and to go to faraway places ... In other cases, the peasants inconspicuously hollowed out the ripe wheat, i.e., they crushed the grain or even cut the ears of corn and hoarded a personal reserve from what had been so unscrupulously stolen from the collectively-owned fields.

This really is a 'new civilisation'? It is hard not to agree with the Webbs, from whose book we have taken these quotes. A new civilisation not only as far as the peasantry were concerned, but also when compared to more ancient times. It is the first time in world history that a famine was artificially caused, on such a large scale; informers, as in the Roman Empire or at the time of the Inquisition, received a part of the deportee's property; the kulaks and the bourgeoisie (6.8 million according to the CUNHU publication: *The Building of Socialism in the USSR)*[45] were liquidated 'as a class' and one hundred and eleven million individual farms were collectivised.

As far as the geographical distribution of population is concerned the repercussions of both collectivisation and deportation led to a decline in some areas, and an increase in others. (See table VII.) The increase in the population figure for the Ukraine, of 2 million in the years 1927-32, is followed by a significant reduction of one million between 1933 and 1938. The number of Ukrainians fell from 31.2 million in 1926 to 28.1 million in 1939. Some demographers[46] attempt to explain this decline by 'a different concept of national identity' at census time. This is evidently not the only, nor even the principal reason. For instance, the Byelorussians have not, during these same years, altered their 'concept of national identity', and their number increased by nearly 30 per cent (1.6 million; see table VI). What is important is that at the time of the 1926 and 1959 censuses, an identical percentage of Ukrainians (87 per cent) remained faithful to their mother tongue. This is significant because it was always on language that 'Russification' had an immediate effect.

In Kazakhstan, one of the main deportation areas, the population varies greatly; sometimes it goes up (by almost 500,000 inhabitants in six months), sometimes it goes down abruptly (see table VII). In all probability, it is not an accident that Kazakhstan registered the highest mortality rate for the whole country, even in 1940. It seems to have affected equally the newly-arrived and the local nomadic population which was adapting uneasily to the 'new civilisation'. Nobody even attempts to explain by 'a difference in concept' the fact that the Kazakhian population fell by 860,000 between 1926 and 1939 (table VI). Other national minorities from that part of the country shared the Kazakhs' fate. The number of Cuighours fell from 108,000 in 1926 to 95,000 in 1959, that of the Altai people from 50,000 to 45,000, the Yakoutes from 241,000 to 237,000, the Toungouses from 39,000 to 25,000, and the whole of the Northern people from 140,000 in 1926 to 129,000 in 1959.

In 1933-4 there was a general fall in population. Conquest quotes the material from the OGPU, which was communicated to Stalin, in which the number of famine victims was estimated to be 3.3-3.5 million. Foreign correspondents in Moscow estimated it to be about 5 million[47]. Urlanis[48] assumes that the population was 158 million at the end of 1933; in other words, that the decline in one year was over 7.5 million (see table II). Even the population of manual workers who were best stocked in food supplies at the time, fell in 1933 (table II).

The 1933-4 famine resulted in the disappearance of an enormous number of children, particularly new-born babies. While the figure for the persons born in 1929-31 appears, in the 1970 census, as 12.4 million approximately, the figure for births between 1932 and 1934 is only 8.4 million. This fall in population cannot in any case be interpreted as an example of conscious birth control on the part of the population. Although 1929-31 were the most intense years of collectivisation, the fall in the birth-rate was relatively low in relation to the previous three years (table II). The 1933 famine was too much of an unexpected event, and furthermore, there was no knowledge of birth control in the Russian villages of the time. It is likely that at least 3 million children, born between 1932 and 1934, died of starvation.

A characteristic feature of that period is the complete prosperity presented to outsiders. The terrifying drop in population was ignored. Planners,[50] foreign visitors, and party leaders never ceased to praise the rhythms of population growth. In January 1934, at the Seventeenth Congress, Stalin mentioned: 'the growth of population in the USSR, which rose from 160 million at the end of 1930 to 168 million at the end of 1933', thus forcing the figure from 8 to 10 million. His famous 'We live better ...' is also dedicated to a powerful demographic increase. 'We live better, we are happier.' This is what was said to the kholkozians who had just lost their relatives, who have been deprived of their land and their cattle. ' ... and this has the effect of the population reproducing much more rapidly than before. Mortality rate has gone down, birth rate has gone up, which brings about a clearly very sharp increase ... at the moment our net population growth is around 3 million people.' (Speech made at a meeting of male and female combine-harvester drivers, with some party members and some Government members in 1935.)

Is it ignorance, or deliberate falsification?[51]

The December 1934 elections were, in themselves, a very revealing index of population losses. There were 91 million registered voters. '2.5 per cent of the whole country's adult population are deprived of the right to vote, which represents a little more than 2 million people.' (Molotov at the Seventh

Panrussian Congress of the Soviets. 'Main results of the Government's activities', *'Osnovnye itogi raboty pravitel'stva'* – Minutes from the Central Committee).

According to the 1926 census, the number of people aged ten and over was 109.4 million and in 1931, 103 million. If the mortality rate of the over-eighteen had remained the same as for the years 1927-31, at the end of 1934 there would have been 99 million electors, which in fact means a drop of 6 million people.[52] Although this figure is fairly rough, it nevertheless shows that the losses suffered between 1926 and 1938 occurred mainly during the first half of that period.

In the years 1935-38, the Archipelago expanded rapidly. 'You know that the economic problems in the Far East are now our top priority,' declared Molotov at the Eighteenth Congress. 'Consequently the problems of organisation relating to the displacement of the Far East populations have become of prior importance.' These problems were resolved. We note, in Siberia and in the Far East, that there was a 25 per cent population increase between the 1926 and the 1939 censuses. The records were witheld by the *oblast'* in Magadan where the population figure was multiplied by 8.4.[53] The newly-arrived people settled mainly in the rural zone (120,000 out of 150,000) and distinguished themselves by a surprisingly low birth-rate (10.9 per cent) and by an even lower mortality rate (8 per cent). It seems nevertheless that the mortality rate here has to do with some peculiar calculations. According to widespread opinion, the 1939 census counted in the Magadan *oblast'* not the prisoners but only their gaolers, the 'Vohrovcy'* and the members of their families.

The Archipelago led at one moment to population expansions in the towns where the work camps were and then to the decimation of the population of these same towns (see table VIII). The drop in population in some old towns in the Urals and Siberia might perhaps be explained by the fact that the influx of population did not compensate for the numbers who were victims of repressive actions (table VIII). We can draw up an indicative estimate of the Archipelago's inhabitants from the results of the 1937 elections. The number of electors, 94 million, was 3.5 million lower than the number of people aged eighteen and over (as calculated in the 1939 census). It is possible that a portion of those who did not vote – they were 3 million – might not have abstained from their own volition.[54]

The official survey does not mention any losses in human lives during that period. It provides almost no clue. The increased mortality rate in 1937, when compared with 1935 and 1938-9 (see table II) gives a tiny indication. It is just possible that the very high mortality rates in various remote areas have borne some relation to the activity of the Archipelago. For instance, in the autonomous Republic of the Komi, the mortality rates for 1940, 1950, 1960 reached respectively 37.1, 14.4 and 6.0, when for the whole of the RSFSR the figures were 20.6, 10.1 and 7.4.[55]

An evaluation of the population trends has been compared to the data from the 1931 and 1939 censuses (see tables IX and X). While in 1931 the official population figure was 900,000 more than the estimates, on the other hand in 1939 6.9 million people aged fifteen and over were not accounted for. Consequently, for this section of the population, taking into account the 0.645 million correction made from the 1931 data (table IX) the figure for the losses reaches 7.5 million (i.e., 5 million men, 2.5 million women). This figure does not include the millions of children who died of starvation (cf. above). According to the already formulated method, to underestimate the losses by between 1 and 3 million is possible (given the inaccurate population count in the 1926 and 1939 censuses), but in the way of overestimation the error would probably not be more than 300,000. The 1934 elections lead one to believe that 4/5 of these losses were between 1932 and 1934 and 1/5 (1.5 million) during the later period.

Human Losses in the Years 1939-1958

Figures do not govern humanity, they only show how humanity is governed.

[Goethe]

There were, in 1939, within the country's borders at that time, about 193.5 million; the 1959 census listed 130.7 million. Gigantic demographic upheavals brought about a deficit of 63 million: annexations of population, war casualties, extermination of the Jews, the communists and partisans by the Fascists, famine amongst the Leningrad inhabitants, rise in mortality rate following a deterioration of living conditions, deportations to Germany (followed by returns as well as non-returns), exterminations in the camps, Stalinist repression against some national minorities, inhabitants of occupied territories, war prisoners, population swap with Poland, Czechoslovakia, Germany and other countries, Armenian immigration, drop in birth-rate, and finally, a consequence of those and the many other causes, a mortality rate twice as low (see table II).

It is estimated that during this period, the population losses reached the high figure of 24.5 million (18.7 million men and 5.8 million women) (see table XI). This figure has been underestimated by at least 2.9 million, given the estimated deficit in the population of the order of 14.4 million, when according to the CSU material, the population fell by 11.5 million[56] for the period 1949-58.

To distinguish between the different causes of the fall in population does not seem to be possible in practical terms; however, in the framework on which we have decided, we will examine a few problems.

1. Losses Due to Migrations

'After the integration in the Soviet Union in 1939-40 of some areas of Western Ukraine, Byelorussia, Bessarabia, northern Bukovina and of the Baltic states – Latvia, Estonia, Lithuania – the population of the USSR grew by roughly 23 million.'[57] This figure has been generally accepted in Soviet reference and propaganda publications insofar as the figure of 20 million was put forward for the population annexed after the 1959 census, excluding, we must believe, from the number of inhabitants in 1939 those who have left the country. The following do not figure in the Great Soviet Encyclopaedia: Tuva (86,000), Transcarpathian Ukraine (0.7 million)[58] and a few other territories which fell to our lot without a population, for the purpose of re-establishing a historical justice on a traditional and legal basis, and for a better protection of the territory. The tragic fate of the conscripts,[59] of the Finnish people (424,000), of the Germans from Konigsberg (1,157,000), of the Japanese and the Ajines (260,000),[60] constitute a special page in the history not only of our people but also of the nearby countries.

Not all the inhabitants of the annexed territories had dreamed of being annexed and quite a few took the first opportunity to leave their new country. As early as 1940, during the period of the Nazi Soviet pact, 392,000 Germans who had been living in the Baltic states, in Bessarabia and parts of Western Ukraine emigrated.[61] In 1943 115,000 Polish soldiers left the USSR with their families. In 1945-6 another 1,526,000 left. There were by 1950 a total of 2,136,000 people in Poland who had come from territories incorporated into the USSR.[62] At that time, Poland was often used by Jews from the Baltic states in transit to Israel (somewhere between 10,000 and 30,000). Apart from the Poles, Rumanians, Czechs, Hungarians and Germans living in the USSR left the country after the war. All in all this involved approximately 400,000 people.[63]

Millions of Soviet citizens were still in Germany at the end of the war; they were either evacuated, left the country or were imprisoned. The figure for civilians deported was probably as high as 3 million people (2.3 million Ukrainians,[64] 338,000 inhabitants of Byelorussia,[65] hundreds of thousands of *oblasti* from the RSFSR and from the Baltic states). The return of these people and of the Soviet prisoners of war was of particular concern to the Soviet government. By 1 September 1945 2,229,000 people had been repatriated by the Allied Forces. They were thanked by General Golikov: 'We must mention with gratitude the considerable help provided by our allies.'[66]

All in all, by 1 January 1953, 5,458,000 people[67] had returned to their own country, under the auspices of the repatriation agencies. A few managed to stay where they were. We know[68] that the international organisations dealing with refugees repatriated 141,000 Baltic states inhabitants between 1947 and 1951, as well as around 128,000 Russians and Ukrainians. In March 1947 Vyshinskii suggested comparable figures; 'In the minutes of the Security Council it is reported that there are at the moment 827,000 displaced people in West Germany, 221,525 of whom are citizens of the USSR.'[69] These figures for refugees and those who did not return are not likely to be very accurate, since a great number were able to escape the vigilant search of the repatriation agents.

There was also a movement in the opposite direction, to the USSR, after the war. Poland sent back 520,000 Ukrainians (probably to avoid a further annexation). 30,000 people came from Czechoslovakia, 15,000 from Yugoslavia.[70] Also tens of thousands of White Russians returned (in Manchuria they totalled 69,000 in 1940); in addition a fairly large group of Armenians returned (120,000). In all it seems that the country lost between 2.5 and 3 million people. Rakovskii[71] estimates the deficit to be 1.7 million, without counting the refugees and others who did not return, and he only covered the population exchanges within the Eastern European countries.

As has been noted above, these migratory phenomena are most probably accounted for by the CSU in its summary of the population between 1939 and 1959, and so they do not enter into our assessment of human losses.

2. Losses Amongst the Civilian Population

The increase in mortality attributable to famine and poor hygiene and sanitation can be measured by the losses amongst children and elderly people. Table XI shows that 566,000 children under ten died in 1939. The number of women over thirty and men over fifty were 1.3 million and 745,000 more respectively than could be foreseen in terms of natural population fluctuations. Altogether there were losses of 2.6 million amongst these particular age groups, which in 1939 represented half of the country's population. If we bear in mind that there were also a considerable number of losses in the immediate post-war years and that the drop in population can be explained by a host of other causes, it is possible to take the figure of 5.2 million as a minimal estimate of the losses suffered by the civilian population. There is no doubt that this figure is inflated, given that we have put together the losses recorded amongst the young and old age groups, whose mortality rates are naturally high, with the losses of the intermediate generation who are sustained by greater vigour. On the other hand, the intermediate generations were involved in actions for and against the partisans, and this certainly brought their losses to a higher level.

The over-all estimation of the losses also includes the victims of the Leningrad famine, (650,000)[72] as well as the Jews exterminated by the Fascists (2.5 million)[73] and those who died in the air raids and military operations.[74]

According to the data of Soviet historians, the Nazis killed 4 million people in the Ukraine (1.3 million of whom were prisoners-of-war),[75] 1.4 million Byelorussians (810,000 of whom were prisoners-of-war)[76] and 100,000 in Latvia;[77] i.e., a total of roughly 6 million people. It must be noted that the accounts which were referred to confirm that it was mostly a matter of large-scale punitive actions against prisoners of war and the Jews, [78] and that there is a lack of concrete proof of the genocide of hundreds of thousands of Russians, Ukrainians and Byelorussians. This is why such high figures for the total losses suffered by the civilian population raise certain doubts. If, however, the figures are accurate, the total estimate – for losses due to war – an estimate that would include the victims of German repression, of the siege of Leningrad and air raids and bombings – amounts to 7 or 7.5 million people.

3. Repressive Action Against National Minorities

The mass removals of people, who as a general rule were neither accustomed to the climate nor to the working conditions, to the difficult conditions of the Kazakhstan and Siberia, cannot have improved the economic situation of those regions. Even where these people did become acclimatised (for example the Koreans in Kazakhstan and

241

Uzbekistan) it was only possible after a long period of adaptation.

[L. Marian'skii: *Population Migrations (Sovremennye migratsii naseleniya)*, Moscow, 1969.]

Between 1938 and 1946 the national minorities were resettled on a massive scale. Koreans, Greeks, Poles, Finns, Germans from the Ukraine and from the Volga were sent away to live in Siberia and Central Asia. Soon they were joined by Tartars from Crimea, Kalmouks, and Moslems from Northern Caucasus, a total in all of between 3.5 and 4 million people (see table VI). If not all, a substantial number of the inhabitants of the Baltic states, the Ukraine and Byelorussia who had lived under occupation or were prisoners, underwent the same treatment. The mortality rate during the resettlement itself, as well as on arrival, was high enough. Marian'skii reports that of the 600,000 Poles who were sent to the eastern regions of the USSR in 1939, 260,000 returned to Poland between 1946 and 1948.[79] Conquest also mentions 600,000 resettled and 44,000 sent to the ITL *(Ispravitel'no-trudovyi lager'*/'Camps for reform through work'); he specifically states that the Poles lost 270,000 people in 1942, i.e., 25 per cent in the space of two and a half years. The fall in the Kalmouk population between 1939 and 1959 (see table VI) and the insignificant increase amongst Tchetchenes, Bachkirs, Ingouches, and Karatchais underline the enormous losses suffered by the resettled communities, when one considers that the people of the Northern Caucasus who were not moved, increased their population by between 30 and 50 per cent during the same period.[80]

The number of Latvians and Estonians (table VI) fell by 14 per cent (400,000). The drop in the Lithuanian population was, it seems, masked by the annexation of the *oblasti* of Vilnius and Klajpeda. The low male population is a striking indicator of the losses suffered by these nationalities (see table XII). Indeed, since these people were not conscripted into the Red Army the losses suffered by the male population are probably mostly linked to the repression of the post-war era. This is confirmed by the fact that in the Baltic states, in

Moldavia and Byelorussia, it was the men between 25 and 29 and between 30 and 34 in 1959 who suffered most and these age groups were scarcely, or not at all, affected by the war. What is more, the losses amongst these men were one and a half to two times higher than the average for the whole country (table XII). While the losses in the next age groups, those of 35 to 39 and 40 to 44, who had been actively involved in the war from the beginning, were substantially more in the RSFSR, the Ukraine, Kazakhstan and the other Republics of Central Asia and the Caucasus, in the Baltic States and Moldavia, on the other hand they were little more than those of the 30 to 34 age group. Neither do we see in the Baltic States a fall in the death-rate among elderly people (those over 60 in 1959), who had not taken an active part in the war. Whereas in the eastern Republics where the losses were mainly to do with the war, there is a decrease of between 50 and 70 per cent (table XII). The fate of the Ukrainians and the people of western Byelorussia and many other areas was very similar to that of the Baltic nationalities, but unfortunately the censuses make no distinctions between the different groups.

If we take as a base figure the official figure for war losses of 20 million to which we add the 3 million emigrants, the mortality rate for the years 1946 to 1949 appears to be 2.3 times higher than that of 1950 (see table II). This would suggest losses in the order of 8 million.

4. Military Losses

The Red Army losses were enormous. The unfavourable light cast by the male-female population ratio on the number of males shows this up, as does the male 'deficit' amongst the intermediate generations (who fought in the war). An attempt to assess the maximum number of military losses, using as a basis the chart of the distribution of the country's manpower, is suggested in table XIII.

The extraordinary scale of the military losses was due as much to the military strategy of the Soviet leadership as to the superiority of German armament. The basic doctrine of Soviet strategy was to begin offensives on various fronts with the maximum concentration of forces in total disregard for loss of human life. The main order received by the Red Army, deployed on a vast front along the western border and, neither well equipped nor ready for battle, was to advance. There was the border to cross, Lublin to seize, all the German forces to surround and so on.[81] 'There was no hint of a strategic retreat,' Halder noted in his diary with satisfaction.[82] Some days later he continued, 'an over-all survey of the situation this morning (25 June 1941) indicates that the Russians are determined to fight decisive battles in the border zone, and that they are only retreating in a few places along the front where our armies have forced them to do so'. Halder's delight is understandable – the German generals had feared that the Red Army would retreat to the East. 'On the other side of the Dnepr-Dvina line, there is the danger of the vast expanses of land absorbing any operation which took place on such an extended front.'[83] But the Soviet armies moved not toward the East, but to the West. They launched twenty attacks on the front during the first five months of the war.[84] After the troops from the western regions, the reserves were thrown into the battle and after them the newly formed units. 'During the summer the supreme commander sent to the front 324 divisions, only 68 of which had the task of organising defences along the lines of retreat:[85] 'During the first forty days of military operations alone, 2.4 million men were sent to the front by rail, and during the summer and autumn of 1941, 291 infantry divisions, 94 infantry brigades and over 2 million foot soldiers also went as reinforcements.'[86] In addition to the regulars, over two million members of the people's militia were thrown in to the battle – 'people of all ages with little physical ability for military action and badly prepared for warfare'.[87] In total, in 1941, 18 million men were mobilised of whom between 10 and 12 million were involved in active service (table XIII).

According to Hopkins,[88] Stalin even had some theoretical basis for the engagement in combat of all available forces. 'He wants the greatest possible number of his divisions to have been in contact with the enemy, so that the troops will know that it is possible to fight the Germans, that they are not supermen ... He wants to train as many troops as possible for the great offensive that will take place next spring!'

This uninterrupted counter-attack which cost the Red Army seven million men (only three million were taken prisoner) took the German command completely by surprise. 'At the beginning of the war we had in front of us 200 enemy divisions. Now we can count 360. Admittedly they are neither armed nor equipped by our standards and tactically their leadership is much weaker than ours. But in spite of all this, these divisions are there. Even if we crush a dozen of them, the Russians will form another dozen,' Halder remarked pessimistically on 11 July 1941.[89] But German tanks continued to advance. An area in which 40 per cent of the country's population lived, i.e., about 80 million people, was already behind their lines. Only 7.5 million were successfully evacuated,[90] of whom between 2.5 and 3 million were from Leningrad and Moscow;[91] and between 7 and 8 million men were mobilised. However, the war industry was re-established in the East: hundreds of thousands if not millions of airmen, tank drivers, and gunners were trained and new commandos were formed. Local mobilisation of workers in the Volga and Urals area considerably pushed up the proportion of non-Russians in active service. 'In May (1942) the troops engaged at the front and in the navy numbered 5.5 million, of whom 1.2 million were Georgians, Azerbaidzhanese, Armenians, Uzbeks, Kazakhs, Kirghizes or Bashkirs, all called up under a general mobilisation.'[92] 'In many units the soldiers of non-Russian nationality represented a high proportion of the forces, and almost one-third of the troops at the front in Stalingrad.'[93] The losses suffered by national minorities from the federal republics were almost equal to those of the Russians, Ukrainians and Byelorussians (see table XII). While for the Slavic peoples the main population losses were not as a result of the war itself, Leningrad and Moscow provided a huge number of troops, both conscripts and volunteers, i.e., 450,000 and 'fifty complete divisions representing a total of over a million men' respectively.[94]

By 1943 the reserves of men who could be called up and who were simply not too old to fight (those under forty-five) were in fact exhausted. The army had two main sources of recruitment for its reinforcements: hospitals and the liberated areas. Only the very badly wounded were sent to the rear for treatment; more than half the wounded were left in areas near the front. Hospitals for light injuries became the object of particular attention, so the army's health service could provide, after six months or a year, reinforcements to swell the number of combatants at the front (see table XIII and notes). Some medical publications issued in the last few years to commemorate the end of the war publicise openly many examples of such cases.[95]

The second source of reinforcements, which was almost as intensively exploited as the first, fed the fighting units in the same direct way. 'Tens of thousands of men and youths from the liberated areas of the Ukraine volunteered to join the Red Army, without waiting to be called up ... in the 13th Army alone as many as 30,000 were recruited.'[96] This took place in the first *oblasti* in the Ukraine to be liberated in September 1943. But, shortly after, 'between the 1st and 23rd of January and during March and April 1944 the troops from the second Ukrainian front absorbed over 330,000 recruits who had lived under occupation for a long time'. 40 per cent of the recruits from the western Ukraine were either totally or partially illiterate and a fairly large number were still under the influence of Nazi propaganda.[97] These 'volunteers', who we must remember were neither properly trained nor equipped and fought just as they were, would be found lying dead in their civilian clothes on the battlefields of their native land.

However the offensives were intensified and demanded more and more soldiers. While slightly over a million took part in the fighting around Moscow and in front of Stalingrad,[98] 177 divisions, i.e., 2.5 million men, were involved in the operations launched on four fronts in the Ukraine. Forces amounting to 2.5 million men were gathered for the Kursk attacks, for the military operations in Byelorussia, on the Vistula-Oder and for the Berlin campaign.[99] Losses too became heavier with between 1.3 to 1.5 million men killed[100] (see table XIII). The number who died would have been even greater if it had not been for the significant improvements in the area of the health service.

In 47 months (1,428 days) of war, 5.5 million were killed in battle, one million died from wounds and about a million perished in captivity either from their injuries or starvation or in military operations on behalf of the Germans;[101] and 18 million were wounded. As far as total military losses are concerned Stalin suggested 7 million soldiers and officers, and Krushchev 10 million. If we take it as referring to losses suffered in military operations, the former is nearer to our own estimate.

It is well known that the winners do not go on trial, even for a Pyrrhic victory. We lost thirty times more soldiers and officers than England or the United States, indeed more than Germany, Austria, Italy, Finland, Hungary, Romania, Japan, Great Britain, the United States and France put together. Our losses were greater than all of those sustained by Russia, France, Great Britain, Germany and Austria-Hungary in the First World War. But however high the figure – more than 7.5 million soldiers and between 6 and 8 million civilians – they do not include the losses of between 9 and 11 million people during those same years which were not the result of Fascist aggression. These were those resulting from Stalinist repression. An investigation of this remains an extremely important area of research.

Examination of the Results

By their fruits you shall know them

So, in the end, how many? The estimated figures are listed in table XIV: 42.3 million victims and 6.5 million emigrants – such is the outcome or, as we might say, the cost of forty years glorious history. During those years nearly one man in two and one woman in four did not not die a natural death. And if we consider the critical years on their own (1918-22 and 1932-49), of the 30 million men who died in those years only 19 million died in their bed and 12 out of 32 women did not live out their lifespan. If we took only the minimum figures, the number of human losses would still represent over one-third of all deaths during those years. The maximum estimate would represent almost half. Is it possible? Has it

247

ever happened before? In absolute terms we can manifestly answer no. Nobody has yet managed to exterminate 40 million human beings in such a short space of time, even if one takes their enemies as well as their own population. Neither Attila, nor Genghis Khan, nor Tamburlaine, nor Hitler was able to pile up such a heap of corpses. All the world's countries added together have had fewer losses in two world wars.

Much higher estimates for the losses attributable to repressive measures have often been suggested, anywhere between 30 and 60 million. Those who have put forward these figures must take into consideration the fact that between 1932 and 1942, 42 million men died altogether (table XIV): This figure constitutes the natural and rational limit for even the maximum estimate and it would be hard to argue that not one man in eighteen years died a natural death. Exaggerating these figures seems to be the normal turn of contemporary thought – anything less than a million is taken to be insignificant. But they do remind us, once again, how far we deviated from a 'child's tear' in building our radiant future.

NOTES

1 After the experience of the Twentieth Congress, perhaps we should add a thousand, or a million.
2 The minimum (not less than ...) appears to be the most important and most trustworthy estimate, and what's more, it can be reached by using official Soviet data. We have not referred to other sources, firstly because we do not have any more reliable data available; secondly because, for a Soviet citizen, it is quite normal and also interesting to analyse the casuistry and the scientific falsification, as well as the official propaganda, in order to extract a few fragments of the truth (assuming, of course, that this is possible).
3 The mortality rate is the relation between the number of deaths in a given group during a year (usually of the same sex and age group) and the average number of people constituting this group during the year. Theoretically it would be safer to use a death probability figure (the number of deaths during the year compared to the living population at the beginning of the same year) rather than the mortality rate in the evaluation. In practice, though, it is preferable to use the former,

since the error involved is slight and can also be taken into consideration during the calculations.

4   S. A. Novosel'skii, V. V. Paevskii, *Tablitsy smertnosti (Mortality Tables)*, Moscow-Leningrad, 1930.

5   Unfortunately the scope of this study does not allow us to cite these tables or to elaborate on the method.

6   S. A. Novosel'skii, V. V. Paevskii, *O svodnykh kharakteristikakh vosproizvodstva naseleniya i perspektivnykh ischisleniyakh (Some General Characteristics of the Reproduction of the Population and some Forecasts)*, Leningrad, 1934, 'Trudy demograficheskogo instituta'. B. Babynin 'Perspektivy rosta naseleniya SSSR v 27-28, 32-33' ('Growth Perspectives of the Population of the USSR in 27-28, 32-33'), *Planovoe khozyaistvo, II*, 1928.

7   Yu. A. Korchak-Chepurkovskii, *Izbrannye demograficheskie issledovaniya (Selected Demographic Studies)*, Moscow, 1970.

8   For the period 1918-1838 we have considered the population within the borders prior to 17 September 1939, and, for the years between 1939 and 1958, within the present borders.

9   S. A. Novosel'skii, V. V. Paevskii, *Tablitsy ...* op. cit. The population figure at the beginning of 1939 is obtained from the annual breakdown of five-year age groups published by the CSU (Central'noe statisticeskoe upravlenie/Central Statistics Office) Cf. *Itogi vsesoyuznoi perepisi naseleniya 959g./Account of the Population Census of the Soviet Union for 1959*, Moscow 1962 and *Naselenie SSSR/The Population of the USSR*, Moscow, 1974). This division into fractions is made by using the results of the estimate for the preceding period (1926-38).

10   The tendency towards a lowering of the mortality rate can probably be explained by several factors: changes in social and medical conditions, the decline in the birth-rate, and above all by the recrudescent periods of losses, which took the lives of many who would have lived longer in more peaceful times.

11   B. C. Urlanis, *Voiny i narodonaselenie Evropy (Wars and the Population of Europe)*, Moscow, 1960. In the 'Peace Manifesto' adopted by the Communist Parties and Workers' Conference held in Moscow in November 1957, we note: 'The Second World War has claimed more than 30 million lives, without even mentioning the millions of wounded and maimed' *(Pravda*, 29 September 1957). We have used this figure which included the civilian losses as a basis for all evaluations. One year later Krushchev remembered another 20 million, and the accepted base figure moved from 30 to 50 millions.

12   B. C. Urlanis, ibid.

13   B. C. Urlanis, 'Dinamika naseleniya SSSR za 50 let' (The Dynamic of the USSR Population in the Last 50 Years), in *Naselenie i narodnoe blagosostoyanie (Population and Social Conditions)*, Moscow, 1968.

14   *Naselenie SSSR*, op.cit.

15   *Zhenshchiny v SSSR (Women in the USSR)*, Moscow, 1975.

16   Unfortunately, the CSU does not provide specific data, or any indication of the method used. It is quite possible that Stalin's threats are still feared.

17 In *Itogi vsesoyuznoi perepisi naseleniya 1959 g,* op.cit., the borders of the
country are defined in the following way: 'The territory of the USSR,
beyond the old imperial borders with the exclusion of Poland, Finland
and Kars, now includes the area which used to be known as Boukhara
and Khiva; Galicia and North Boukovinia, which became part of the
USSR in 1939; the Tuva territory included in 1944; Transcarpathian
Ukraine; the town of Konigsberg (now Kaliningrad) and the surrounding area; as well as the south of Sahalin Island and the Kuriles
Islands included in 1945.' One always has to say 'beyond the old
imperial borders', because even the old borders were never established
at any one time.

18 E. Z. Volkov, *Dinamika naseleniya za 80 let (The Population in the Last
Eighty Years),* Moscow, 1930.

19 *Perepis' naseleniya 1970 g. (1970 Population Census)* Moscow, 1969.

20 'The population census was supposed to be the reflection of the
number and composition of the great soviet people, the reflection of
the giant conquest of socialism in our country, which led, in
November 1936, to the adoption of the Stalinist constitution by the
Seventh Extraordinary Pan-Russian Soviet Congress. But some
Trotsko-Bukharinist agents of Fascism infiltrated the leadership of the
CUNHU and the census office' *(Planovoe khozyaistvo, II, 1938).* 'The
enemies of the people have done all they can to distort the real
population figures. They gave malicious instructions to the census
agents, which made numerous groups refuse to fill in the census forms.
The Soviet intelligence service, led by the Stalinist Commissar of the
People, I. I. Fezov, has destroyed the viper's nest of traitors who had
sneaked into the Soviet statistics machinery' (Decisions of the Peoples'
Commissars on the 1939 census). It is interesting to note· that this
quotation has been taken from the book of the 'saboteurs' P. I.
Pustokhod and V. K. Voblyi, *Perepisi naseleniya (Population Censuses),*
Moscow, 1940. In 1936, they commented in detail on the excellent
methods and organisation of the census and on the value of the
Stalinist guidelines, but in 1940, still safe and sound and having got
their second wind, they altered in places the names of the authors and
republished the book after having changed, it is true, the reserv-
ations/criticism made about the 1937 census. (Stalinist/
saboteur, exact/erroneous ...).

21 See the preceding note.

22 *Itogi vsesoyuznoi perepisi naseleniya 1959 g.* op.cit.

23 S. A. Novosel'skii, V. V. Paevskii, *Tablitsy,* op.cit: Id., O. svodnykh,
op.cit.

24 I. G. Venetskii, *Matematicheskie metody v demografii (Mathematical Methods
in Demography),* Moscow, 1971.

25 B. Babynin, art.cit.

28 The USSR population has fallen upon a similar problem in the last
few years. The increase in the mortality rates for several male age
groups (those over fifteen) and female ones (those over forty) is due to
a large extent to the systematic decline in infant mortality in the

preceding years. The fall in the post-war mortality rate resulting, as we have already noted, from the losses of the previous years, certainly plays an important part. (cf. G. Bakhmeteva, 'Dozhivzemost' i smertnost' naseleniya SSSR'/'Life expectancy and mortality of the Soviet population', in *Prodolzhitel'nost' zhizni (The lengthening of life)*, Moscow, 1974.

27 *Narodnoe khozyaistvo SSSR v 1967 godu (The National Economy of the USSR in 1967)*, Moscow, 1968.

28 S. A. Novosel'skii, V. V. Paevskii, op.cit.

29 I. G. Venetskii, op.cit.

30 *Itogi Vsesoyuznoi perepisi naseleniya 1970 g. (Results of the 1970 Population Census)*, Moscow, 7, 1974.

31 L. S. Kaminskii, S. A. Novosel'skii, *Poteri v proshlykh voinakh (Human Losses during the Past Wars)*, Moscow, 1947.

32 A. G. Rasin, *Naselenie Rossii za 100 let (The Population in Russia during the Last 100 Years)*, Moscow, 1965.

33 Zinger, *Evreiskoe naselenie Rossii (The Jewish Population of Russia)*, Moscow, 1932.

34 E. P. Pletnev, *Mezhdunorodnaya migratsiya naseleniya i razvitie sovremennoi kapitalisticheskoi sistemy (International Migration and the Development of Contemporary Capitalism)*, Moscow, 1962.

35 L. S. Kaminskii, *Meditsinskaya demograficheskaya statistika (Medical Demographic Statistics)*, Moscow, 1962.

36 V. G. Avraamov 'Zhertvy imperialisticheskoi voiny v Rossii na I sent. 1917 g.' ('The Victims of the Imperialist War in Russia on September 1st, 1917'), *Izvestiya Markomata zdravookhraneniya*, 1-2, 1920.

37 E. Z. Volkov, op.cit.

38 G. A. Batkis, *Sotsial'naya gigiena (Social Hygiene)*, Moscow, 1936.

39 E. Z. Volkov, op. cit.

40 B. C. Urlanis, op.cit.

41 B. C. Urlanis, art.cit.; A. Ya. Boyarskii, *Naselenie i metody ego izucheniya (Population and the Methods Used to Study It)*, Moscow, 1975.

42 S. G. Strumilin, *Nashi trudovye resursy i perspektivy (Our Labour Resources and the Future)*, Moscow, 1922.

43 ibid.

44 Sidney and Beatrice Webb, *Sovetskii kommunizm – novaya tsivilizatsiya? (Soviet Communism – A New Civilisation?)*, Moscow, 1937.

45 CUNHU, *Sotsialisticheskoe stroitel'stvo SSSR (Socialist Construction in the USSR)*, Moscow, 1934.

46 A. I. Gozulov, M. G. Grigor'yants, *Narodonaselenie SSSR (The Population of the USSR)*, Moscow, 1969.

47 ' ... one of the greatest catastrophes known by mankind since the World War, which caused an increase in the number of deaths resulting from disease and exhaustion, an increase that involved 4 or 5 million more than could normally be expected'. (V. G. Chamberlain, 'The Iron Century in Russia', 1935; cited in S. and B. Webb, op. cit.)

48 B. C. Urlanis, *Problemy dinamika naseleniya (Problems of the Dynamics of the Population)*, Moscow, 1974.

49 CSU, Aborty (Abortions), Moscow, 1927. Koseleva, 'Opyt sotsial'noi

gruppirovki dannyh po abortam' ('Essay on the social interpretation of data on abortion'), *Vestnik statistik*, 5, 1928.

50 Even authors as serious as Novosel'skii and Paevskii were several millions from the truth when they published their forecasts for 1934. Cf. S. A. Novosel'skii, V. V. Paevskii.

51 Apparently Stalin is nearer the latter, with his subtle mind and biting humour. He even described collectivisation in the following way: 'We understand that the peasants have seized upon the proposals of the Soviet government, set out to turn their patch of land into large fields, taken tractors and other machinery and thus got involved in agriculture on a large scale.' *(Sochineniya/Works,* 13, p. 267). And what use is the ambiguous appeal addressed to the Party workers in 1937? 'It is vitally important to suggest to our Party leaders – from cell secretaries and secretaries of the organisations to the level of the *oblasti* and the Republics – that they must enlist the services of two people for a given period, two Party workers, capable of replacing them effectively.'

52 There were 14 million people who voted against. It would seem we were then still some way from the present 99.9 per cent. But it was not very far away because this percentage was reached in the middle of 1938.

53 *Naselenie SSSR,* op.cit.

* Member of the VOHR; Voiska vrutenei ohrany respubliki

54 Usually much higher figures are suggested. The well-known demographer F. Lorimer, after the 1939 census, estimated the difference between forced and paid workers to be 6.8 million. Conquest suggested a figure of 12 million for people affected by the repressive measures from the end of 1938 (15 million if we include common-law criminals), of whom 3 million perished either in prison or in the camps in 1937-9.

55 *Narodnoe khozyaistvo RSFSR v 1967 godu (The National Economy of the RSFSR, in 1967),* Moscow, 1968.

56 The population was 178.5 million on 1 January 1950 and, according to the 1959 census, 167 million before 1950; we estimate the number of children born in 1949 to be 4.5 million, a figure calculated from the birth-rate figures for 1949-53; cf. table II.

57 *SSSR (USSR), Bol'shaya sovetskaya entsiklopediya (Great Soviet Encyclopedia),* Moscow, 1947.

58 I. Lyalikov, *Geografiya naseleniya SSSR (The Geography of the Soviet Population),* Moscow, 1947.

59 Besides, we don't know if it is so tragic. Who are the happier, the 7 million Germans uprooted from their country in 1945-6 or the million who remained in the Western territories and who are now gradually being brought back by the German Federal Government?

60 L. Marian'skii, *Sovremennye migratsii naseleniya (Contemporary Migration of the Population),* Moscow, 1969.

61 ibid.

62 ibid.

63 Yu. L. Pivovarov, *Naselenie sotsialisticheskikh stran zarubezhnoi Evropy (The Population of the Socialist Countries of Europe)*, Moscow, 1970.

64 *Vtoraya mirovaya voina (The Second World War)*, Moscow, 1966.

65 *Prestupleniya nemetsko-fashistskikh okkupantov v Belorussii 1941-44 gg (The Crimes of the German Fascists Occupying Byelorussia from 1941 to 1944)*, Minsk, 1965.

66 *Vneshnyaya politika Sovetskogo soyuza 1945 g. (The Foreign Policy of the USSR in 1945)*, Moscow, 1949.

67 *Istoriya velikoi otechestvennoi voiny Sovetskogo soyuza (History of the Great Patriotic War of the Soviet Union), (IVOVSS)*, Moscow, 6, 1966.

68 L. Marian'skii, op.cit.

69 *Vneshnyaya politika ...* op.cit., (1947).

70 S. I. Rakovskii, 'Vnutrennyaya migratsiya naseleniya i sdvigi v etnograficheskoi geografii zarubezhnykh sotsialisticheskikh stran Evropy' ('Internal Migration and Movement of the Population in the Ethnographic Geography of the Socialist Countries of Europe'), *Sovetskaya etnografiya*, 4, 1969.

71 Ibid.

72 D. V. Pavlov, *Leningrad v blokade (Leningrad during the Blockade)*.

73 L. Marian'skii, op.cit.

74 4l0,000 German civilians were killed during the bombings and 20,000 in the zone near the front. Cf. B. C. Urlanis, *Voiny ...* , op.cit.

75 *Vtoraya mirovaya voina*, op.cit.

76 *Prestupleniya nemetsko-fashistskikh ...* , op.cit.

77 *Istoriya Latviiskoi SSR (History of the Latvian Republic)*, Riga, 1971.

78 *Vneshnyaya politika SSSR vo vremya velikoi otechestvennoi voiny (The Foreign Policy of the USSR during the Great Patriotic War)*, Moscow, IX, 1949, 1-3.

79 L. Marian'skii, op.cit.

80 *Itogi vsesoyuznoi perepisi ...* 1959, op.cit.

81 *Dokumenty vneshnei politiki Sovetskogo soyuza v period velikoi etechestvennoi voiny (Foreign Policy Documents of the Soviet Union during the Great Patriotic War)*, Moscow, I, 1949.

82 *Dnevnik nachal'nika General'nogo shtaba sukhoputnykh voisk Germanii gen. Gal'dera za period avgust 1939 – sentyabr' 1942 (Diary of General Halder, the Commanding Officer of the German Infantry, August 1939-September 1942)*, Moscow, 7, 1959.

83 D. M. Proektor, *Agressiya i katastrofa (Aggression and Catastrophe)*, Moscow, 1972.

84 *Voennaya strategiya (Military Strategy)*, Moscow, 1962.

85 *IVOVSS*, 2.

86 *Vo glave zashchitu sovetskoi rodiny (Leading the Defence of the Soviet Nation)*, Moscow, 1975.

87 A. Vert, *Rossiya v voine 1941-45 gg. (Russia during the 1941-45 War)*.

88 *Dnevnik ... gen. Gal'dera ...* op.cit., 8.

89 *IVOVSS*, 6.

90 *Vtoraya mirovaya voina*, op.cit.

91 *IVOVSS*, 3.

92 *Vo glave zashchitu* ... op.cit.
93 *IVOVSS*, 3.
94. *Vtoraya mirovaya voina*, op.cit.
95 *Voenno-meditsinskii zhurnal*, 5, 1975; *Materialy konferentsii voenno-meditsinskoi akademii 22.4.75 (Documents from the Conference of Military Medicine, 22.4.75)*, Leningrad, 1975.
96 IVOVSS, 3.
97 *Vo glave zashchitu* ... op.cit.
98 *Vtoraya mirovaya voina, Voenno iskusstvo (The Second World War, Military Art)* Moscow, 1966.
99 Ibid.
100 As surprising as it may seem, the Sovinformbiuro has given a comparable figure: 1.1 million for the third year of the war. Cf. *Vneshnyaya politika SSSR vo vremya otechestvennoi voiny*, op.cit.
101 These figures are extremely approximate, since they are obtained from scattered information and biased speculation (see the explanation of table XIII). Nevertheless it seems to us that they give an accurate overview and exaggerate rather than minimise the military losses.

ANNEXE

TABLE I

**MORTALITY RATES PROVIDED BY THE CENSUS AND
USED IN THE ESTIMATES (IN %)***

Census	1897**			1926	1939***			1959
Estimated period		1917-22	1923-26	1927-38		1939-49	1950-58	
		1926 rate x1.5	1926 rate x1.2	1926 rate x1.0		1926 rate x0.9	1959 rate x1.2	
Age								
0-4	133.0	118.0	94.7	78.9	75.5	71.0	14.3	11.9
5-9	12.9	9.9	8.8	7.3	5.6	6.6	1.2	1.0
10-14	5.4	4.7	8.7	8.1	2.6	2.8	1.0	0.8
15-19	5.8	5.6	4.4	8.7	8.4	8.8	1.6	1.8
20-24	7.6	8.4	6.6	5.5	4.4	5.0	2.2	1.8
25-29	8.2	9.2	7.3	6.1	4.7	5.5	2.6	2.2
30-34	8.7	9.5	7.6	6.3	5.4	5.7	8.1	2.6
35-39	10.3	11.3	8.9	7.5	6.8	6.8	8.7	3.1
40-44	11.8	13.5	10.8	9.0	8.1	8.1	4.8	4.0
45-49	15.7	16.4	13.1	10.9	10.2	9.8	6.5	5.4
50-54	18.5	21.0	16.8	14.0	13.8	12.6	9.5	7.9
55-59	29.5	27.2	21.7	18.1	17.1	16.3	13.4	11.2
60-64	34.5	37.1	29.4	24.7	24.4	22.2	20.5	17.1
65-69	61.6	54.8	43.8	36.5	35.0	32.8	80.2	25.2
70 +	89.0	119.0	95.4	79.5	78.6	71.6	76.6	63.8
Pop. total	32.4 ****	80.5	24.4	20.3	17.4	18.3	8.5	7.4

*For the estimate we have not used the exact rates indicated
in this table: not the cumulative rates but the annual rates
which distinguish men and women. For the new-born (aged
0) the estimated rate is lowered to take account of the

monthly mortality. The rate for one-year-old children is also somewhat reduced.

** The high infant mortality rate of 1897 compared to 1917-22 is perfectly explicable. In fact between 1897 and 1926 infant mortality diminished by 40 to 50 per cent. Is it not normal to assume that part of this decrease (less than half) took place during the first, comparatively quiet, twenty years?

*** A slight rise in the mortality rate of elderly people in the estimate for 1939 is compensated by a lower mortality in the other age groups. What is more, the 1939 table has not included the population of the annexed territories where there was a lower mortality amongst the older age groups.

**** In 1910-13, the mortality rate was established to be 30.2 per cent.

TABLE II
POPULATION TRENDS BETWEEN 1913 AND 1958
(1913-39 within the borders prior to 17 September 1939,
after 1940 within the existing borders)

Year	Rate in %			Number in millions of men at the end of the year		
	BIRTH	MORTALITY	GROWTH (−LOSS)	IMMIGRATION/ EMIGRATION BALANCE	POPULATION OF THE COUNTRY	WORKERS & EMPLOYEES
1913	47.0	30.2	2.4	−0.1	139.3	—
1914	43.7	27.2	2.3	1.2	142.8	—
1915	35.9	28.8	1.0	0.3	144.1	—
1916	27.1	25.4	0.3	−0.6	143.8	—
1917	26.3	29.1	−0.4	0.1	143.5	—
1918	34.7	44.2	−1.4	−1.0	141.1	—
1919	31.7	46.7	−2.2	−0.6	138.3	—
1920	32.2	43.3	−1.5	0	136.8	—
1921	37.3	29.7 ?40*	−0.4	−1.9	134.5	—
1922	38.2	29.6	1.2	−0.1	135.6	6.3
1923	45.5	25.5	2.7	—	138.3	—

1924	42.2	23.5	2.8	–	141.1	7.4
1925	43.9	24.5	2.9	—	144.0	8.6
1926	42.5	21.5	3.1	—	147.1	10.0
1927	43.4	21.0	3.5	—	150.6	10.7
1928	42.2	18.2	3.8	—	154.4	11.4
1929	39.8	20.3	3.3	—	157.7	12.4
1930	39.2	20.4	2.9	—	160.6	15.4
1931	38*	—	2.9	—	163.5	20.2
1932	(29)*	—	2.3	—	165.8	24.2
1933	(20)*	—	-7.8	—	158[1]	23.5
1934	80.1	—	1.3	—	159.3*	24.8
1935	29.6	16.3	2.1	—	161.4*	25.9
1936	—	—	2.4	—	163.8	27.2
1937	38.7	18.9	3.2	—	167.0	28.6
1938	37.5	17.5	3.6	—	170.6	29.9
1939	36.5	17.3	3.4	—	174.0	31.6
1940	31.2	18.0	2.4	23	199.4	33.9
1941	29*	—	—	—	—	29.0
1942	12*	—	—	—	—	19.4
1943	11*	—	—	—	—	20.4
1944	15*	—	—	—	—	25.0
1945	15*	—	—	-3	176.4*	28·6
1946	23.8	22*	—	—	—	32.0
1947	25.7	22*	—	—	—	33.5
1948	24.1	22*	—	—	—	35.0
1949	28.5	22*	—	—	178.5	37.6
1950	26.7	9.7	3.1	—	181.6	40.4
1951	27.0	9.7	3.3	—	184.9	42.3
1952	26.5	9.4	3.1	—	188.0	43.9
1953	25.1	9.1	3.0	—	191.0	45.4
1954	26.6	8.9	3.4	—	194.4	49.1
1955	25.7	8.2	3.5	—	197.9	50.3
1956	25.2	7.6	3.5	—	201.4	51.9
1957	25.4	7.8	3.9	—	204.9	54.9
1958	25.3	7.2	3.5	—	208.8	56.0

* Data calculated from the censuses (births) or estimated (deaths, population figure).

Sources: B. C. Urlanis, *Voiny i narodnaselenie Evropy (Wars and the Population of Europe),* Moscow, 1960; B. C. Urlanis, 'Dinamika naseleniya SSSR za 50 let' (Population dynamics in the last 50 years) in *Naselenie i narodnoe blagostoyanie (Population and Social Conditions).* Moscow, 1968.

The figures in brackets correspond to the number of babies who survived the famine, rather than the birth-rate. It is hardly likely that the birth-rate in 1932-3 was below 30-35 per cent.

The unattributed data of one contributor has been taken from the works cited below [1-13]. The birth and mortality rate for 1914-26 are taken from the calculations of A. Ya. Bojarskii [1]. The mortality rate in 1921 must have been much higher, since Bojarskii made no allowance for the famine, which cost, according to several researchers, 5 million lives [2, 3].

The immigration/emigration balance is taken from E. Z. Volkov [4]. For 1914-17 it is the result of the difference between 4.7 million refugees from western regions and foreign prisoners of war on the one hand, and 3.7 million Russian prisoners in Germany on the other hand. In 1918-23 populations on the move included 4.7 million people from the western regions and foreign prisoners of war who had left the country, according to the central organisation in charge of prisoners and refugees, 3.17 Russians back from captivity and 2 million 'White' emigrants [4, 5].

The data covering birth and mortality rates for the years 1926-30, 1937-40, 1946-9, 1950-8 are regularly summarised in CSU directories [6, 7]. Figures for 1933-6 are taken from the findings of Urlanis and other authorities [8, 9].

The figures for workers and employees are taken from the work of E. D. Grazhdannikov [9] and for the war years from *The History of the Great Patriotic War (Istoriya velikoi otechestvennoi voiny)* [13].

All the data include quite a significant degree of error and therefore table II gives only a general outline.

[1] A. Ya Boyarskii, *Naselenie i metody ego izucheniya (Population and Methods Used to Study it)*, Moscow, 1975.

[2] 'Golod' Famine, in *Bol'shaya sovetskaya entsiklopediya (The Great Soviet Encyclopaedia)*, Moscow.

[3] S. G. Strumilin, *Nashi trudovye resursy i perspektivy (Our Labour Resources and the Future)*, Moscow, 1922.

[4] E. Z. Volkov, *Dinamika naseleniya za 80 let (Population Trends in the Last 80 Years)*, Moscow, 1930.

[5] B.C. Urlanis, 'Dinamika naseleniya SSSR za 50 let' (Population trends in the USSR in the last 50 years), in Naselenie i narodnoe blagosostoyanie (Population and social conditions), Moscow, 1968.

[6] *Narodnoe khozyaistvo SSSR. Ezhegidnik 1956-1975 gg. (The National Economy. Directory 1956-1975).*

[7] *Zhenshchiny v SSSR (Women in the USSR),* Moscow, 1975.

[8] B. C. Urlanis, *Problemy dinamiki naseleniya (Problems in the Population Trends),* Moscow, 1974.

[9] E. D. Grazhdannikov, *Prognosticheskie modeli sotsial'no-demograficheskikh protsessov (Models for Forecasting Demographic and Social Development),* Novosibirsk, 1974.

[10] *Itogi Vsesoyuznoi perepisi naseleniya 1959 goda (Summary of the 1959 Population Census),* Moscow, 1962.

[11] *Naselenie SSSR (Population of the USSR),* Moscow, 1974.

[12] *Sotsialisticheskoe stroitel'stvo SSSR (Socialist Construction in the USSR),* Moscow, 1934.

[13] *Istoriya velikoi otechestvennoi voiny Sovetskogo Soyuza za 1941-45 gg. (History of the Great Patriotic War of the Soviet Union, 1941-45),* Moscow, 6.

TABLE III

CHANGES IN THE POPULATION FROM 1914 TO 1918

(in thousands of people; in the 1923 borders)

	1914	1915	1916	1917	1918
Total population at the 1st Jan.	139,912	142,588	142,260	142,472	140,903
Conscripted into army (mobilised since 1913)	4,441	5,540	9,895	12,960	15,685
Active Service	—	4,153	5,158	5,168	—
Domestic Service	375	774	1,406	1,742	2,005
Deserters and Demobilised	—	13	59	117	4,357
Disabled soldiers	—	61	297	546	784
Freed from captivity because of illness	—	—	141	417	724
Prisoners	—	241	1,328	2,900	3,409
Killed in action from the beginning of the war to 1st Jan.	—	68	345	642	685
Died from wounds	—	30	110	200	300
Died from disease	—	—	—	—	230
Died from various causes	—	—	—	—	63
Died in captivity	—	—	—	—	285
Refugees*	—	885	3,065	5,929	7,429
Foreign prisoners of war	—	200	1,150	1,830	2,260

* The findings of E. Z. Volkov seem exaggerated.
Sources: 1. E. Z. Volkov, *Dinamika naseleniya za 80 let (Population Trends in the Last 80 Years)*, Moscow, 1930.
2. *Trudy komissii po obsledovaniyu sanitarnykh posledstvii vojny 1914-23 gg. (Studies of the Commission of Inquiry on the Medical Consequences of the War 1914-23)*, Petrograd, 1923.

TABLE IV
TYPHUS CASES BETWEEN 1917 AND 1924 (IN %)

	1917	1918	1919	1920	1921	1922	1923	1924
Exanthematic typhus	1.0	2.1	34	34	6.0	11	1.8	0.9
Recurrent typhus	0.7	0.3	4	113	6.9	12.1	1.8	0.4

Source: G. A. Batkis, *Sotsial'naya gigiena (Social Hygiene)*, Moscow, 1936.
According to Health service statistics fatalities reached 20 to 30 per cent in 55 *gubernii*.

TABLE V
TOTAL POPULATION BETWEEN 1896 AND 1926
(in millions of people; in the borders prior to 17 September 1939)

	1926	1922	1920	1917	1913	1896
Evaluation	147.1	136.55	133.18	129.69	123.80	89.8
Estimate of the CSU	147.1	136.10	136.81	143.50	139.31	103.9
Difference	—	+0.45	–3.63	–13.81	–15.51	–14.1
Losses for the period considered	+0.45*		–4.08	–10.18	–1.7	+1.41*

* The plus signs indicate an exaggeration in estimating the level of the 'natural mortality' rate.
Sources: CSU information.

TABLE VI

POPULATION OF THE NATIONALITIES IN THE USSR

(IN THOUSANDS OF PEOPLE)

Nationality	1926	1939	1959	1970	1939-59 (Increase in %)
Russians	77,791	100,931	114,114	129,015	13.6
Ukrainians	31,195	35,611*	37,253	40,753	4.6
Byelorussians	3,928	8,275*	7,913	9,052	-4.4
Lithuanians	41	2,032	2,326	2,665	14.4
Latvians	151	1,628	1,400	1,430	-14.1
Estonians	155	1,143	988	1,007	-13.5
Poles	782	1,730*	1,380	1.168	-20.3
Jews	2,600	4,628	2,267	2,151	-51.4
Germans	1,239	1,427	1,619	1,846	14
Finns	135	—	93	85	—
Karelians	248	—	167	147	—
Yakoutes	241	—	233	296	—
Peoples of the North**	140	—	129	151	—
Kazakhs	3,968	3,101	3,622	5,299	16.8
Ouighours	108	—	95	173	—
Kalmuks	133	134	106	137	-20
Chechens	318	407	419	613	8
Ingouches	74	92	106	158	15
Balkars	33	43	42	60	-2
Karatchais	55	76	81	113	6
Crimean Tatars	180	—	—	—	—
Koreans	170	—	313	358	—
Total Population	147,028	190,678	208,827	241,720	9.5

* In the borders prior to 17 September 1939, there were 28.1 million Ukrainians, 5.3 million Byelorussians and 626,000 Poles.

** It is instructive to compare the changes amongst certain small nationalities or peoples who live both within and outside the borders of the USSR. Cf. *Chislennost' i rasselenie narodov mira (The Number and Distribution of the Peoples of the World)*, Moscow, 1965. Cf. table VIa.

Sources: Census results.

TABLE VIA

Nationality	Country	Total 1926	1959	Increase (%)
Saami	USSR	1,729	1,790	0.12
	Finland	2,300 [a]	3,000	1.6
Eskimos	USSR	1,290	1,120	−0.4
	USA and Canada	25,800 [b]	30,000	1.8
Aleutians	USSR	352	420	0.8
	USA and Canada	3,900 [b]	5,000	3.1
Evenki	USSR	37,500	24,700	−1
	China	5,000 [c]	6,000	8.8
Ainy	USSR	1,450	80	—
	Japan	16,000 [d]	20,000	0.6
Bouriats	USSR	237,000	252,000	0.2
	Mongolia	25,000 [e]	28,000	4

a 1940
b 1950
c 1953
d 1897
e 1956

TABLE VII

CHANGES IN THE POPULATION OF CERTAIN REGIONS
(IN THOUSANDS OF PEOPLE)

	Area in 1926 [a][1]	1926 Jan.[1]	1931 Jan[2]	1931 July[2]	1933 Jan[3]	1939 Jan[4]
SSR of Ukraine	452 [b]	29,043	—	31,608	31,901	30,960
SSR of the	2,853	6,074 [c]				6,146
Kazakhs		6,170	6,780	7,260	6,797	
Northern Caucasus [d]	271	9,151	—	10,280	10,064	10,511
Siberia and the Far East	11,150	11,382	—	13,307	14,394	16,674

Population Losses in the USSR 1918-1958

a. In thousands of square km.

b. The borders of the Ukraine were somewhat reduced, in 1935, by 440,000 square km.

c. The top line is the population within the 1939 borders, and the lower line within the 1930 borders. In 1926 the borders were extended a little and the census indirectly counted 6,196,000 (excluding the autonomous Republic of Kara-Kalpak). The figures on the lower line were all taken from the same study.

d. The following made up part of the Northern Caucasus in 1926-33: the *kraya* of Krasnodar, Ordzhonokidze, Rostov, the autonomous Republics of Daghestan, Kabardino-Balkar, Checheno-Inguch, Severo-Osetinsk, Adygeisk, Karachaevsk and Cherkess. (To make the comparison easier we have excluded the autonomous Republic of the Kalmuk.) In 1939 the territory of northern Caucasus was clearly extended. Thus in the book, *The Population of the USSR,* the surface area is listed as 355,000 sq. km. and the population is listed as being 10,332,000. Consequently it is clear that the increase in the population of northern Caucasus was partly or totally due to the extension of the territory.

Sources: 1. *Vsesoyuznaya perepis' naseleniya 1926 g. (Population Census in the USSR in 1926)*, Moscow, 1928.

2. *Narodnoe khozyaistvo SSR (National Economy of the USSR)*, Moscow-Leningrad, 1932.

3. *Sotsialisticheskoe stroitel'stvo SSR (Socialist Construction in the USSR)*, Moscow, 1935.

4. S. Sul'kevich, *Naselenie SSSR po perepisi 1939 g. (The Population of the USSR according to the Census of 1939)*, Moscow, 1939.

TABLE VIII

THE NUMBER OF INHABITANTS OF CERTAIN
TOWNS IN THE URALS AND SIBERIA
(IN THOUSANDS OF PEOPLE)

	1926 17 Dec	1931 1 July	1936 1 Jan	1939 1 Jan
Sverdlovsk	140	223	446	423
Chelyabinsk	59	117	293	273
Nizhnii Tagil	39	—	170	160
Zlatoust	57	—	111	99

263

	1926 17 Dec	1931 1 July	1936 1 Jan	1939 1 Jan
Berezniki	19	—	80	51
Andzhero-Suzhensk	80	—	82	69
Omsk	162	178	286	289
Tomsk	92	—	158	145
Krasnoyarsk	72	170	189	190
Prokop'evsk	10	—	121	107
Kemerovo	21	—	140	133
Magnitogorsk	—	—	224	146
Stalinsk	4	—	217	189
Barnaul	74	—	146	148
Karaganda	—	—	141	156

The data for 1926 and 1939 is provided in the census material of these years. In fact they are published without alteration in several publications of the CSU, such as *Results of the 1959 census (Itogi vsesoyuznoi perepisi 1959 goda)*, Moscow, 1962, and *The Population of the USSR (Naselenie SSSR)*, Moscow, 1974. Data for 1931 is provided in the statistical compilation, *The Economy of the USSR (Narodnoe khozyaistvo)*, Moscow-Leningrad, 1932. Data for 1936 is taken from the annual statistics of CUNHU. *Socialist construction in the RSFSR (Sotsialisticheskoe stroitel'stvo RSFSR)*, Moscow, 1937. It is typical that this information was published by the same 'CUNHU saboteurs' who had made so many efforts to reduce the population figure at the time of the 1937 census, i.e., just at the time when the annual statistics were about to be printed. However, we can see here a numerical exaggeration which has 'the character of sabotage'.

TABLE IX
POPULATION TOTALS ON 1 JULY 1931
(IN THOUSANDS OF PEOPLE)

Age Group	Census	Estimate	Difference*
0-2	15,348	—	—
3	4,779	—	—
4-6	12.667	12,412	255
7	4,238	4,231	7
8-10	10.566	10,633	–67
11	2,964	2,975	–11
12-14	8,501	8,467	34
15	2,833	2,825	8
16-17	7,125	7,173	–48
18-19	7,313	7,252	61
20-39	50,673	50,032	641
40-44	7,761	8,209	–448
45-49	6,668	6,.276	392
50-59	10,112	9.994	118
60 +	10,605	10,648	–43
4 +	142,036	141,127	899
7 +	129,360	128,715	644

*   The alternation of the discrepancies can be explained by the inaccurate age-group breakdown in the 1926 and 1931 censuses. Using another scale (as do Novosel'skii and Paevskii), we observe a different positive or negative balance; the over-all difference, however, is even greater (787,000 for the groups over the age of seven).

Source: *Sotsialisticheskoe stroitel'stvo SSSR (Socialist Construction in the USSR)*, Moscow, 1932.

TABLE X

POPULATION TOTALS ON 1 JANUARY1939

(IN MILLIONS OF PEOPLE)

Age Group	1939 Census Data	Estimate using 1926 Census	Difference
0-7	31.7	—	—
8-11	16.5	—	—
12-14	13.4	11.8	1.6
15-19	15.2	16.2	-1
20-29	30.9	31.9	-1
30-39	25.5	26.2	-0.7
40-49	15.3	16.7	-1.4
50-59	11	11.9	-0.9
60 +	11.2	13.1	-1.9
Tot. 15 +	109.1	116	-6.9

Source: 'Predvaritel'nye itogi perepisi 1939 g' (Preliminary Summary of the 1939 Census), *Planovoe Khozyaistvo*, 6, 1939.

The subdivision by age group in the official publication neither includes the inhabitants of the remote areas (1.2 million), nor 0.2 million people who have crept into CSU publications in the last few years. These 1.4 million have been spread throughout the different age groups, proportional to their importance.

TABLE XI

POPULATION TOTALS BY SEX AND BY AGE IN 1959

(IN THOUSANDS OF PEOPLE)

Age Group	Est.	Men Census	Diff.	Est.	Women Census	Diff.
20-24	10,058	10,056	2	10,126	10,287	-161
25-29	9,281	8,917	364	9,475	9,273	202
30-34	11,172	8,611	2,561	11,282	10,388	894
35-39	7,867	4,528	3,339	8,268	7,062	1,206
40-44	6,825	3,998	2,827	7,510	6,410	1,100
45-49	7,905	4,706	3,199	8,649	7,558	1,091

Age Group	Est.	Men Census	Diff.	Est.	Women Census	Diff.
50-54	6,531	4,010	2,521	7,030	6,437	593
55-59	4,748	2,905	1,843	6,052	5,793	259
60-69	5,444	4,099	1,345	7,617	7,637	–20
70 +	3,285	2,540	745	6,046	5,432	614
Tot. 20 +	73,116	54,370	18,746	82,055	76,276	5,779

The total of men and women, according to our estimate, is 24,525,000 more than the census.

TABLE XII

IMBALANCE OF THE MALE POPULATION IN RELATION TO THE FEMALE POPULATION, BY AGE GROUP, IN 1959. IN %

	25-29	30-34	35-39	40-44	45-49	50-54	55-59	60-69	70-+
RSFSR	2	16	37	38	40	43	55	53	60
Ukraine	7	22	37	40	39	36	46	44	51
Byelorussia	13	26	35	41	39	32	45	42	50
Uzbekistan	7	3	30	34	23	17	37	23	20
Kazakhstan	–5	12	32	31	30	28	48	34	35
Kirghizie	5	10	31	32	26	29	50	32	27
Tadjikistan	9	0	23	27	10	16	29	21	22
Turkmenie	5	8	30	30	22	23	41	24	20
Armeinia	6	5	31	32	25	19	37	26	29
Azerbaidjan	1	3	29	33	23	29	47	29	40
Georgia	9	10	34	37	26	25	44	28	28
Lithuania	12	25	26	30	33	–2	28	30	49
Moldavia	14	19	22	21	17	16	36	40	46
Latvia	8	30	37	32	26	23	36	46	52
Estonia	9	25	35	30	31	32	38	48	59
USSR	4	17	36	38	38	38	50	46	53

The number of men and women in the Republics reflects the losses, the migrations and certain national idiosyncracies, as well as the greater number of men than women in the Moslem regions before the war.

Source: 1. *Itogi vsesoyuznoi perepisi naseleniya 1959 g. (Results of the 1959 Population Census in the USSR),* Moscow, 1962.

Men	Germany [a]			USSR				
	1941	1943	1944	1941	1942	1943	1944	1945
Age [b]								
Born before 1939	—	—	—	88	87	86	85	84
65 and over	—	—	—	3.2	3.2	3.5	3.6	3.7
14-16	—	—	—	7.2	7.5	7.6	7.5	7.3
17-65	—	—	—	54.5	55.9	57.3	58.6	60.3
46-50	—	—	—	3.6	3.8	3.9	4.3	4.5
17-45	—	18.5	19	43.4	44.5	45.1	46.4	48.2
18-36	—	—	—	31.1	31.6	32.2	32.8	33.6
In liberated areas								
17-65	—	—	—	41.5	42	43.3	55	60.3
17-45	—	—	—	34	34.5	34.8	44	48.2
17-45 able bodied [c]	—	15.8	17	30.5	31	31.5	40	43
Occupations [d]								
Workers and Employees	—	15.5	13.5	25	10	10	12	13
Farmers	—	—	—	17	8	6.5	8	8
Teachers	—	—	—	2	1	1	1.5	1.5
Other	—	—	—	2	1.5	1.5	1.5	
Army [e]								
Mobilised[1]	7.5	—	13-15	18	23	28	32	—
Armed Forces	7.5	9.8	10.7	11	12	14	14	13.7
Active Army	3.8	3.4	2.7	4.2	6.1	6.5	6.5	7
Losses [f]								
Killed[1]	0.17	0.34	1.8	1.2	2.4	3.5	5	5.5
Wounded[1]	0.62	1.2	4.4	2.5	6.5	10.5	16	18
Died following wounds[1]	—	—	0.2	0.2	0.4	0.6	0.9	1
Demobilised[1]	—	—	2.2	0.8	1.8	2.8	4.2	4.7
Wounded and hospitalised	0.1	0.2	0.4	0.4	0.8	1	1.3	0.5
Sick and hospitalised	—	0.2	0.3	0.4	0.6	0.5	0.5	0.5

Men	Germany			USSR				
	1941	1943	1944	1941	1942	1943	1944	1945
Recovered	—	0.4	0.6	0.6	1.2	1.4	1.7	1
Prisoners[g]	0.04	0.07	1.9	3	4	4.2	4.3	—
Definite Losses	0.3	0.5	5.9	5.2	8.6	11.1	14.4	7.5
Provisional losses	—	—	1.3	1.4	2.6	2.9	3.5	—

1. Cumulative from the beginning of the war.

a. The data for the German population has been taken from the documents of the German military command [1, 2, 3].

b. The figure for the age groups between 1941 and 1945 has been calculated from the 1939 census, i.e., it has already taken into account the 'natural death'. The real figure was apparently smaller, since between 1939 and 1941 the mortality rate of the population was higher (camps, Finnish war). The number of men between 17 and 65 in the German occupied territory in 1941 was approximately 22 million. A decree of the Praesidium of the Supreme Soviet of the USSR, dated 22 June, announced the conscription of all men born between 1905 and 1918 in fourteen military regions [4]. The swift German advance impeded the mobilisation: some of those called did not manage to show up (especially in rural areas), others could not be evacuated, and others who were already in the army were dispersed to their homes, (particularly the Ukrainian units fighting in the Ukraine). In fear of desertion the Latvian and Lithuanian units were dissolved [5]. There were in all probability not more than 9 million men between 17 and 65, of whom 7.5 million called up for military service had fled from the occupied *oblasti*. The number of those called up in 1944 shows the size of the male population living in occupied territory.

c. 85.9 per cent of those wounded were less than 40 [15], which clearly indicates the proportion of these age groups in the active army. The percentage of those fit for military service was very high (about 90 per cent, mainly due to the considerable number of volunteers (4 million) [6]. In the German army in 1942, 85 per cent of those called up who were aged between 18 and 45, were considered fit for service, and in 1945 it was almost 90 per cent [1].

d. The economy demanded specialists. At the beginning of 1943, 15.5 million men were employed in the German economy (of whom 5.5 million were fit for active service, but who were instead mobilised locally as skilled men or specialists). Furthermore 6.3 million foreigners were made to work. In 1944 the number of men with special skills fell to 4.1 million [1, 14]. The employment structure of the USSR before the war, established using the data from the 1939 census [10], is shown in the table as 1941. Between 1942 and 1945, the number of workers and employees in the whole country was between 19 and 29 million [9, 13] of whom between 10 and 12 million were men [11, 12]. Men constituted 29 per cent of the active population involved in agriculture in 1942. In 1945 men between 18 and 54 made up only 8.3 of the rural population [9].

e. We include in the number of those mobilised all men between 17 and 65 who were not working in industry. The camps, aptitude for military service and special assignments greatly reduced the contingent, which had already been weakened by the losses between 1939 and 1941.

By fighting forces, the figures for which are listed in *IVOVSS*, we mean the army (377 divisions in 1945), and the navy. The armed forces also included: the anti-aircraft defence, 4.7 of the total numbers [9]; the airforce, by the end of the war larger and probably more powerful than the German airforce (The German VVS numbered 1.9 million men in 1943) [1]; the health staff (200,000 doctors and 500,000 nurses) [16]; the staff of the military schools (323,000 in Germany in November 1944) [1] and their pupils (The Red Army recruited around 500,000 officers per year, 2.5 million men had received some sort of military training before their call up) [9]; the administrative and rail staff (for whom it is difficult to suggest an accurate figure); the garrisons and troops stationed abroad (in the Far East, in the Caucasus, in Iran); the reserve troops (general headquarters provided for the different fronts tens and even hundreds of divisions from the reserves) [3]. At the time of the 1943-5 offensives, the army at the front was completely renewed, which required a huge reserve. From the end of 1942 onwards a large part of these forces were made up of units withdrawn from the front (either to make up the numbers, or for reorganisation or because of the need for rest). It seems that the over-all total of men in the Red Army (and the German army too) was several times the number of the forces involved on the ground.

f. The losses resulting from wounds were much higher than the number of men killed (They were six times more in the Russian and German armies during the First World War [2, 17]. In 1944 on the western front the loss ratio was 1 to 5 or 6 for the Germans). The loss ratio of wounded and killed in the German army on the eastern front was 3:4-3:7 in 1941-2 [2], 3:6 in 1944 [1], i.e., the ratio is more or less the same whether the army is on the attack or in retreat. Sovinformbiuro information shows that the ratio in the Red Army, even at the beginning of the war, was roughly identical. In November 1941 the figures were 230,000 killed and 720,000 wounded, i.e., a ratio of 3:1 [4]. A great number of wounded soldiers, however, were left on the battlefield at the beginning of the war. This is what explains the relatively low mortality during the first twenty-four hours following the wound: in 1941, 24.4 per cent of the total died from wounds; this percentage went up to 44-5 per cent in the second and third year of the war; and up to 56.4 per cent in the fourth year [18]. Research has shown that even in 1943, only 52.2 per cent of those mortally wounded were killed on the spot, the others either died as a result of haemorrhage or other causes [8]. The stabilisation of the front line and the improvements in the health service lead us to believe that the ratio between wounded and killed amongst Soviet troops was the same as that amongst German troops during the second half of the war. For 1941 and 1942 lower coefficients were adopted in the table.

The number of seriously wounded increased as the war went on, due to improvements in both the evacuation facilities from the battlefield and medical care. During the first six months of 1942, 13 per cent of the wounded

271

underwent some form of surgery; this percentage increased to 32 per cent in 1943, 53 per cent in 1944 and 57 per cent in 1945 [19]. The death rate in the evacuation hospitals, where the number of wounded men placed ranged from 65 per cent in 1942 to 35 per cent in 1944, was 1.1 per cent and 0.7 per cent respectively [24]. Given that of the soldiers who died from their wounds, between 75 per cent and 90 per cent died within the first seventy-two hours, i.e., before their arrival in hospital, one can estimate the mortality rate in the Red Army to be about 5 per cent of the wounded. It was virtually the same for the Germans.

The sick represented 34.7 per cent of the total losses caused by defects in health and medical care (between 28.1 per cent and 39.2 per cent according to the period) [20]. From the official records we know that the death-rate amongst the sick was extremely low. 90.6 per cent of the sick and 72.3 per cent of the wounded resumed military activity. These figures are the pride and glory of Soviet medicine and they are constantly remembered [18, 23]. However because of their apparently sacred character there is no attempt to obtain any proof or confirmation. In the several volumes of the *Encyclopaedia* devoted to the effects of the war [22], it is stated that 'The number of wounded men who resumed military activity during the great patriotic war was, according to official sources, over 70 per cent.' It is well known, though, that 'official data' is never queried and no proof is provided. Considering the period in which these figures were published, the fact that they were never varied during the course of the war [32] and their discrepancy when compared to overall figures, one has to treat them with caution (according to the Soviet data, the figure for the Germans was 40 per cent [33], and 50 per cent for the Russian army during the First World War, even though the wounds were often not so serious).

During the war years, 2,990 evacuation hospitals were created, with 1,340,000 beds [16]. With the military hospitals [9 to 35 per cent of the beds] [22] and the health units in the country, overworked as they were (sometimes the demand was between 2 and 5 times the capacity of the service), at any one time over 2 million people could be treated in hospital. The period of time spent in hospital became gradually longer

(106 days in 1942, 149 in 1945) [23]. Those not seriously wounded, making up 40 per cent of the total number of injured men, recovered more rapidly (between 40 and 50 days [9]. The Health Service treated annually between 5 and 8 million people. Figures of this order are understandable when one considers the number of wounded and sick from the various fronts during the numerous military campaigns. Between October 1941 and April 1942, the number of sick and wounded on the Leningrad front was 353,000; this was more than the total number of soldiers in the front-line units (32 divisions whose complement was then between 35 and 45 per cent, and who incorporated at the same time 180,000 reinforcement troops, 125,000 conscripted soldiers, 30,000 from the navy and 25,000 who came from the surrounded areas) [15]. 'On the first front in the Ukraine, during the first half of 1944 286,000 wounded were recalled when they left hospital. This number was sufficient to complete the numbers of some tens of divisions at the time. The health service on the second front in the Ukraine provided reinforcements during the last couple of years of the war of 1,055,000 recovered soldiers' [15]. Taking into account the casualties evacuated to the hospitals behind the lines (35-40 per cent) [22] and also those who died from their wounds we can say that there were, on those two fronts respectively, around 400,000 and 1.5 million casualties. When extended to the army as a whole fighting on 11 or 12 fronts that would amount to 6 or 8 million wounded each year. Taking into account the differing intensity of the military operations in different areas, we can put forward a figure of between 5 and 7 million wounded. We also know [23] that the daily contingent leaving the hospitals behind the lines was around 2,500 men. At that time, about a third of the wounded were admitted to these hospitals and about half resumed military activity; consequently the total number of wounded reached approximately 4.5 to 5 million.

g. The German generals [2, 24, 25] mention 3.5 to 4 million prisoners at the beginning of the war. 'So at the beginning of 1942 Rosenberg drew Keitel's attention to a scandalous situation: of the 3.6 million Soviet prisoners, only a few hundred thousand were in a fit state to work' [26]. They recalled that the Germans had sent the Ukrainian prisoners back to their homes (this would be between a few hundred thousand and a million). Soviet historians claim the German data to be exaggerated and absurd, but as they in turn move on to list the Fascist atrocities, they claim the following numbers died in prison: in Byelorussia, 810,000 men [9], in the Ukraine, 1.3 million [15], in Lithuania, 165,000 [4]; in Poland, 434,000 died and 63,000 escaped [27]; in Latvia and Estonia, hundreds of thousands [5]. Moreover, of the 5.7 million who were repatriated or who did not return home [4], about 3 million, as has been noted above, were submitted to forced labour and so nearly 3 million were prisoners of war.

Trying to pull together both the Western and Soviet point of view, the historian Calvacoresi has written: 'All in all, the Germans took about 5.5 million Soviet officers and soldiers prisoner. In the middle of 1944, 3.5 million were either dead or killed, 800,000 had been freed, one million were employed in productive work who were either non-Russians or willing to work for the Germans' [28]. Several hundred thousand Soviets served in the German auxiliary troops (between 0.7 and a million) [29]. We know the size of the Vlasov army (about 50,000 men) [30], the Cossack section, the Estonian and Latvian legions (6,500 and 15,000 men in 1942) [30], the Caucasian legion (110,000 men), the Tatars from the Volga (35,000 to 40,000 men), the Crimean Tatars (20,000 men), and the Kalmuks (5,000 men) [31]. The hostile attitude of the Fascists towards the problems of the Soviet nationalities did not allow these units to play an important part. These losses amongst these troops and the mortality of the prisoners of war in the camps seem to be near a million (many of the prisoners were wounded). We add to that figure the military losses.

[1] *Voenno-istoricheskii zhurnal,* 4, 1959; 5, 1960; 12, 1965; 9, 1968.

[2] *Dnevik nachal'nika General'nogo shtaba sukhoputnykh voisk Germanii gen. Gal'dera za peroid avgust 1939-sentyabr' 1942 g. (Diary of General Halder, the Commanding Officer of the German Infantry, August 1939-September 1942),* Moscow, 1-2, 1959.

[3] *Vtoraya mirovaya voina, Voenno iskusstvo (The Second World War, Military Art)* Moscow, 1966.

[4] *Vneshnaya politika Sovetskogo soyuza v period velikoi otechestvennoi voiny (The Foreign Policy of the Soviet Union during the Great Patriotic War),* Moscow, 1, 1949.

[5] *Istoriya Latviiskoi SSR (History of the Latvian Republic),* Riga, 1971.

Population Losses in the USSR 1918-1958

Istoriya velikoi otechestvennoi voiny Sovetskogo soyuza 1941-45 gg. (History of the Great Patriotic War of the Soviet Union) / (IVOVSS), Moscow, 2.

[7] *IVOVSS*, 3.

[8] *IVOVSS*, 4.

[9] *IVOVSS*, 6.

[10] *Itogi vsesoyuznoi perepisi naseleniya 1959 g. (Results of the 1959 Census of the Soviet Population)*, Moscow, 1962.

[11] N. Voznesenskii, *Voennaya ekonomika SSSR v period otechestvennoi voiny (The War Economy of the USSR during the Patriotic War)* Moscow, 1948.

[12] A. V. Mitrofanova, *Rabochii klass Sovetskogo Soyuza v pervyi period Velikoi otechestvennoi voiny 1941-2 gg. (The Working Class in the Soviet Union during the First Part of the Great Patriotic War, 1941-2)*, Moscow, 1960.

[13] E. D. Grazhdannikov, *Prognosticheskie modeli sotsial'no-demografìcheskikh protsessov (Forecasting Models in Socio-demography)*, Novosibirsk, 1974.

[14] V. I. Dashichev, *Bankrotstvo strategii germanskogo fasizma (The Bankruptcy of the Strategy of Fascist Germany)*, Moscow, 1973.

[15] *Vtoraya mirovaya voina, op.cit.*, 'Obshchie problemy'.

[16] *Sovetskaya medetsina*, 5, 1975.

[17] V. Avraamov, 'Zhertvy imperialisticheskoi voiny v Rossii' ('The Victims of the Imperialist War in Russia'), *Izvestiya Narkomata zdravookhraneniya*, 1-2, 1920.

[18] *Opyt sovetskoi meditsiny v velikoi otechestvennoi voiny 1941-5 gg. (Soviet Medicine during the Great Patriotic War 1941-5)*, Moscow, 35.

[19] *Organizatsiya zdravookhraneniya v SSSR (The Organisation of Public Health in the USSR)*, Moscow, 1962.

[20] A. A. Vishnevskii, 'Proshloe i nastoyashchee sovetskoi voenno-polevoi khirurgii' ('Surgery in Campaigns, Past and Present'), *Sovetskaya meditsina*, 5, 1975.

[21] V. D. Kuvshinskii 'Voenno-polevaya terapiya i sovremennye problemy sovetskoi meditsiny' ('Therapy in Wartime and the Contemporary Problems of Soviet Medicine'), *Terapevticheskii arkhiv*, 5, 1975.

[22] *Opyt sovetskoi meditsiny, op.cit.*, 1.

[23] *Trudy 4-go plenuma gospital'nogo soveta (Work of the 4th Plenum of the Hospitals Council)*, Moscow, 1946.

[24] *Rokovye resheniya (Fatal Decisions)*, Moscow, 1958.

[25] K. Tippel'skirkh, *Istoriya vtoroi mirovoi voiny (History of the Second World War)*, Moscow, 1956.

[26] A. Vert, *Rossiya v voine 1941-5 gg. (Russia during the 1941-5 War)*, Moscow, 1967.

[27] *Voprosy istorii*, 2, 1961.

[28] R. Calvacoresi, *Total'naya voina. Prichiny i sledstviya vtoroi mirovoi voiny (The Total War. The Causes and Consequences of the Second World War)*, Rome, 1972.

[29] R. Gelen, *Sluzba. Vospominaniya 1942-71 gg.* (Service. Memoirs from 1942 to 1971), Mayence-Wiesbaden, 1971.

[30] D. Littlejohn, *Patrioty-predateli. Istoriya kollaboratsionizma v okkupirovannoi Germaniei Evropy 1940-5 gg. (The Patriot Traitors. History of Collaboration in German-Occupied Europe, 1940-5)*, New York, 1972.

[31] P. Milen, *Mezhdu svastikoi i sovetskoi zvezdoi. Natsionalizm sovetsikh narodov vo vremya Vtoroi mirovoi voiny (Between the Swastika and the Soviet Star. Nationalism of the Soviet People during the Second World War)*, Dusseldorf, 1971. (German)

[32] *Vo glave zashchitu sovetskoi rodiny (Leading the Defence of the Soviet Nation)*, Moscow, 1975.

TABLE XIV

RESULTS OF THE ESTIMATE OF THE LOSSES IN POPULATION

BETWEEN 1918 AND 1958

(IN MILLIONS OF PEOPLE)

	1918	1922	1926	1927	1932	1938	1939	1949	1958	Total
Population total	140.9		112.6	147.1		122.5	190.6		130.7	
Annexation		2.6					23			
Fall	30.9				24.6		63		118.5	
Departure	3.5							3		6.5
Natural Death:	9.2		7.9	8.9		8.2	21.1	14.4*		69.7
Men	4.7		4.1	4.6		4.2	10.5	7.7		35.8
Women	4.5		3.8	4.3		4	10.6	6.7		33.9
Losses:	10.3					7.5	24.5*			42.3
Men	6.2					5	18.7			29.9
Women	4.1					2.5	5.8			12.4
Losses Curve	10-15					7-10		21-29		38-54*
Increase due to birth-rate		34.5			48.1		78.2			
Census Total				147.1			170.6	208.8		

* The actual mortality rate between 1950-58 was 2.9 million lower than the forecasted figure, and consequently the losses have been that much greater. We have not included this correction, since we suspect that the 1950 population figure is reached with less accuracy than the 1959 figure (taken from the census) and it also seems a little dangerous to diverge from the minimum estimate.

For the periods 1918-26 and 1927-38 we take into account those alive in 1929, and for the period 1939-59 those alive in 1939. Infant mortality between the beginning and end of a period, i.e., after 1926 and 1938, has not been taken into account. As has been noted in the text, infant mortality during certain periods has been very important, being about 3 million between 1932 and 1934, for example.

On A. D. Sakharov's Book 'My Country and the World'

ROY MEDVEDEV

Translated by M. Colenso

Academician Sakharov's political views have changed significantly in the last seven or eight years, and this has recently
brought him back into the sphere of political publishing. I
refer to Sakharov's book *My Country and the World*, which
appeared in the West in 1975. This short work is not a piece
of research, nor does it claim to present a scientific analysis of
current problems. Indeed, Sakharov admits 'how poorly
qualified he is to probe complex questions of social relations'
(p. 7). Unlike Solzhenitsyn, Sakharov does not speak as a
prophet who claims to hold the key to all the world's
problems. His book has none of the virulence and frenzied
incisiveness which are so typical of Solzhenitsyn's recent
utterances. This book is written rather in the vein of an
exhortation than of a demand, and the author comes across as
extremely gentle and well-meaning, but no less irreconcilable
to evil in whatever form it manifests itself.

Anyone studying the problems of international relations or
of Soviet society will find in Sakharov's book not only a
number of bold judgements, interesting arguments and
justifiable criticism, but also a great many one-sided, tendentious and plainly erroneous statements. He or she will be
struck by the *naïveté* of Sakharov's standpoint on certain
difficult issues and by the lack of what is normally referred to
as 'sober realism'.

If *My Country and the World* had been published anonymously or under a pseudonym, it would probably not have attracted much attention. Neither in this work nor in his earlier articles and 'memoranda' has the author produced any original political concepts. Much of what he writes may be found much more concisely expressed in the works of other, mainly Western authors. Sakharov himself refers in his introduction to the works of 'noble and profound thinkers – physicists and mathematicians, economists, lawyers, public figures, philosophers' such as Einstein, Bertrand Russell, N. Bohr and R. Cassen. In his Nobel lecture Sakharov speaks of Schweitzer, the German physician, humanist and philosopher. One could add to these names that of the great American-Russian sociologist Pitirim Sorokin or the American mathematician A. Rapoport. In the final analysis Sakharov neither is nor claims to be a political thinker. But then the right to express one's views and debate the political issues of the moment is surely not the sole prerogative of professional politicians.

Sakharov's great virtue is his courageous and unrelenting struggle for man's freedom, for the recognition of Soviet citizens' elementary democratic rights, and his defence of political prisoners. Whilst being one of today's most eminent physicists and a front-ranking contributor to Soviet science – both in the creation of the Soviet hydrogen bomb and in various non-military areas of nuclear energy use – Sakharov has neglected his status and privileges for the cause of human rights in the USSR and in other countries. This effort, combined with a relentless campaign for peace and international *rapprochement,* was justly crowned at the end of 1975 with the award of the Nobel Peace Prize. It is precisely because Sakharov's voice will now ring louder in everyone's ears, both at home and abroad, that I consider it important to appraise critically the political content of Sakharov's book.

Where Sakharov is right

There are many points on which I cannot agree with Sakharov, and I shall return to these. Any objective evaluation of his book, however, should begin not with criticism, but with a list of those points on which one must agree with the author. Can one refute, for example, Sakharov's descriptions of the crimes of Stalinism and the horrors of the terrorism which prevailed in our country during the Stalin years? Can we doubt Sakharov when he asserts that many remnants of that regime have survived into the present, that Soviet society remains in many respects closed and undemocratic? Can we seriously challenge his criticism of the Soviet electoral system and of the harsh, indiscriminate censorship of political, scientific and artistic works? Can we disagree with his comments on the excessive brutality of the Soviet penitentiary system, the systematic infringement of many basic civil and political rights and freedoms such as the freedom of the press and of speech, freedom of political association and the freedom to receive and distribute information?

We cannot argue with Sakharov's statements concerning the harsh treatment of the Crimean Tartars, the Volga Germans and the Meskhi, discrimination against the Jews and the government's disregard for certain important aspects of the national life of various other minority groups. Sakharov rightly speaks out for the removal of all artificial barriers to the free exchange of information and ideas and personal freedom of movement. He has clearly never been opposed to a détente based on growing trust between all countries and peoples and on a *rapprochement* of all the parts of our fragmented world. Neither in his book *My Country and the World*, nor in his Nobel lecture, does Sakharov challenge the basic ideas and proposals of the Helsinki conference on security and collaboration in Europe. The Soviet press is clearly deceiving its readers when it presents Sakharov as an opponent of the All-European Conference in Helsinki. 'The final act passed at the Helsinki conference', declared Sakharov in his Nobel lecture,

is especially important for us because it is the first official formulation of the only viable approach to problems of international security. It goes far in establishing the connection between international security and the protection of human rights, of the free exchange of information and of personal freedom of movement, and the important obligations of member-countries towards the guarantee of these rights. We are not, of course, talking about a guaranteed result, but about new possibilities which may be realised through the persistent and systematic efforts of all the member-countries working on a unified and consistent basis ...

Where, then, is Sakharov's denial of the importance of the Helsinki conference? Where is his affirmation of Solzhenitsyn, who in the summer of 1975 so vehemently attacked the very idea of an All-European conference and labelled President Ford's visit to Helsinki as 'treachery'.

We cannot refute what Sakharov says about mutual and balanced arms limitation, especially on the missile and nuclear side. Moreover, he is dealing here with problems about which he knows far more than the average newspaper reader. Unlike Solzhenitsyn, Sakharov never mocks the Western liberal and left-wing radical intelligentsia. Whilst criticising the mistakes which it makes, he stresses the reasonableness, the inner honesty and altruism of the main body of the Western intelligentsia. One can only welcome Sakharov's appeal for demilitarisation, an end to arms supplies to under-developed countries, for internationalism and national altruism, for increased economic and cultural aid for the Third World.

Although Sakharov on a number of occasions paints an excessively gloomy picture of Soviet provincial life (there are not *that* many villages and settlements where the working day begins in a long bread queue, or where the whole neighbourhood heads straight for the shop because there's some frozen cod to be had), he is quite right about the scanty provision of food products and consumer goods to provincial towns and villages. The Italian correspondent from *Giorno* newspaper who wrote an open letter to his Chief Editor (*Za rubezhom* No. 45, 1975), praising Moscow's milk and butter, should have talked to inhabitants of Kalinin, Kaluga, Kursk and other regional centres not so far from Moscow, who often travel to the capital just to stock up with sausage, meat, condensed milk and even good quality macaroni, things which are unavailable in their own shops.

Sakharov is absolutely right when he says that the Soviet economy is over-stretched and devoid of reserves, when he talks about the rape of nature, bad hospital facilities and growing alcoholism. He is quite justified in his criticism of excessive centralised state control of the economy, the lack of autonomy in even the larger industrial enterprises and on Collective and State Farms. He is right to condemn the various forms of persecution against non-conformers and the political repression which, although noticeably scaled down, continues to weigh heavy in the life of our society. Although not himself a religious person, he laments the degradation of all religions, churches and sects.

In the final part of his book Sakharov tries to offer a positive programme of democratic reform. Although one could argue on some of the twelve points he proposes, his programme as a whole is quite sound. I personally feel that in the present phase of centralisation and huge-scale production the freedom to strike is not the foremost requirement for democratisation. It is much more important to guarantee all working people the right to assemble and to demonstrate and petition. But Sakharov's programme evokes in me and my colleagues sympathy rather than objection.

Sakharov's book does, however, contain a lot of rationalisations and suggestions which are either tendentious or incorrect. It is these which mainly give cause for the sharp attacks which he suffers in both the Soviet and the Western Communist press.

The lack of objectivity and the tendentiousness and partiality of Sakharov's judgements

Concluding his survey of Soviet society today, Sakharov himself remarks: 'This chapter has turned out, by our usual standards, rather "malign". In the agonising hours after work I occasionally feel an involuntary twinge of uneasiness, almost shame. Am I really fighting this cause?' (p. 36.)

I think that Sakharov is fighting a very important and useful cause. The normal functioning of our socialist society demands criticism – resolute criticism which does not retract

itself in the face of countless taboos, criticism which embraces every aspect of our life and all levels of our state
government. I consciously omit to qualify criticism here by
the words 'responsible', 'objective' or 'just'. In the first place
our society became accustomed, over the long years of Stalin's
terror and Krushchev's period of 'subjectivism', to keeping
quiet and acquiescing, while our leaders, studiously protected
from any checking or criticism from below, forgot how to
listen calmly to words of criticism and react reasonably. Thus,
even the more just and calm criticism comes to be regarded as
'malign'. Secondly, many people have over the same period
forgotten how to criticise. And now, when some of them have
broken their vow of silence and are beginning to censure the
shortcomings of our society, their criticism often emerges as
excessively biased, tendentious and subjective. This sort of
criticism then becomes even easier to destroy, by labelling it
'slander' and 'calumny'. This is exactly what happens so often
to Sakharov.

It is not that Sakharov deliberately focuses his attention on
the negative aspects of Soviet life and its shortcomings and
gives only passing credit to its undisputed achievements. Any
criticism naturally looks primarily to the shortcomings. It is
more a question of the 'accents' which Sakharov places on his
critical rationalisations. And although he does not in the
majority of cases violate the truth, his book might paint not
merely a one-sided, but an incorrect picture of Soviet life for
many of its readers abroad. Sakharov unwittingly uses the
same simplistic jargon which Soviet propaganda typically uses
when it talks about the West. Let us take an area in which the
Soviet Union has made enormous strides: housing. There are
different ways of describing the successes achieved in this
area. One could mention, for example, that in the twenty
years from 1956 to 1976 the housing stock increased by just
over two thousand million square metres of habitable space,
that in excess of fifty million apartments were built, that over
85 per cent of town dwellers improved their housing conditions and that not less than 70 per cent of families now have
their own apartment. One might write that the quality of
apartments and of housing construction generally had greatly
improved over these two decades, that the planning of

apartment blocks and the services had become more rational, and that public transport now functioned better, and so on. One would have to say, of course, that the quality of housing in the USSR still lagged behind Western standards, that each person in the USSR had less living space than in the USA or Western Europe, that the telephone system was inadequate, that there were many instances of abuse in the system of apartment allocation, that the architectural style of most new housing was shabby and unexpressive, and that many construction problems still needed to be solved. Sakharov, however, opens his comments on Soviet housing with a list of its shortcomings. He states that not all families yet have their own apartment, that getting one is a matter of chance which for many families takes a lifetime. He observes that even in family apartments not every member of the family has his or her own room, and that domestic services in the USSR are even worse than those in the 'homes of poor families' in the USA (not a very convincing statement from someone who has never seen these 'homes of poor families'). Sakharov notes only in passing that 'a great deal of construction work is going on' in Soviet towns. To attempt to reach a true picture of the housing situation in the USSR from Sakharov's book would be a risky matter. By getting carried away with criticism, Sakharov commits certain glaring inaccuracies and errors. He writes, for example, 'It is not true that our country has the cheapest housing prices in the world. The cost per square metre in terms of the average wage is no lower than in the majority of developed countries' (p.15). Sakharov does not give any evidence or calculations in support of this dubious statement. Firstly, it is false to talk about an 'average wage' without mentioning apartment rent levels in absolute figures. Even communal flats in the USSR are two to three times cheaper than *similar* flats in the West. As for state-owned apartments, rent rarely accounts for more than 10-12 per cent of any family's budget. This rent does not cover even a half of the total cost to the state for building and services. Rent levels in the USSR are certainly lower than in the West both absolutely and relatively, and the same may be said of the majority of communal facilities: gas, heating, lighting, public transport fares, postage and other amenities.

It does Sakharov no credit to deny these facts. His calculations of average earnings in the USSR and the USA are also highly spurious. Everyone knows that an American worker earns considerably more than his Soviet counterpart. But for the sake of remaining objective we must mention the high levels of state and local taxation in the USA, high property taxes, large deductions for social insurance, a higher level of inflation than in the USSR, huge rents and expensive and inadequate public transport which makes a private car a necessary evil rather than a luxury.

Sakharov is plainly wrong when he says that neither education nor medical services are free in the USSR because the whole society pays for them. Schools and hospitals and the means to finance their staffing cannot, after all, be created out of nothing. This was well understood by those socialists who in the last century campaigned for the abolition of medical and schooling fees. This demand implied by its nature that society as a whole must foot the bill for education and health services. Hospitals and schools would not send bills to their clients, and the less well-off families and those with few children would thus be able to receive the treatment they needed at state expense. Whilst this has come about in the socialist countries, the quality of education and health services leaves much to be desired, as Sakharov says. In his book, alas, he is equally tendentious and subjective about the state of Soviet science and many other aspects of the life of Soviet society.

The futility of theoretical reasoning

I doubt whether Sakharov would approve the efforts of someone who, without having any knowledge in the field of modern theoretical physics, boldly proceeded to discuss the nature of elementary particles, magnetic fields or quanta. In his book, however, Sakharov launches into a discussion of theoretical problems of society about which he has not even an approximate idea. He uncritically adopts the view of a number of Western ideologists in stating, for example, that 'modern Soviet society can best be summed up as a society under state capitalism'. He asserts that the Soviet party elite is 'virtually inalienable' and 'has lately become hereditary' (p. 19). He later goes on to talk about the socialist countries and about socialist society without putting the word 'socialist' in inverted commas. Moreover, at the end of his book he answers the question 'What is socialism?' by honestly declaring 'I don't know.' But does he know what state capitalism is? Obviously not. He does not even trouble to give evidence of the 'inalienable' or 'hereditary' nature of the party elite. I do not intend here to argue a Marxist position with him, since he now condemns Marxism. I shall merely refer to an article by Yu. Orlov, a friend of Sakharov who also does not consider himself a Marxist. The article, entitled 'Is Untotalitarian Socialism Possible?', contains many contentious points. Orlov is right, however, when he says that 'the special nature of so-called state ownership consists particularly in the fact that personal profit is not the motive behind the leaders' activities'. He argues that the control of production in the USSR and the 'monopolisation of initiative' are not hereditary, and for this reason the elite of the state apparatus is merely a temporary holder of state property. The share of profit which passes to the private use of this collective owner is thus relatively small. Orlov sees Soviet society not as one of 'state capitalism' but as a 'society of totalitarian socialism'. A transition from the present form of 'totalitarian socialism' to a humane, democratic socialism will, he says, be difficult, but possible. These formulations are closer to reality than Sakharov's implausible theorising.

It is even more realistic to describe Soviet society as one of 'state socialism' or 'state-bureaucratic socialism'. The majority of nineteenth-century socialists thought that a socialist society would be a society without the state and would not need any political compulsion. This view was shared by the Marxists, who recognised the importance of a socialist state or proletarian dictatorship for only a historically brief transitional period during which the growth of socialist relations and the withering of the state would take place as parallel processes. 'The proletariat needs only a withering state,' wrote Lenin just several months before the October Revolution, 'i.e., a state so constructed that it would immediately begin to erode and could not resist this process'. In reality the October Revolution created a state which not only failed to 'immediately erode', but which continued for many decades to grow steadily more complex and powerful. It was natural that the fabric of socialist society in the USSR should have become distorted in many ways by the existence of an all-powerful state with a sizeable bureaucracy and a strong military and police machine. The removal of these distortions is not helped at all by the existence of a single political party whose ruling elite has fused with the ruling elite of the state apparatus. This type of 'state socialism' inevitably embodies features of both true socialism and bogus socialism. It may bear some affinity with state capitalism, but this is more a superficial affinity than an inner identity. Sakharov and his adherents, unfortunately, see only this purely superficial side of the questions they raise.

Sakharov's idealisation of the West and of Western democracies

In the third chapter of his book, 'Problems of Disarmament', Sakharov rightly stresses the special importance of creating a variety of means for policing disarmament or arms limitation agreements. He does not, however, tire of repeating that even when a checking system has been established, the West cannot trust the Soviet Union until an 'open' and democratic society has been created. 'The Nixon-Brezhnev and Ford-Brezhnev agreements', writes Sakharov,

> are very important. But I want to stress first and foremost the parts of them which seem to me inconclusive, even dangerous. Speaking generally, they pay insufficient attention to policing problems, they fail to appreciate fully the peculiarities of our totalitarian state and the potential of its strategic secrecy. The Soviet side has in all negotiations on disarmament consistently taken a very hard line on questions of policing. This hard (and ultimately unreasonable) line must be contrasted with the resoluteness of the West which is based on real strength and goodwill.

[pp. 45-6]

I do not wish to dispute the importance of the policing of existing or future agreements on disarmanent. The Soviet line on this matter has often appeared to me to be hard and unreasonable. If the desire for disarmament is genuine, then why put up so many artificial barriers to effective checking? And if the checking were equal on both sides, then why put considerations of state prestige and fears of espionage in its way? It is quite obvious, however, that the question of thorough and effective checking is real not just because of the 'closedness' of Soviet society. We may suppose that an 'open' country like the USA cannot conduct many secret processes and manoeuvres which her own or the foreign public do not get to hear about sooner or later. The recent exposure of a number of secret acts of the CIA and FBI confirms this. But those who see such exposures as one of the strengths of American democracy should not forget that many of the deeds of the CIA and FBI which are now coming to light actually took place ten or even fifteen years ago. Of course, freedom of the press in the USA made it easy for D. Elsberg and the New York Times to publish a great deal of secret material from the Pentagon. Clearly, such publicity is impossible and unthinkable in the USSR. But even in the United States, Elsberg's revelations demonstrate not only the strength but also the weakness of independent public opinion and an independent press. They show just how many crucial decisions and actions which affect the life of the nation can be kept secret from both the American public and from Congress. We must presume also that the Pentagon, the White House, the CIA and the FBI have made their own conclusions from these discomforting revelations and will now be more careful about guarding their secrets. One should not overstate the 'openness' of American society or of Western society in general; in many cases this is no more than a common myth sustained by propaganda. In Western Europe recent decades have seen the continuing growth of huge monopolies and supra-national corporations whose activities and decisions are especially carefully protected by a cloak of secrecy. Some of these corporations have a budget which exceeds that of Belgium or the Netherlands. They sometimes operate their own 'foreign policy' by organising not only political campaigns but even *coups d'état*. They expend tens of millions of dollars on bribing individual politicians and even whole political parties and they can carry out a great deal of research and experimentation which is unseen by the public and even by government bodies. Even greater secrecy surrounds the operations of the majority of the large private banks and financial institutions in the West, whose scope for manoeuvre both in economic and political areas should not be underestimated. I believe that in many respects modern Western society is no less 'closed' than Soviet society, and this makes Sakharov's idealisation of Western 'goodwill' and 'openness' not merely a strange illusion, but a dangerous one.

The West, unfortunately, has by no means solved all the problems of political, civil, economic and social rights and freedoms. The matter of policing disarmament and of scrupulously enforcing both existing and future agreements is equally urgent on both sides. Both East and West have far to go in making their social systems more 'open' and democratic.

A word on the 'unfortunate' Hess

I am often asked whether Sakharov's book actually contains the phrase about the sufferings of the 'unfortunate' Hess on which the Soviet press has commented so much. Unfortunately it does, and it is not merely an accidental slip. Sakharov tells us of the sad fate of the teacher Peter Paulitis, a Lithuanian nationalist who was arrested by Hitler's forces during the war for having rescued a group of Jews and sent to an annihilation camp. Subsequently the Soviet authorities sentenced him to twenty-five years' imprisonment, and then a further ten years for publishing a 'nationalist' newspaper. Sakharov proclaims that the fate of such people, 'reminiscent of the lot of prisoners in mediaeval times, and in our time the unfortunate Hess, cannot fail to shock' (p. 32). And so that there can be no suggestion that this comparison is accidental, Sakharov adds that he mentions Hess, 'knowing of his complicity in the cruel workings of Nazism, but believing that life imprisonment is almost equivalent to capital punishment, which I oppose on principle and irrespective of the gravity of the crimes committed' (p. 32).

I do not know what is contained in the charges against Peter Paulitis or his fellow-countryman Ludwig Simutis, whose sentence continues till 1980. But if it is true to say that these are people who are deeply respected by their friends for their honesty and integrity, as Sakharov attests, then any comparison between their fate and that of Hess is, I suggest, totally irresponsible – I feel tempted to say blasphemous. The case of people who suffer for their convictions (Sakharov calls them 'prisoners of conscience') should certainly not be paralleled with the cases of people who are put away for their grave criminal and wartime offences. Capital punishment and life imprisonment are in no way synonymous, and the words 'almost equivalent' do no credit to either the logical or the legal thinking of the author. The majority of Western European countries have long since abolished the death penalty but have retained life imprisonment or sentences of forty, fifty and even ninety-nine years. Several years ago Sakharov, myself and some other scholars signed an address to the Praesidium of the Supreme Soviet of the USSR requesting legislation to abolish the death penalty in the USSR. However, as I remember it, the petition contained a reference to the peacetime conditions of the present day. There are periods in any country when the death penalty seems a just punishment for especially serious crimes. Should one censure the Israelis for their execution of Eichmann, or Krushchev and Bulganin for executing Beria or Abakumov? Can one call the Nuremberg judgements excessively severe? If we adopt Sakharov's formulation, Hitler, Himmler and Goebbels could all have lived freely in our midst had they not decided to commit suicide!

Further on the freedom of emigration

In his new book Sakharov reaffirms his solidarity with American political figures such as Henry Jackson and George Meany and with the US Senate. He brings the question of trade with the USSR in direct line with the question of freedom of emigration from the USSR. He appeals to the US Congress not to make any compromises on this matter, as this would be unforgivable 'capitulation'. He issues the warning that if the American people adopts the line of President Ford or Secretary of State Kissinger, who prefer to make the compromise, 'there will never again be any room for manoeuvre against Soviet blackmail in any other area of détente; the long-term consequences could be terrifying' (p. 41). Sakharov severely censures the European countries and Japan for their lack of support for the US Congress line on emigration and for allowing the USSR the credits originally sought from the USA. He appeals to the whole of Western Europe to keep up the pressure on the USSR on the emigration question, even if this involves accepting temporary restrictions, which would be 'minimal in our terms' (p. 42). Sakharov's attitude on this matter seems strangely to contradict his own principles. At the end of his work he stresses that he is a 'convinced evolutionist and reformist'. He has declared more than once in the past that in the USSR, indeed throughout the world, change can and should only come about gradually, springing not from revolution but from reform. But how can a reformist and evolutionist be against any form of compromise, especially when such a complex problem as the free choice of the country of residence is at issue? How can he demand that the USA and the Western countries adopt an 'all-or-nothing' policy on this question?

Even the introduction of complete freedom of movement within the USSR requires time and gradual change, let alone the freedom to move around the world. As a first step we must distinguish two issues: the right to political refuge and the right to choose one's place of domicile on non-political grounds. At present such great differences in standard of living exist between different countries and continents that it will take several generations to overcome them. Even in Western Europe the present relative freedom of movement and choice of domicile has taken decades, even centuries to evolve, and present levels of migration from one European country to another create quite a few problems. But how should we regard unlimited world-wide migration? Demographers predict, for example, a doubling or trebling of the population over the next thirty years in the poorest countries of Asia, Africa and Latin America. Would not the complete freedom for all people to choose their domicile under these circumstances bring about the destruction of many of the nation states which are economically more advanced? Sakharov makes a special point of the fact that he is in favour of free emigration not only for the Jews, but for people of any nationality and from any totalitarian state. Quite clearly he is very unrealistic about this question.

Sakharov's biggest mistake

Sakharov's biggest – and least forgivable for a Nobel Prizewinner – mistake is his position regarding the war in South-East Asia. In the Introduction to his new book he recalls his famous article 'Reflections on Progress, Peaceful Coexistence and Intellectual Freedom', written and published in 1968. He remarks that he has 'not significantly departed from the position which he formulated in that article' (p.6). But this is quite untrue. On many fundamental questions he now holds views which are directly opposite to those of seven or eight years ago. In 1968, for example, he wrote of Vietnam:

> The reactionary forces in Vietnam are fighting a cause which cannot hope for the support of the people and are using military force, breaking all legal and moral codes and committing scandalous crimes against humanity. A whole nation is being sacrificed to the alleged purpose of 'stemming the tide of communism'. The American people are being kept in the dark about the role of personal and party prestige, the cynicism and cruelty, the short-sightedness and ineffectuality of the American anti-communist effort in Vietnam and the damage this war is doing to the true wish of the American people, to contribute to the struggle of all humanity for a stronger peace. An end to the war in Vietnam would mean firstly the sparing of many lives. But it would mean also the restoration of peace throughout the world. Nothing so

undermines the possibility of peaceful coexistence than the continuing war in Vietnam.

[*A. Sakharov in the Struggle for Peace*,
Frankfurt-am-Main, 1974, pp. 17-18]

And here is what Sakharov writes about the situation in Vietnam today, now that the war is finally over and the American troops have been evacuated from the whole of the Indo-Chinese peninsula:

I believe that with greater determination and persistence on the part of America in the military and especially the political sphere tragic developments could have been avoided. Political pressure could have been put on the USSR not to supply arms to North Vietnam, a strong expeditionary force could have been sent there at the right time, the UN could have been brought in, more effective economic aid could have been made available and other Asian and European countries could have been involved; all these things could have so influenced events as to avert the war with its horrific consequences for both sides ... But even when the war had reached a state of deadlock, a combination of diplomatic and determined military effort, if explained to the American people and the rest of the world, could have stabilised the situation ...

[pp. 54-5]

This was, however, prevented by a 'whole army of much more vociferous and irresponsible critics, deserters, saboteurs and hack politicians who were using the war for their own narrow political ends. Even more disturbing was the attitude of the many Europeans who did not lift a finger to give real aid but who often distorted the facts of the situation and its historical perspective' (p. 55). Quite frankly this is not the language worthy of a Nobel Prizewinner. What does Sakharov mean by 'more determined military effort'? How can he advocate that the countries of Western Europe, Japan and even Third World countries should assist the USA 'in the difficult, almost hopeless attempt to resist the totalitarian threat in South-East Asia'? In *My Country and the World* he writes that the war in Vietnam meant not only the deaths of soldiers on both sides, but also awful bombardments and 'the murder of innocent civilians with napalm and phosphor and other evil inventions of modern warfare' (p. 54). Whilst realising all this, Sakharov recommends more determined military effort and even the involvement of all America's Western and Eastern allies.

Sakharov is advocating here a 'pacification' programme for Vietnam which even the most fervent American 'ultra-right' did not arrive at. It is well known that both President Johnson and President Nixon were determined not to let communism win in Vietnam and they invested a great deal of military effort in fighting it. But it emerged only gradually that a war in the jungles of Vietnam, a country twice as far from the USA as Korea, a country with front lines of enormous length and extensive guerilla zones, requires much greater effort than Macnamara and his Pentagon anticipated. One could, of course, argue that if the USA had sent to Vietnam not a 500-thousand-strong but a 1,500-thousand-strong expeditionary force supported by 500-600 thousand European and Japanese soldiers, if she had sent to South-East Asia several large air-force units and given 'aid' to South Vietnam to the tune of several millions of dollars, then the 'situation' might have been 'stabilised' and a solid line of defence established, as happened in Korea. But even the majority of the 'ultra-right' in America soon realised that this was too high a price for the victory over communism in South-East Asia. By concentrating almost half her land army and her air and naval forces in Indo-China, and spending half her defence budget and more than half her aid fund on a war against a comparatively small Asian country, America would have tied her hands firmly and lastingly in South-East Asia and forfeited her freedom of manoeuvre in all other parts of the world. America's military commitments in Europe, Latin America, the Middle East and other parts of Asia would not have been met. Could not world communism have made use of this situation? It is a fact that Cuba's attempts at guerilla warfare in parts of Latin America in the mid-1960s were aimed at weakening America's position in

293

view of her commitment in Vietnam. 'We must give the USA a second Vietnam to contend with in Latin America' – this was the message from some Latin American communists. I heard these words also at the lecture in Moscow. But they were not merely words. Sakharov writes: 'American critics of the Vietnamese war could see clearly that victory was not getting any nearer. They believed – wrongly, in my view – that victory was not possible unless the sort of determined action were undertaken which would have jeopardised our entire world order' (p. 54). No, it was not the American critics who were mistaken on this point; it was Sakharov himself. And it is he who with hindsight advocates the kind of programme of action in South-East Asia which really could upset world order. The path which Sakharov's views have followed cannot but outrage and alarm all those who have so far had a deep respect for him.

Dostoevsky once said or wrote: 'If I had to choose between Christ and truth, I would choose Christ.' I feel, however, that it would be more appropriate to be guided by the ancient adage: 'Plato is my friend, but truth is dearer to me'. I have tried to make these words my guiding principle in this article.

Solzhenitsyn: Truth and Politics

(A Discussion of *Gulag Archipelago*, Volume III)

ROY MEDVEDEV

Translated by George Saunders

Two and a half years after the publication in the West of the first volume of *Gulag Archipelago*, with the sensation that produced and the subsequent expulsion of the author from the USSR, the third volume of this monumental work has come out in Paris, in both Russian and French.

One might have thought the first two volumes would have exhausted the basic theme of Solzhenitsyn's literary investigation. Not only the history and structure of Gulag but all aspects of the life of the prisoners and of their keepers, the types of concentration camps, and the character of the different 'waves' of unfortunates who replenished the 'population' of this fearsome Archipelago by the millions – all this was dealt with in the first two volumes of Solzhenitsyn's book. But the author was right when he said in the Preface to his second volume that even with the help of hundreds of former zeks who had provided him with their letters, memoirs, stories and statements he had been able to open only 'a peephole into the Archipelago, not the view from the tower'.[1] Many books and memoirs were written about the Stalin camps even before Solzhenitsyn's study: more than thirty have been published in the West alone. But all these, put together, still do not exhaust the dreadful subject. It is not surprising, therefore, that Solzhenitsyn found himself at no loss for materials for his third volume.

One of the important subjects treated in the third volume

is the post-war history of the Gulag Archipelago: the revival of the hard labour of Tzarist times *(katorga)*, even as a juridical category, and the establishment on the basis of the former 'corrective-labour camps', of the system of Special Camps *(Osoblagy)*, where most often the inmates consisted exclusively of politicals from the various 'waves'. Solzhenitsyn also gives a detailed description of the various types of penal exile *(ssylka)*. Here, going back into history again, he tells of the deportation of the wealthy peasants and the 'kulak supporters' in the years of collectivisation, and the deportation to the East of the many nationalities Stalin found 'inconvenient'. Solzhenitsyn began the first volume of his book with the chapter 'Arrest' and he now concludes Part Six with the chapter 'Zeks in Freedom' – a description of the release of those prisoners who managed to survive into the 1955-7 period of rehabilitations. The last, relatively brief section, Part Seven, gives the reader a picture of the present system of Gulag, where relatively few 'politicals' still remain but where, as before, we are far from the justice and humaneness that even the criminals deserve – those Solzhenitsyn writes of with such distate in the first two volumes of his book. It is unquestionably to the author's credit that he has given the first detailed description of the tragic events in Novocherkassk in 1962 and of a number of other hushed-up tragedies of the post-Stalin years.[2]

However, the main theme of the new volume is a detailed description of the gradual, slow, but steadily intensifying change of mood and behaviour among the prisoners, the various forms of passive and active resistance, beginning with escape attempts and protest actions and ending with armed uprisings. It is with emotion that we read the scrupulously detailed descriptions of several escape attempts known to Solzhenitsyn (usually unsuccessful ones). As for the revolt of the prisoners at Kengir[3] – apparently the biggest revolt in the entire history of Gulag – the description of that event is the central and most important part of the third volume. Solzhenitsyn takes satisfaction in reporting that the majority of informers uncovered by the zeks in the Special Camps were secretly killed. He is delighted at every instance of resistance to arbitrary rule. He does not conceal his feeling of triumph in recounting the story of the Kengir uprising and regrets only that not all the barracks and not all categories of prisoners took part. The chapter headings speak for themselves: 'The Wind of Revolution', 'When the Earth Is Ablaze in the Compounds', 'We Break the Chains Barehanded', and 'The Forty Days of Kengir'. And it would of course be unfair to Solzhenitsyn to do more than comment that in this case (departing from the theories he expounded in the second volume) he himself defends the right of the oppressed to rise up against their oppressors, meeting violence with violence, the right of slaves to make a revolution in the name of freedom and justice.

In my reviews of the first and second volumes of *Gulag Archipelago* I have already given my estimate of this book as one of the most valuable documents of our era, one of the greatest books of the twentieth century.[4] I have no reason to change this assessment after reading the third volume. Solzhenitsyn himself, in his Afterword, apologises to the reader for the unwieldy size of this work and for certain artistic failings. But these apologies are needed least of all in regard to the third volume. For it is based, to a much greater extent than the earlier volumes, on the personal experience of the author, and this gives it more the quality of an artistically crafted memoir than a 'literary investigation'. And as a writer Solzhenitsyn is especially strong precisely in describing events he himself has seen. That is what makes the central chapters of the third volume the most satisfying artistically and the most powerful. Nevertheless, despite the fact that the third volume is a worthy conclusion to this tremendous work, the general attitude toward the book has subtly changed during the last year or year and a half in the West and in the USSR. The appearance of the third volume no longer caused a sensation; in many Western countries the press took only brief notice of the event. And though the entire finished work of Solzhenitsyn now stands before the reader – a work that I am convinced will remain the *chief* work of his life – there is less being said and written, and there is much less controversy, about it than there was when only the first volume had appeared. There are apparently several reasons for this.

Does Solzhenitsyn tell the truth?

It is logical to wonder how such a question could arise. After all, we know Solzhenitsyn as a passionate lover of truth, author of the appeal 'Do Not Live by the Lie',[5] fearless critic and exposer of the crimes and lies he saw around him. Despite that, the question arises, especially in Western Europe, where he now lives and has the opportunity to say what he thinks for all to hear and to publish everything produced by his pen

Solzhenitsyn himself has declared more than once that he imagined the West quite differently than he now finds it, at first hand. But the West, too, has in many respects begun to look at Solzhenitsyn differently in recent years, and this is especially true of the students and intellectuals, not to mention the politically active elements of the working class. In his numerous political articles, press conferences, letters, television and other appearances, and speeches during the past two years Solzhenitsyn, as everyone knows, has voiced many reactionary and utopian ideas and advanced some obviously absurd theories, revealing his lack of knowledge of the elementary facts of both Russian and world history. He has discredited himself as either politician or prophet precisely with that part of the Western public that reads the most and is traditionally liberal.

'Is the author of *Gulag Archipelago* a reactionary?' asks Yefim Etkind in one of his articles.[6]

This question is being asked more and more often. Solzhenitsyn sometimes angers his audience by flinging out spurious slogans or provocative assertions, plainly contrary to the truth. But is Balzac judged by his anti-republican and legitimist articles? It was Victor Hugo who, with good reason, regarded him as a revolutionary writer.

[*Le Monde*, 10 March 1976.]

However, this covers only part of the truth. For Solzhenitsyn has been speaking out in the West less and less as an *artist and writer* and has more and more involved himself directly in politics, taking positions that at times are shocking even to the most right-wing political figures in the Western world. In fact virtually all of the *purely literary* works that Solzhenitsyn has published in the last three years (including *Gulag Archipelago*) were written in the USSR before the writer was expelled.

But unfortunately it is not only Solzhenitsyn's reactionary and utopian views that are at issue. There is also the question of Solzhenitsyn's way of defending his views, the polemical methods he permits himself to use in combating his political opponents. Solzhenitsyn is outraged at the Bolsheviks for many of the unworthy means they employed to achieve a goal they considered worthy, but he is not at all hesitant in his own choice of means. In his polemical ardour he has frequently resorted to flagrant distortion, juggling of the facts, deliberate omission or hushing things up, and the use of smear techniques against people he does not agree with. This disdain for moral considerations on the part of Solzhenitsyn the politician undermines the trust of a good part of his readership in Solzhenitsyn the artist. And that is why many of them ask, Isn't he exaggerating in *Gulag Archipelago?* Isn't he resorting to falsification here too? It would seem that this is one of the chief reasons for the decline in Solzhenitsyn's popularity and in that of *Gulag Archipelago.*

While I am not one of Solzhenitsyn's co-thinkers and do not share his political views, I must attest that all of the basic facts about the Gulag Archipelago presented in the third volume do correspond to the truth. Solzhenitsyn paints a grim picture of the Stalinist concentration camps, and it is sometimes hard to believe. But the reality was precisely as he shows it. A great deal was even worse, for there are more than a few 'islands' of the Archipelago that Solzhenitsyn did not describe, that he does not even know about.

There are, to be sure, a number of inaccuracies in the third volume, cases where something is presented as a fact that was actually just one of the camp myths. For example, there is an erroneous legend, which Solzenitsyn himself presents only as a *rumour* without citing any evidence, having to do with disabled veterans of the Great Patriotic War. 'And what necklace should we weave this into?' he writes. 'What category of exile should we assign this to – the exile of disabled veterans of the Patriotic War? *We know next to nothing about this, and those who know are very few.*' (Emphasis added. – R.M.)

> They were sent to some northern island – they were sent off because, for the glory of the fatherland, they had let themselves be disfigured in the war, and the aim of sending them off was to contribute to the health of the nation, which was putting on such a winning performance in all types of athletics and ball games. There on an unknown island, these unlucky heroes of the war were held, naturally without the right of correspondence (an occasional letter got out, that is how this became known), and just as naturally, they were kept on meagre rations because only their labour could warrant a lavish one. And it seems they are living there to this day.

[p. 390.]

It is true the war left many disabled veterans. I remember, even at the end of the first year of the war, how many of these unfortunates were begging on the trains, near the markets and tearooms, or simply on the streets. Released from the hospitals, they did not know where their families were or often did not want to return to their wives or sweethearts as cripples. At the end of the war, it is true, these people somehow disappeared unnoticed from the streets of the big cities. But they were not shipped off to some unknown northern island to die in order to 'contribute to the health of the nation'. Toward the end of the war, in all the major cities of the country, a network of special hospitals was organised for chronic invalids and helpless disabled veterans who had no families or did not wish to live with their families. When I was studying at Leningrad University in the first years after the war, our department was a 'sponsor' for one of these hospitals for 'chronic cases', as the war invalids were called. The fate of these people was, of course, hardly enviable; only a few of them were able to work in the shops attached to the hospital. However, none of them starved because they did not 'warrant a lavish ration'.

The only other inaccuracy I will mention is Solzhenitsyn's remark, made in passing but highly meaningful, that he had met quite a few people from the Baltic countries and Western Ukraine in the Special Camps, but hardly any Georgians, and although in exile there had been 'some people from the Caucasus, no one could recall a single Georgian among them' (p. 389). A great deal of evidence can be cited, however, to show that the terror of the 1930s raged even more furiously in Georgia than in most of the other republics, that it was precisely the death sentence that was handed down there most often, and that the methods of torture there were notorious for their refined cruelty. During the disastrous battle of the Kerch Penninsula in the summer of 1942, several Georgian regiments fell into encirclement and thousands of Georgian soldiers were taken prisoner. After the war most of these men were sent to the Archipelago. And if Solzhenitsyn met few Georgians in exile, that is mainly because these people of Southern birth and sensitive temperament nearly all died in the camps well before the end of their term.

Such inaccuracies are perhaps even fewer in the third volume than in the first and second. Yet if one were to follow the formula used in the American court system (and apparently the British, too), 'Do you swear to tell the truth, the whole truth, and nothing but the truth?' Solzhenitsyn would not be able to assent to the last two parts of this formula. For the terrible truth the great artist has revealed to the world in his book bears within it a layer of untrue and tendentious argument that, though not great in size, is rather obtrusive in substance. This has its source primarily in certain concepts new to Solzhenitsyn (at least, they are expressed for the first time in *Gulag Archipelago*) and in his attempts to twist reality to fit these concepts.

New motifs and influences in 'Gulag Archipelago'

In his Afterword the author writes: 'I must explain that never once was this entire book, with all its parts, on one and the same desk!' (p. 579). But that was written in 1967. And the present volume has come out in 1976, with the author preparing it for publication in Zurich, where his desk was not 'burning up beneath him', nor the ground under his feet. Although Solzhenitsyn nowhere speaks of it, it is not hard to conclude, by comparing the first and third volumes, that by this time the author did have the entire book before him 'on one and the same desk' and that quite a few pages, even the better part of the first chapter, were inserted during the past few years in the West.

In my review of the first volume of *Gulag Archipelago,* I wrote that Solzhenitsyn nowhere tried to whitewash, justify, or praise the Vlasovites,[7] let alone all the other former Soviet citizens who fought on Hitler's side against the Soviet army. Solzhenitsyn merely tried to show some of the circumstances that would seem to mitigate the guilt of these people and render the post-war reprisals against them excessively harsh. In the third volume, however, the author has decisively altered his conception. Now he quite plainly whitewashes and justifies the Vlasovites. Moreover, he particularly singles out the Soviet soldiers and commanders who went over to the fascist side not in 1943 but in 1941, right after the outbreak of the war, in the months when the German army was moving rapidly and victoriously eastward.

Solzhenitsyn painstakingly gathers information about the military and semi-military formations that were created long before the Vlasov units, and about the establishment of 'people's militia' in Byelorussia for 'defence' against the partisans. He is ready to understand, forgive, and justify the collaborationist 'burgomasters', 'elders', police, and even those who served in punitive detachments recruited and formed by the Germans, not to mention the Cossack regiments and divisions organised by Hitler's forces in the Don and Kuban regions. While he uses the term 'foolish calves' *(telyata)* for the Soviet young people (including himself) who rushed eagerly to the front lines to defend their homeland, he regards those who went over to the enemy side as heroes rising up in an epic struggle against the Stalinist tyranny, people whose noble impulses, unfortunately, were neither understood nor made use of by Hitler and the German General Staff, owing to German obtuseness.

A question involuntarily occurs to the reader: how to explain this striking shift in the author's position? But Solzhenitsyn gets around the problem very simply. He writes:

In the first part of this book the reader had not yet been prepared to receive the full truth ... There, at the beginning, when the reader had not yet walked with us the full length of the road through the camps, he was only asked to perk up his ears and invited to think a little. Now after all the prison transports, transit prisons, logging details, and camp rubbish heaps, perhaps the reader has become more inclined to agree.

[p. 30.]

It is impossible to believe that this is a sincere explanation. It gives rise to an involuntary feeling – at least for most Soviet readers, even Solzhenitsyn's admirers – of protest and mistrust towards the author.

It is generally known that after Hitler's attack on the USSR even the old White Guard emigrés split in their attitude toward the war. One section of the emigré community, headed by General Denikin and the Cadet leader Milyukov,[8] favoured the victory of the USSR; another section took a neutral position; and only a small section went along with the fascists. All of Solzhenitsyn's sympathy is now on the side of the last group, and he regrets only that there were too few of them and that they did not have the full confidence of the German occupationists. Solzhenitsyn understands very well that Hitler's forces wished to destroy not only Bolshevism but Russia as a state, and that in our pre-war newspapers not everything was untrue. He understands very well that 'for the new arrivals Russia was even more insignificant and loathsome than for those departing. The vampire only wanted Russia's vital juices; let the body fall lifeless wherever it might' (p. 28). Nevertheless, in this very book one can find more than a few pages with apologies for treason that are surprising to hear from a Russian writer. For example, here is what Solzhenitsyn writes about the members of the police and punitive forces that served the Germans:

Where did they come from? Why? Can it be that the civil war was still smouldering and had flared up again? Are these Whites who were never completely beaten? No! It has already been mentioned that many White emigrés (including the foul and accursed Denikin) took the side of Soviet Russia against Hitler ... These tens and hundreds of thousands of police and punitive troops, elders and interpreters, all came from the ranks of Soviet citizenry. And there were even quite a few young people, including those who had grown up after October.

What made them do it? Who were these people?

Above all they were people whose families, or who themselves, had been run over by the tank treads of the 1920s and 1930s. Who had lost parents, relatives, loved ones in the murky waves that washed down our sewage disposal system. Or who themselves had sunk and re-emerged in camp or in exile ...

And let us not forget [Solzhenitsyn continues] that among these our countrymen who came against us with the sword and made speeches against us, there were completely unselfish people whose property had not been taken, who had not sat in the camps, and who did not have family in the camps, but who had for a long time felt stifled by our entire system – the contempt for the fate of the individual, the persecution of people for their beliefs, the mocking song 'Where people breathe so freely', the worshippers bowing to the Great Leader, the official yanking at the pencil, 'Hurry up and sign the loan!' and the applause rising to an ovation.

[pp. 18, 22.]

All this is quite enough, in Solzhenitsyn's eyes, to drive good, sometimes even noble, people into collaborating with the occupation regime, serving as 'burgomasters' and punitive troops, and to cause them to prefer the devout worship of another Leader, the Führer, and another song, 'Deutschland über alles'. Somehow it is awkward even to refute these arguments that Solzhenitsyn piles up, one upon the other.

To be sure, life was not easy for our people in the 1920s and

1930s and the terrible crimes of the Stalin regime inflicted wounds upon millions of Soviet people that have never healed. However, only a small minority of those who suffered turned to collaboration with the enemy, and that element was not the best but precisely the worst among those who had been victimised. Hundreds of thousands of people could be named – from Vera Khoruzha and Nina Kosterina to S.V. Rudnev and Konstantin Rokossovsky[9] – who had also been 'run over by the tank treads' of the 1930s but who fought courageously to defend their homeland from Hitler's forces. But for today's Solzhenitsyn this is no argument – to him these people are either 'calves' or 'Orthodox loyalists'. He takes his stand entirely on the side of the people for whom indignation and outrage at Stalin's crimes, natural to any honest person, had passed over into blind hatred and brought them into a dead end of unreasoning embitterment, so that they no longer thought of changing or removing the bad or evil system in their own country but were ready, out of hatred for one satanic tyrant, to surrender their entire country to another kind of fiend. The only problem was that this other fiend for some reason was in no hurry to buy up their souls and regarded their intentions with suspicion. Just think of it – Solzhenitsyn indignantly tells us – the fascists, in their fear, disbanded the 'people's militia' in Byelorussia, and when 739 people in one of the prisoner-of-war camps for officers expressed their desire to join Vlasov's army, the Germans released only eight for military duty. 'How typical of German obtuseness,' Solzhenitsyn writes (p. 34).

Solzhenitsyn is wrong in thinking that collaborationism was a phenomenon peculiar to the USSR. The fascists recruited quite a few traitors in all the occupied countries of Europe. One can say with certainty that if there had been no mass terror in our country in the 1930s, no forced collectivisation, and no famine of 1932 -3, the occupying regime would not have been smaller if the fascists had not followed a captured Soviet territories. Likewise, the partisan movement might have been smaller if the fascists had not followed a policy of such total terror and pillage in the parts of the USSR and the countries of Eastern Europe they conquered. But after all, Hitler went to war in order to establish German

305

domination over all of Europe and to extend Germany's *Lebensraum* at the expense of the 'inferior' Slavic nations, which were in fact scheduled for partial annihilation, removal to the East, denial of any form of state or independent status, and conversion into the slaves of the 'superior' race of 'Aryans'.

Solzhenitsyn knew this when he fought bravely as an officer in the Soviet army; he still knows it today. It is all the more incomprehensible, then, that he should write so inspiredly about treason, not only by individual soldiers, but by entire Red Army units in the first weeks of the war, portraying this treachery as heroism and even as the salvation of Russia's national honour.

Solzhenitsyn expresses this quite openly:

And so the Soviet-German war – to our pride and joy – showed that we were not such slaves as we were written off to be in all the liberal historical studies. Slaves would not strain themselves to bring Father Stalin's head within reach of a sabre ... These were people who had borne twenty-four years of Communist happiness on the skin of their backs, who knew as far back as 1941, when no one else in the world knew, that nowhere on the planet and never in history was there such a cruel, bloody, and at the same time sly and tricky regime as that of Bolshevism, ... that no other regime in the world would compare with it, not even the raw and immature Hitler regime, which at that time had blinded every eye in the West. And here a time had come when weapons were placed in these people's hands. And were they supposed to sit still and let Bolshevism survive its final hour, to grow again in all its savage oppression? And were they supposed to take up the struggle against it only afterwards (a struggle that has not begun anywhere in the world to this day)? No, the natural thing to do was imitate the trick used by Bolshevism itself. Just as it had buried its teeth in the body of a Russia weakened by the First World War so the thing was to smash Bolshevism in a similar situation in the Second World War.

[p. 31.]

Solzhenitsyn continues:

> I will be so bold as to say that the Russian people would
> have been worth nothing, would have been a nation of
> hopeless chattel, if they had let slip the chance, during war,
> at least to draw back and fire a few curses at the Beloved
> Father. In Germany there was a conspiracy of the generals,
> but what did we have? Our top generals were worthless,
> corrupted by party ideology and self-seeking; they had not
> even kept alive the national spirit that one finds in other
> countries. Only the rank and file of peasants, soldiers, and
> Cossacks raised their fists and struck a blow. It was entirely
> a movement of the ranks – so close to the vanishing point
> was the part played by the emigré former gentry, the
> former wealthy elements, and the intelligentsia. And if this
> movement had been given its head when it surged up in
> the first days of the war, it would have become a new
> Pugachov rebellion[10] – in the breadth and depth of the
> social layers involved, in the popular support it had, in the
> part played by the Cossacks, in its aim of 'settling the score
> with the high and mighty criminals', in its elemental
> driving force, despite weak leadership ... It was not fated,
> however, to develop to the full, but to perish in dishonour,
> branded with the words 'Betrayal of our sacred homeland'.

[p. 35.]

All of this is fantasy and imagining, based on no reality
whatsoever. If the moods that Solzhenitsyn attributes to the
'rank and file', that is, the majority of the population, had
really existed the army could never have won the war or even
continued to function. Solzhenitsyn, who fought in the war
himself and more than once has shown a certain feeling of
pride in his own military record (this can be felt even in the
first volume of *Gulag Archipelago*), must have seen how
self-sacrificingly the Soviet soldiers fought against the fascist
armies. Despite casualties that were *ten times* greater than in
the First World War, despite battles that were incomparably
more terrible than the Samsonov disaster of 1914,[11] despite
the loss of almost half of Russia, our people did not fall for

the false promises of Hitler's fascists. They not only stood up against the massive German military machine, which was backed by the economic resources of all of Europe and by dozens of divisions from countries allied with Hitler, but they overcame the enemy.

A vicious ideological mishmash like this, the idea of a 'Pugachov rebellion' headed by Hitlerites, was bound to develop among those who fled to the West after serving Hitler as police, punitive troops, and hirelings of other sorts. They seek in these hallucinations some justification for their rather tainted performance under the Fascist occupation and wish now to present themselves as 'ideological opponents' of Soviet power. Apparently Solzhenitsyn's present circle of intimates consists largely of such people. And apparently that is the reason his three years in the West have not had a very beneficial effect on Solzhenitsyn the artist.

We are inclined to attribute to Solzhenitsyn's new milieu many of the other pages in the third volume, for it is simply hard to believe that he wrote them in the USSR or that he gave them to some of his friends to read while still there, as he claims in his second Afterword (p. 581).

For example, Solzhenitsyn apologises totally for the principals and teachers who continued to run the schools in the occupied towns and villages according to the programme dictated by the fascists. What is wrong with that? he asks.

Of course one had to pay a certain price. The portraits with the big whiskers had to be taken out of the schools and, perhaps, portraits with the little moustache brought in. An evergreen had to be decorated, not for New Year's, but for Christmas, and on that occasion (and on some imperial anniversary instead of October), the principal had to give a speech praising the wonderful new life, when in fact things were pretty bad. But they had to give speeches before in praise of the wonderful life when that too had been pretty bad.

[p. 16.]

And this is written by the author of 'Do Not Live by the Lie!'

Yes, it is true that much of what teachers and principals told their pupils in the 1920s and 1930s did not, to put it mildly, correspond to the truth. But the overwhelming majority of educators at that time believed what they said; they believed as much in the verities of Marxism-Leninism as the young Solzhenitsyn did then. And they knew as little about the crimes of the Stalin clique as Solzhenitsyn did, with all his intelligence and the doubts he had even then about Stalin and the 'public' political trials organised in 1936-8. But not to know about the crimes of the occupation regime, while living in the fascist-held territory, was impossible. Children as well as teachers knew about them. That is why the best of them, like the hero of Basil Bykov's short novel *Obelisk*, joined the partisans and did not give speeches in praise of the occupation.[12]

Solzhenitsyn does not overlook the fate of the young women who became the mistresses of German soldiers and officers. This is an ancient theme, and Maupassant, for one, handled it brilliantly as long ago as 1880 in his celebrated *Boule de Suif*. Here too, however, Solzhenitsyn holds to a unique point of view. This is what he writes:

> First, about the women, who as we know are now emancipated ... But what is this? Didn't we create a worse Kabanikha for them by accusing them of anti-patriotic and criminal behaviour for freely disposing of their bodies and selves?[13] Hasn't all of [pre-Stalinist] world literature glorified love that is free of national bonds and the wills of generals and diplomats? ... Above all, what age were these women when they met the enemy not in battle but in bed? Not older than thirty, it would seem, perhaps even twenty-five. That means their earliest childhood impressions were formed after October, in Soviet schools and by Soviet ideology! Are we so quick with anger at the work of our own hands? Some of these young women had been stirred up by our constant screeching for fifteen years that there is no such thing as one's homeland, that the idea of the fatherland is just a reactionary invention. Another type of these women were bored with the pristine puritanism of our meetings, rallies, and demonstrations, cinematography

309

without kisses, and dances without embraces. A third group was overcome by politeness and gallantry, by the little things in a man's personal appearance, the outward show of courtship, which no one had taught our lads during the five-year plans or under the commanders of our army, cast in the Frunze mold. Those of a fourth group were simply hungry, with a primitive kind of hunger, that is, they had nothing to put in their mouths. A fifth group, perhaps, saw no other way to save themselves or their relatives and not to be parted from them.

[pp. 13-24.]

It is strange to think that all this was written by a Russian, an officer who went through the war, who in 1943-5 must have seen clearly, as he passed through the liberated Russian towns and villages, what the 'politeness and gallantry' of the German officers and soldiers amounted to then. Moreover, it was not only the women who slept with Hitler's men (and with the camp bosses in the camps) whose 'earliest childhood impressions had been formed in Soviet schools and by Soviet ideology'; that was also true of the women who died of hunger without selling themselves for a bar of chocolate or a pair of stockings. And there were many more of these – millions of them! Certainly none of the women who 'met the enemy not in battle but in bed' deserved the long terms in hard-labour camps many of them received. But they deserve the derisive term 'German bedstraw' with which their former friends and fellow villagers labelled them in the years of occupation. Solzhenitsyn emphatically disagrees. True, he does write something vague about moral censure, qualifying it with a 'perhaps'. But those he considers most to blame are 'all of us, their contemporaries and fellow countrymen. What were we like', he writes, 'if our women were attracted to the occupation troops?' (p. 14.)

Once more on the Communists in the camps

Throughout Solzhenitsyn's book, and the third volume is no exception, we find revulsion and hatred not only toward

Communists in general but toward party members who spent up to ten years, or as many as eighteen, in Stalin's camps and who suffered torments incomparably greater than those Solzhenitsyn himself underwent. He calls the majority of party members nothing less than 'the Orthodox' and contends that after the Twentieth Congress these 'Orthodox' Communists returned to freedom no different than they had been before they went into the camps. In general, he claims, the Orthodox want to forget about the camps and prisons and avoid any acquaintances from the camp days.

> After all, what kind of 'loyalists' would they be if they couldn't forgive and forget, and go back to the way they had been? Why, they had sent petitions to this effect four times a year 'Let me go back! Let me go back! I'll be good; I always was!' What did going back mean to them? First of all it meant reclaiming their party cards, their service records, their seniority, the honours they had been awarded ... And they came flooding back in 1956, as though from a musty old trunk, bringing with them the air of the 1930s, wishing to take up where they had left off the day of their arrest.
>
> [p. 479.]

Both the tone and the content of this tirade call for strenuous objections. Solzhenitsyn knows very well that the Communists arrested in the 1930s came back, not from a 'musty old trunk' but from the same dreadful labour camps that he writes about, bearing the marks of torture and harsh trials. And though the majority of them had not betrayed their convictions, their attitudes toward the reality of our life was quite different. (We do not refer to the isolated cases of 'forgetful people', who are found in all the categories and 'waves' of former zeks.) And they did not come 'flooding back' from the camps, but returned to freedom in a thin, straggling line, for most of the Communists arrested in the 1930s were shot or died in the camps.

Solzhenitsyn's biased and ungracious attitude does him no

311

honour. If a Communist conducted himself or herself in a
worthy manner, he mentions it only in passing. For example,
he reports that the committee that led the Kengir uprising
included women, among them 'Shakhnovskaya, an economist
and party member, a woman already grey'. On the other
hand, if a coward, traitor, or artful dodger is a Communist, he
spares no detail in writing about it. But here a difficult figure
confronts Solzhenitsyn – Kapiton Kuznetsov, leader of the
camp uprising, head of the forty-day government, president
of the committee elected by the prisoners. He was a former
Red Army colonel, a graduate of the Frunze Academy,[14] a
man well on in years. He had commanded a regiment in
Germany after the war and was given a prison term because
'someone under him had escaped to the Western Zone'. At
the time the uprising began he was in a camp prison for
having 'blackened the reality of camp life' in letters sent out
through free women workers. Presumably Kuznetsov was a
party member, but Solzhenitsyn says nothing about this. He
has no facts to compromise Kuznetsov with. On the contrary,
we learn from Solzhenitsyn's account that Kuznetsov
behaved admirably throughout the forty-day uprising. He
refused release from prison, his term having come to an end
during the uprising; he organised the effort to break open the
walls, take out the bars, and make spears from them; in
the negotiations with the 'important generals' who flew to the
camp, Kuznetsov's command 'Off with your head-
gear!' forced even the MVD generals to remove their hats
to show respect for the corpses of the zeks who had been
killed.[15] In reply to the threats of these generals, according
to Solzhenitsyn's own testimony, 'Kuznetsov rose. He
spoke smoothly and easily and held his ground firmly. "If
you march into the compound with your weapons," he
warned, "don't forget that half the people who took Berlin
are here. And they will overcome your weaponry too"'
(p. 328).

What reproach, one wonders, could be brought against this
man? This is how Solzhenitsyn concludes his account:

Kapiton Kuznetsov! The future historian of the Kengir
revolt will have to explain this man for us. What did he go

through during his imprisonment and what was his attitude toward it? What was the status of his case? ... Did he only feel the pride of the professional military man in maintaining such good order in the rebellious camp? Did he take the leadership of the movement because he was caught up in its spirit? (I reject this idea.) Or, knowing his ability as a commander, did he do it in order to calm the flood, bring it back into the riverbanks, and when the movement had spent itself, to lay it at the boots of the bosses? (That is what I think.)

[p. 328.]

The trial of the ringleaders [Solzhenitsyn writes twenty pages later] was held in the fall of 1955: naturally, it was a closed trial and we do not know anything definite about it ... We do not know what the sentences were. Probably Sluchenkov, Mikhail Keller, and Knopkus were shot.

[p. 347.]

But what of Kuznetsov, who was tried by the same court? The author of *Gulag Archipelago* no longer has anything to say about him. Does that mean Kuznetsov proved to be a provocateur? No, Solzhenitsyn does not assert that in so many words; but it is precisely what he is hinting at. Can you write this way about a person who in all likelihood died a hero's death – especially when you have no evidence for your suspicions? As far as Solzhenitsyn is concerned, if a Communist is involved, you can. And this is not the only example of the double standard Solzhenitsyn applies when he writes about Communists who distinguished themselves in the camps.

On the 'liberal' Russian autocracy

Another typical feature running though the entire third volume, and through the book as a whole, is the tone of constant ridicule in reference to the supposed 'savagery' of the Russian Tzars and, balancing that, the scornful attitude

313

toward the Russian revolutionaries and liberals who considered the autocratic regime in Russia 'intolerable'. I have
already had occasion to state in print that the savagery of
Stalin's terror cannot be compared with that of the Russian
Tzars, with the exception of Ivan the Terrible. But Solzhenitsyn does not leave it at that. Constantly returning to this
theme, he apparently regrets that the last Russian autocrats
were so excessively 'liberal'. For example, Alexander II and
the Okhrana did not hunt down the People's Will members
the way they should have. Of course, they arrested them now
and then and jailed them, but 'just long enough to give them
a taste of prison and put a halo around their heads' (p. 87).
Alexander III also was essentially a 'liberal'. Although he had
about a dozen members of the People's Will executed, he
didn't go after the relatives and friends of the executed, or he
punished them too lightly, 'in a fatherly way', as may be seen
especially in the fate of young Vladimir Ulyanov. And
Nicholas II was in general a 'weakling'; he couldn't deal
properly with the workers in January 1905, and in 1917 he
shamefully lost his self-possession and his crown.[16]

> This Tzar and all those who controlled him no longer had
> the determination to fight for their power. They no longer
> suppressed anyone, but simply squeezed them a little and
> then let them go. They kept looking over their shoulder –
> What will public opinion say? We ... can make the bold
> assertion that the Tzarist government not only failed to
> hunt down the revolutionaries but tenderly nurtured them,
> bringing on its own destruction.
>
> [p. 87.]

Elsewhere, in telling of the persecution and trials of Baptists
in the 1960s, Solzhenitsyn cannot help exclaiming: 'The trial
of the 193 Narodniks,[17] by the way, was a hundred years ago.
But Lord, what a fuss was made over their sufferings! It's even
in the schoolbooks.' [p. 567.]

It is obvious how wrong this position is. Just because the
crimes and injustices of the period from the 1920s to the 1950s
were greater than those of earlier centuries and decades, that

does not make a virtue of the injustice of former times, nor do those who fought injustice cease to be heroes in the grateful memory of humanity. But Solzhenitsyn's entire tone, when he deals with this topic, is one of *regret* that the Tzarist repression was *not harsh enough.* Oh, what a shame that so few revolutionaries were trampled on, and so mildly: How good if they had all been strangled in the cradle! Solzhenitsyn's confidence that repression tenfold or a hundredfold stronger would have saved Russian Tzarism leads one to ask, why would he want that so much? If millions had rotted in prison and at hard labour, if tens of thousands had been shot, not under Stalin but under Nicholas II or Alexander III, would *those* corpses have smelled sweeter?

East and West

Another favourite theme of the author of *Gulag Archipelago,* a kind of persistent refrain mixed in with his truly awe-inspiring scenes of the crimes of the recent past, is his jeering at the West, not only the Western leftists and liberals whom he hates but even the right-wing circles, the West as a whole. This scorn for Western political figures is perhaps most blatant in the third volume.

The West, in Solzhenitsyn's opinion, did not help Russia as it should have back in the First World War or in the fatal year 1917. This brought the weakened Romanov monarchy, and after it the Provisional Government, to disaster. The West allowed the Bolsheviks to come out on top in the Civil War and then greeted the millions of Russian emigrés with hostility. The West took no note of the starvation of millions of peasants in 1932-3, nor of the dreadful sweep of the Stalin terror. Then, at the end of the war in 1945, the West gave in to virtually every demand Stalin made.

These reproaches most often flow from a failure to understand that the West itself, since the turn of the century, has been torn by numerous internal and external contradictions and never had the strength or resources to carry out the programme Solzhenitsyn now outlines for it after the fact.

But what is absolutely astounding is that Solzhenitsyn

takes the West to task (above all, the United States) for not
starting a new world war against the USSR and China after
the outbreak of the Korean War and for not using its
monopoly of atomic weapons to wage such a war.

Just as the generation of Romain Rolland was weighed
down in its youth by the constant expectation of war,[18] so
our convict generation [Solzhenitsyn writes] was burdened
by the absence of such an expectation. And only that is the
full truth about the atmosphere in the Special Political
Camps. That's what they drove us to. A world war could
have brought us a quicker death (to be shot down from the
towers, or poisoned by bread or bacilli, as was done by the
Germans), or it could have brought us freedom. In either
case deliverance would have come sooner than the end of
our terms, in 1975.

[p. 51.]

Here once again Solzhenitsyn presents his *own* feelings as
those of all the prisoners. I have had occasion to meet
hundreds of former inmates of the Special Camps, people of
the most varied political views, but I have never heard any of
them say they had longed for a third world war.

Solzhenitsyn apparently senses that his words may shock
his readers and in a temper he exclaims:

Are people astounded at such a cynical, such a desperate
state of mind? Didn't you think, they say, what calamities
this would bring to the vast world out in freedom? – But
those who were free never thought a bit about us! – So
what did you do, they say, start dreaming of a world war?
How could you! – But when they gave these people prison
terms in 1950 that would last to the mid-1970s, what
choice did they leave them except to wish for a world war?

[p. 50.]

Solzhenitsyn is wrong, of course, in maintaining that those
who were free never thought about those in the camps. The
majority of relatives and friends kept alive the memory of

their imprisoned husbands, brothers, and dear ones, waited for them, wrote them letters, and put together packages for them. Nevertheless, Solzhenitsyn takes up this theme again at the end of his book:

> No safe and happy person, either in the West or in the East, can understand or sympathise with the mood of those days behind bars, and it may be that none can forgive us for it ... What kind of crippled life must have been built in order to make thousands and thousands in the cells, in the Black Marias, and in the railroad cars pray for a war of atomic annihilation as their only way out?
>
> [p. 413.]

Indeed it is hard to forgive such an attitude. Solzhenitsyn lived through difficult and terrible times, when even very strong people were crippled or broken. Solzenitsyn's own fate is evidence of that. He was a victim of those times, which taught the author of *Gulag Archipelago* not only firmness and courage, not only extraordinary persistence and stubbornness. They also fostered and developed in him such traits as bitter intransigence bordering on fanaticism, fierce attachment to a single, narrow idea, inability to feel anything but hatred for people with other views or convictions, incapacity to see life and reality in all its multiplicity, and indifference in regard to the means chosen to attain one's ends. Although Solzhenitsyn's efforts are now focused entirely on combating socialism and the 'Progressive Doctrine' that he hates, the techniques he uses in this struggle are all too reminiscent of everything he justly denounces in *Gulag Archipelago*.

In the third volume Solzhenitsyn tells about a former brigade commander, I. S. Karpunich-Braven, who during the civil war had signed quite a few death sentences without even reading the lists handed to him by the Special Section. After twenty years in Kolyma,[19] this brigade commander settled down in a remote village and refused to submit the necessary forms for rehabilitation. He cultivated his garden and in his spare time copied various aphorisms out of books, for example, 'It is not enough to love humanity; you must be able to tolerate people.'

'And just before he died,' Solzhenitsyn tells us, 'he wrote words of his own, such words as to make you tremble – What is this, mysticism? old Tolstoy? "I lived and judged everything in terms of myself," he wrote. "But now I am a different person and I no longer judge from myself alone." '

Unfortunately, Solzhenitsyn has not yet learned to tolerate people and continues to live and judge in terms of himself alone.

NOTES

1 *Zek* – Camp slang for 'prisoner', abbreviated from the Russian word *zaklyuchenny.*

2 *Novocherkassk* – On 1 June 1962, the Soviet government announced sharp increases in the prices of meat and butter. A number of disturbances and protests occurred as a result in many parts of the USSR (similar to the more recent and better-known outbreaks among Polish workers, in 1970-1 and again in 1976). The biggest of the June 1962 protests was apparently in Novocherkassk, a city near Rostov in the Kuban region of south-eastern European Russia. A number of accounts of the Novocherkassk events have been published in several Western countries, including some by writers sympathetic to the Soviet system, but Solzhenitsyn's account seems to be the first detailed description compiled by Soviet dissidents. According to this account, which agrees in most respects with those published earlier, workers at a large electric-locomotive plant outside Novocherkassk, whose pay rates were cut the same day the price rises were announced, began a spontaneous strike that lasted all day and through the night. Signs were up on the factory walls: 'Down with Krushchev! Send Krushchev for Sausages!' On the morning of 2 June, the strike spread to other plants in the city; a demonstration of workers, with portraits of Lenin and posters with peaceful demands, marched to the party headquarters in the central square. The local authorities had fled. The population turned out in large numbers. Workers addressed the crowd from the second-storey balcony of the abandoned party building. Meanwhile, the authorities cordoned off the city and began a troop build-up inside it. Around noon, troops took over the party building, removing the workers. A line of sub-machine gunners pushed the crowd back from the building: they fired warning shots in the air. But there were children in the trees, and they were hit. As they began to fall from the trees, the crowd grew angry. Tensions mounted. A massacre ensued, with at least seventy to eighty of the crowd killed, most by dumdum bullets. During the afternoon, ferment continued. Word spread that top party leaders had flown in from Moscow, including Frol Kozlov and Anastas Mikoyan, and a delegation of

workers had gone to tell them about the massacre. Toward evening a crowd reassembled in the central square, larger than ever. The workers' delegation was allowed to speak to the crowd from the party-building balcony. They reported that the Central Committee members promised an investigation and punishment of the guilty. Still the mass meeting in front of the party headquarters did not disperse. Only around midnight, after the crowd had slowly dwindled, was it finally broken up by pressure from tanks and troops firing in the air.

On 3 June speeches by Mikoyan and Kozlov were broadcast on the local radio. They claimed that the events had been provoked by 'enemies'. Instead of punishing those who committed the massacre, the authorities arrested and deported to Siberia many of the participants and the families of those killed or wounded. A series of trials was held, both secret and 'open' (to officials only). At least nine male defendants were sentenced to be shot and two women to fifteen-year prison terms.

3   *Prison-camp revolts: Kengir* – In the early 1950s a wave of protest actions began in the camps for political prisoners. In 1951, for example, there was a five-day hunger strike in the Vakhrushevo camp on Sakhalin; in January 1952, 3,000 prisoners at Ekibastuz in eastern Kazakhstan held a three-day work stoppage and hunger strike (described by Solzhenitsyn a participant); and in September 1952 at the 'Ozerlag' camp complex there were disorders protesting the killing of a prisoner by guards. Stalin's death in March 1953 intensified the movement, especially when it was followed by an amnesty for prisoners (criminals only) and then the fall of Beria in July 1953. There was a big strike in Norilsk in May 1953, another in Vorkuta in July and August 1953 (and additional ones there in the summer and fall of 1954), one in Taishet in early 1955, and one in Khabarovsk in December 1955. After the Twentieth Soviet Communist Party Congress in 1956, largely under the impact of these revolts, the bulk of political prisoners were released and most the large camp complexes dismantled. However, labour camps for political prisoners continue to exist, on a reduced scale, notably those in Mordovia (Dubrovlag) and the Perm region.

Kengir was, in 1954, a settlement, with an adjacent labour camp: it is now part of the city of Dzhezkazgan in western Kazakhstan. The Kengir revolt involved some 8,000 prisoners and lasted from 16 May to 25 June, according to Solzhenitsyn's account. The revolt was provoked by the unwarranted killing of a prisoner by guards. The prisoners took over the five sectors of the camp compound, from which all guards withdrew. However, the authorities retained control of the machine-gun towers and surrounded the camp with troops, cutting it off from outside. The prisoners maintained an orderly routine in the camp, providing themselves with the necessities of life and making rudimentary weapons and defences. They elected their own governing body and presented the following demands: punishment of the guards guilty of killing and beating prisoners; return of prisoners taken from the camp because of an earlier work stoppage; removal of bars from barracks windows and numbers from prisoners' clothing and an end to the locking of barracks doors at night; elimination of barriers between different sectors of the camp compound; an eight-hour workday (instead of eleven hours); increased pay; freedom to correspond with relatives; review of all prisoners' cases; and direct negotiations with members of the Central Committee of the Soviet Communist Party.

In the uncertain post-Stalin atmosphere, the authorities hesitated and negotiated, cajoled and promised, for a long time. The prisoners tried to communicate the truth about their revolt to the free workers in Kengir and to get support from prisoners in the nearby camps of the Dzhezkazgan copper mines. But that effort failed. Finally the authorities stormed the camp with tanks and sub-machine-guns. In the Attica-like denouement, more than 700 prisoners were killed and wounded. But in the ensuing months conditions were greatly liberalised, and in 1956 the camp itself was dismantled.

3 Roy Medvedev's review of the second volume appeared in the Spring 1976 issue of Dissent, also in George Saunders's translation.

4 *'Do Not Live by the Lie'* – An appeal circulated by Solzhenitsyn in *Samizdat* (uncensored material passed from hand to hand) on the eve of his expulsion from the Soviet Union in February 1974. It called on Soviet citizens, especially young people, to break from conformity and stop complying with the hypocritical rituals imposed by the regime, such as voting 'unanimously' at meetings for things they do not believe in, stating views they do not hold, etc.

6 *Yefim Etkind* – Soviet dissident, taught literature and language at a pedagogical institute in Leningrad from 1951 to 1974. His books on French poetry, German drama (Brecht), Russian stylistics, and problems of translation were published in the USSR in the 1960s and 1970s. A friend of Solzhenitsyn since the early 1960s, he helped hide the manuscript of *Gulag Archipelago* for several years. When the authorities discovered this, in the latter half of 1973, at the time when Solzhenitsyn was forced to publish the book, they brought pressure against Etkind. In April 1974 the faculty council at his institute 'unanimously' voted to remove him from his post as professor, later that year he left the Soviet Union. Medvedev quotes from Etkind's review of *Gulag Archipelago*, vol. 3, on the day of its publication in France. *Le Monde* identifies Etkind at that time as 'professeur associé à l'université de Paris'.

7 *Vlasov.* Andrei A. Vlasov (c. 1900-46) – One of Stalin's top generals until July 1942, when he was captured by the Germans. He agreed to collaborate with the Nazis and formed a 'Free Russia Committee' whose anti-Stalin propaganda was used by the Nazis for psychological warfare. Vlasov's 'Russian Liberation Army' existed largely on paper until late in 1944, when the Nazis allowed anti-Soviet Russians to form units with their own officers under Vlasov, two and a half divisions strong. As the Nazi regime collapsed in April 1945, Vlasov struck out on his own, supported the Czech uprising in Prague against the Nazis, and surrendered to American forces in Bavaria. Turned over to the Soviet authorities, Vlasov and his subordinates were

executed in August 1946. 'Vlasovites' (those who fought under him) who fell into Soviet hands were sent off to the camps of Gulag, if not executed for war crimes.

8 *Denikin: Milyukov* – Anton I. Denikin (1872-1947). Tzarist general in the First World War, one of the main White leaders in the Russian Civil War, 1918-20. Emigrated to Constantinople, then France. In 1939 appealed to White emigrés not to support Nazi Germany in the event of a war between it and the Soviet Union. Pavel N. Milyukov (1859-1943). Russian historian and politician, central leader of the liberal Cadet (Constitutional Democratic) Party, which he helped found in 1905; briefly foreign minister of the Provisional Government in 1917, he cooperated with the Whites in the Civil War. A leader of anti-Soviet emigrés. He edited a Russian paper in Paris, 1921-40.

9 *Kosterina: Khorusha: Rudnev: Rokossovsky* – Nina *Kosterina* (1921-41) – daughter of veteran Bolsheviks who had fought in the Civil War, she remained a Communist activist despite the arrest of her father and uncles in the purges: volunteered for duty in the early months of the Nazi-Soviet War and died, in a partisan operation. Often called the 'Russian Anne Frank' because of her diary, published in *Novy Mir* in 1962, available in English (New York, 1968). Her father, Aleksei Kosterin, held in the camps for eighteen years and rehabilitated in the mid-1950s, became a prominent figure in the dissident movement. He died in 1968 after resigning from the party to protest repression and the invasion of Czechoslovakia. His funeral became the occasion for an oppositional rally by hundreds of dissidents.

Khoruzha: Rudnev: Rokossovsky – all active Communists from the Civil War days, all arrested in 1937 and 'rehabilitated' after the Eighteenth Congress (March 1939), which brought a let-up in the purges on the eve of the Second World War. Despite arrest and imprisonment, all three fought zealously on the Soviet side after the June 1941 Nazi invasion. Khoruzha (1903-42) served as a partisan and in the underground of her native Byelorussia, where she was captured and killed by the Germans. Rudnev (1899-1943) organised and led a big partisan unit in his native Ukraine, where he died in battle. And Rokossovsky (1896-1968) became famous as one of Stalin's top generals in the war, being made a Marshal in 1944. Stalin placed him at the head of the armed forces of 'fraternal' Poland in 1949, a post he left after the Polish October of 1956. Continued to hold prominent posts in the USSR until his death.

10 *Pugachov rebellion* – Peasant revolt of 1773-4 in the Volga region during the reign of Catherine II. Supported by discontented elements of the lower classes – serfs, Cossacks, oppressed nomadic natives – it was led by the adventurer Yemelyan Pugachov (1726-75), who claimed to be Tzar Peter III and decreed an end to serfdom. After his defeat, he was taken to Moscow and publicly executed.

11 *Samsonov disaster* – Defeat of Russian army under Gen. Aleksandr V. Samsonov (1859-1914) in the first big battle between Russian and German forces in the First World War. Samsonov's army invaded East

Prussia, but the offensive was poorly prepared. His army was surrounded and virtually annihilated (losses of 250,000 or more) at the battle of Tannenberg, 27-30 Aug. 1914; Samsonov shooting himself on the field of battle. This major setback to the Tzarist war effort is the central subject of Solzhenitsyn's novel *August 1914*.

12   *Vasil Bykov* (born 1924) – a Byelorussian writer who fought in the Soviet army against the Nazi occupation of his homeland. He is a favourite of Soviet liberals and a frequently published author, though his writings, mainly about the war, are often at variance with officially approved views. His short novel *The Dead Feel No Pain*, for example, depicts Stalinist officers who shot their own soldiers rather than let them be taken prisoner. That novel, published in the Moscow literary monthly *Novy Mir* in 1966, was denounced by *Pravda* and other official publications. *Obelisk* (published in 1973) deals with the rural teacher Moroz, who during the war cooperates with Soviet partisans but continues to run the Byelorussian village school. His purpose is to keep democratic and humanist (Tolstoyan) ideas alive in the minds of the peasant chilrdren, previously uneducated under Polish rule, and to shield them from the brutal teachings of the Nazis. When a group of his favourite students is arrested for sabotage, Moroz shares their fate of execution rather than abandon them. The 'obelisk' of the title is a modest village monument commemorating the youths.

13   *Kabanikha* – Character in Ostrovsky's play *The Thunderstorm*. 'Kabanik-ha' is the disparaging nickname (literally 'female wild pig') by which the wealthy widow Marfa Ignatyevna Kabanova, upholder of morals, is known in her small Volga town. In the Russian literary tradition, Kabanikha came to symbolise heartless despotism clothed in a rigid and backward observance of the proprieties.

14   *Frunze and Frunze Academy* – Mikhail V. Frunze (1885-1925), Bolshevik activist who rose to prominence as a Red Army commander in the Civil War. Briefly commissar of war in 1925. Revered in official Soviet history as a model of military virtue. The Frunze Military Academy in Moscow, one of the top Soviet staff and command colleges, is named in his honour.

15   *MVD* – Ministry of Internal Affairs; this ministry, which had its own troop units, was in charge of the camps.

16   *Okhrana: People's Will; Vladimir Ulyanov; January 1905* – Okhrana (literally 'protection'; short for the Tzarist Department of Police's 'division for the protection of public security and order') was the general term for the political police under the last three Tzars (Alexander II, who ruled 1855-81; Alexander III, 1881-94; and Nicholas II, 1894-1917). *The People's Will* was a revolutionary terrorist organisation that emerged from the Narodnik movement in 1879, dedicated above all to assassinating Alexander II, which it did in 1881. Fierce repression followed; five of the top leaders were executed; and by 1894 the organisation was destroyed. In 1887 some students revived the name, and began a poorly organised conspiracy to assassinate the new Tzar. They were discovered, arrested, tried; five of them were executed,

among them Alexander Ulyanov, whose younger brother was
Vladimir Ulyanov, the future Lenin. When this younger brother of the
executed 'regicide' became involved in radical activities, he was
banned from attendance at universities and later imprisoned and
exiled to Siberia. But Solzhenitsyn is right that the kind of brutal and
drastic measures that Stalin later applied to families of his opponents
were not used by the Tzarist regime of that time. January 1905 refers
to the 'Bloody Sunday' of 9 January 1905, when troops fired on a
crowd of St. Petersburg workers, killing more than a hundred, a
massacre that helped set off the mass strikes and disturbances of the
unsuccessful 1905 revolution.

17   *Trial of the 193* – Public trials staged by the Tzarist authorities from
     October 1878 to March 1879 with the aim of showing there was a
     widespread radical conspiracy. Most of the defendants had not
     previously known one another, but had taken part, in the early 1870s,
     in a spontaneous movement 'to the people,' 'to the Narod'; hence the
     term Narodnik, or 'populist'). The effect of this, and the earlier Trial
     of the Fifty, was to publicise the radical movement and win it broader
     sympathy.

18   *Romain Rolland (1866-1944)* – Nobel Prize-winning French author,
     humanitarian, pacifist and opponent of the First World War, in the
     1930s was regarded by the Stalin regime as one of its best friends in
     the West. Rolland apologised for the purge trials.

19   *Kolyma* – Subarctic region of north-eastern Siberia, named after the
     Kolyma River. It was the site of a labour-camp complex, mainly for
     mining gold, that was the largest in the area and most notorious for its
     murderous conditions.